IMAGES
of America

El Dorado and Union County

On the Cover: This photograph is of the south side of the El Dorado courthouse square, taken around 1950. The city and Union County had prospered during World War II by producing both oil and munitions, and it was in the midst of postwar prosperity that this image was made. Not a parking spot seemed empty and shoppers filled the sidewalk, including in front of the iconic small-town store Woolworth's. In years to come, shopping centers built at the edge of the city drew away commerce, leaving the city center largely empty. Readers of this book will learn how the city of El Dorado was revived, to become a model Main Street for the entire nation. (Author's collection.)

IMAGES
of America

El Dorado and Union County

Ray Hanley
Foreword by Darrin Riley

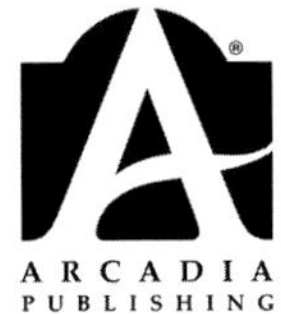

ISBN 978-1-4671-6274-6

Published by Arcadia Publishing
Charleston, South Carolina

Printed in the United States of America

Library of Congress Control Number: 2025932965

For all general information, please contact Arcadia Publishing:
Telephone 843-853-2070
Fax 843-853-0044
E-mail sales@arcadiapublishing.com

Visit us on the Internet at www.arcadiapublishing.com

This book is dedicated to the men whose names are etched in the stone of the war memorial monument on the lawn of the Union County Courthouse. Serving from World War I through the wars in Iraq and Afghanistan, almost 200 Union County men did not make it home but gave their lives in service to their country.

Contents

FOREWORD

The history of El Dorado runs as deep as the precious minerals that lie under its crust. Its early inception as a pioneer town in the Missouri Territory, near the edge of what was then the western border of a very young nation, tested the mettle of the Celtic and European immigrants who sought new beginnings. Her story is a quagmire of myths and facts, legends and reality with something resembling truth rising to the surface. She is a twin city that has held many titles. She has been referred to as "the Queen," an original "Boom Town," and now, "It's Showtime!"

It is the stories of her denizens who truly carve out her tale—those who fled the pestilence and disease-ridden community of Champagnolle, Arkansas, seeking refuge from "bad air" and the prospects of fresh, fertile soil. Young immigrant families leaving the homesteads of Alabama and Georgia soon arrived, bearing hopes of reestablishing a life out of the wilderness. Her citizenship has encompassed the gauntlet, from farmer to oil baron, from famous to the infamous. Her story is a testament to the true pioneering spirit of those who have called her home.

—Darrin Riley
Researcher and curator
South Arkansas Historical Preservation Society

ACKNOWLEDGMENTS

No book like this is possible on an author's efforts alone, as the history of an area is scattered among multiple sites and in the memories of many. Great thanks go to Jimmie Lunsford and Darrin Riley of the South Arkansas Historic Preservation Society. They provided many photographs and answered dozens of questions while touring me through the society's wonderful museum. Thanks to all the participants on the Facebook groups of the towns of El Dorado, Strong, Huttig, and Junction City for their help with questions and photographs. My appreciation goes to the invaluable Encyclopedia of Arkansas, an online history resource that is a part of the Central Arkansas Library System. Thanks also go to Bedford's Photo in Little Rock for scanning services and problem-solving. Deep thanks to my friend Jon LeMay of LeMay Photography, Little Rock, who provided expert help with problem photographs. Special thanks to Richard Mason, who has done so much to revive downtown El Dorado, for his conversation and the use of his image. Thanks to my wife, Diane, who, as she did for my previous 20 books, edited my sometimes-tortured text. Lastly, I would be remiss not to thank my editor at Arcadia Publishing, Caroline Vickerson, for approving my book proposal and for her help and advice as this volume came together. Credit for photographs from the South Arkansas Historic Preservation Society are abbreviated SAHPS. If no credit is listed, images are from the author's collection.

Introduction

An unverified legend of El Dorado's founding is that one day around 1830, Matthew F. Rainey was making his way through the deep woods and glades of southern Arkansas when his wagon broke down atop a low forested hill. The man erected a rough log shed on the hilltop and put his goods up for sale to passing travelers. The resourceful Rainey next claimed the surrounding 160 acres under the Homestead Act. He was thus set to be an early success in recently formed Union County, which had been created by the Arkansas territorial legislature in 1829, carved from parts of Hempstead and Clark Counties.

Between 1829 and 1843, parts of the original Union County had been further sliced away, due to population growth in the region. In the settled lines of Union County after that, the residents' focus turned to choosing the best location for the county seat. The county commissioners convinced Matthew Rainey to surrender his original 160 acres on the ridge, and by 1843, the town of El Dorado was platted out and named the county seat of Union County, Arkansas.

Immigrants arriving from eastern states gave rise to a rapid population gain between 1840 and 1860, though in 1860, half the recorded 12,288 population were slaves. Most of these slaves worked the larger farms where cotton was prominent, but they labored on crops like peas, beans, and sweet potatoes as well. Slaves actually outnumbered the free White citizens of Union County by a few hundred just before the Civil War.

Some 1,500 Union County men marched off to fight in the Civil War for the Confederacy. Some of the wealthy landowners, however, took their slaves and went to Texas. After the war, the cotton economy suffered as prices fell. It is interesting that, through immigration, the county's Black population exceeded that of the White populace for a time, and Black land ownership in Union County exceeded that of most other places in Arkansas.

The railroads arrived in the 1890s and gave rise to a booming timber industry, as trains provided a way to haul out logs and ship the lumber to distant markets. Spur rail lines gave rise to the founding of towns like Smackover and Junction City. The Union Saw Mill Company opened one of the biggest lumber mills in the country, at the little town of Huttig in eastern Union County. The population of Union County surpassed 22,000 in 1900.

Momentous change impacted the county for decades to come, when in 1921 oil was struck outside El Dorado. An even larger strike came the next year in tiny Smackover, a few miles to the north. Union County numbered 29,691 people in 1920, but by 1930, the census had jumped to 55,800 as thousands poured into the area seeking wealth from black gold. World War II saw a continued manufacturing expansion fueled by the county's natural resources. El Dorado even gained air service in the 1940s, as companies like the Great Lakes Corporation moved in to use underground brine for a variety of products. The great heady days of the oil boom were in the past, but Union County diversified its industry for the future.

Despite all this progress, the population of Union County declined steadily after World War II, dropping to a modern-day low of some 45,000 by 1970. Yet the manufacturing base managed to hold, and local leaders began to market the area for tourism. The 1990s spurred a revitalization of downtown El Dorado so that it is now held out as a model for other communities. The Murphy Arts District and the excellent museum of the South Arkansas Preservation Society provided new attractions in the city.

A huge boost to the area came in 2006 when the Murphy Oil Company, then headquartered in its town of origin, donated $50 million for "the El Dorado Promise," which provides college scholarships for all graduates of El Dorado High School. By 2024, another big "strike" in Union County and south Arkansas was approaching, not of oil but of lithium mined from the rich brine deposits left by the oil wildcatters. The future of Union County is poised to be as exciting and interesting as its past.

It is a pleasure to tell the fascinating story of El Dorado and Union County through postcards, photographs, and residents' recollections of days gone by.

One

El Dorado and Union County before Oil

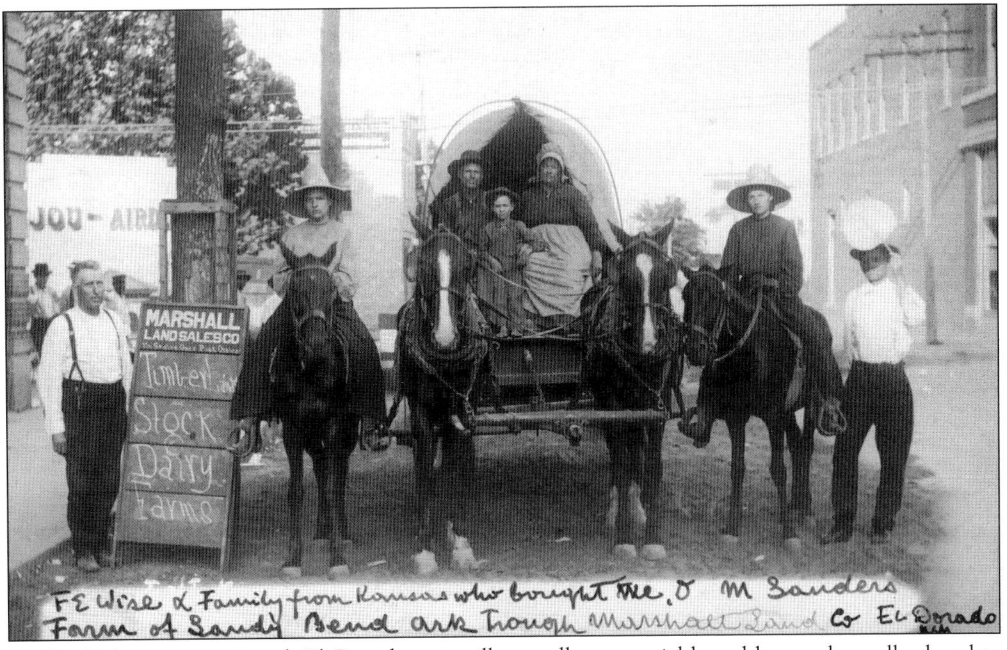

As the 20th century opened, El Dorado was still a small town neighbored by much smaller hamlets scattered across Union County. El Dorado's population in 1900 was under 2,000 and would double to 4,000 by 1910. The major industries in that year remained timber and agriculture, as had been the case for the previous 60 years. Among the new arrivals was the F.E. Wise family, who arrived in El Dorado from Kansas in a covered wagon around 1910.

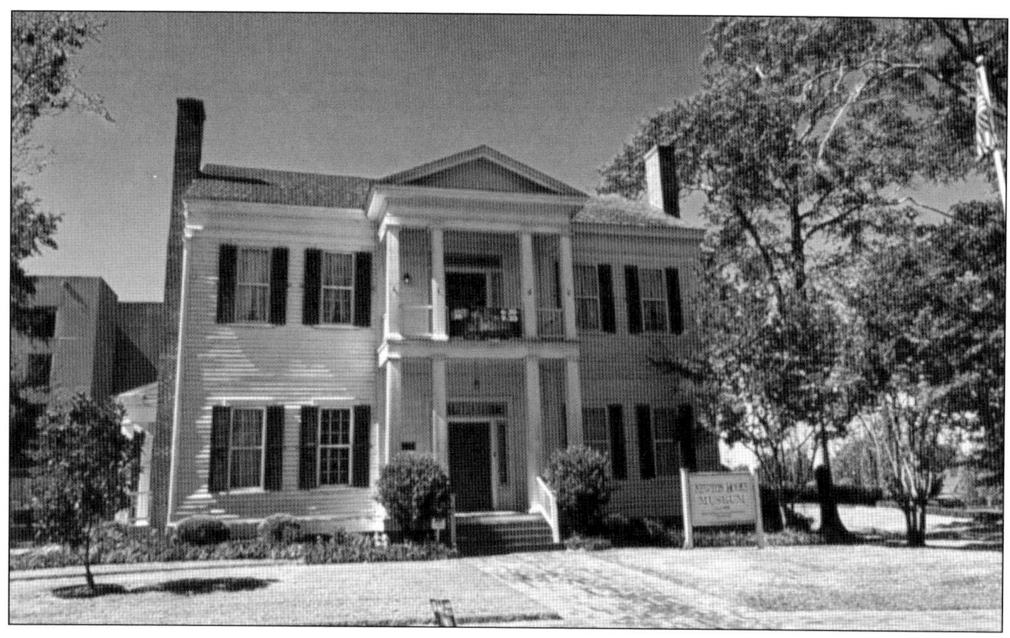

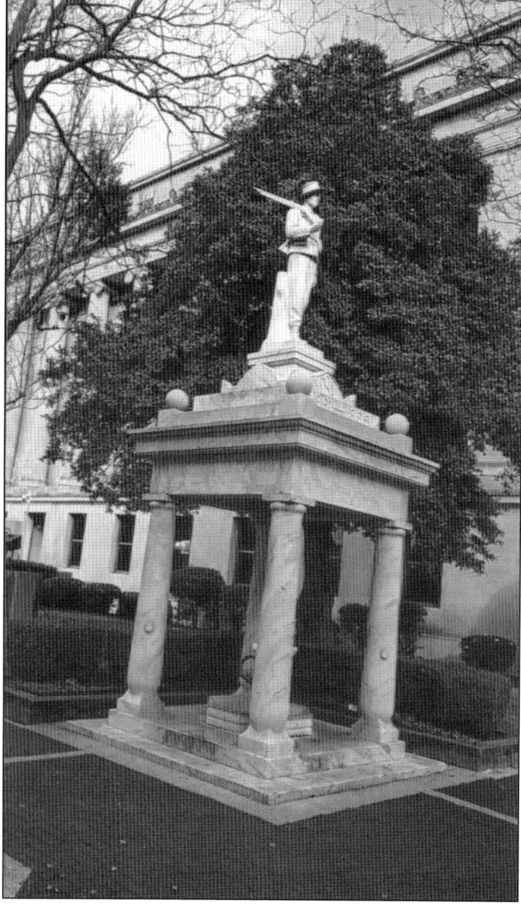

The oldest surviving home in El Dorado is the Newton House, built by the Newton family in 1849 in a Greek Revival vernacular style. It was thought that the family, while having a plantation several miles outside town, built this home in order for their children to attend schools in town. In 1910, it was moved from Peach Street to its present location on Jackson Street. Rescued from disrepair in the 1970s, it was restored and is today the Newton House Museum.

"One might as well go into a Catholic Church and holler to hell with the Pope as to say anything against the Gray in this part of the country." This was penned in 1911 on a postcard view of the Confederate monument on the courthouse lawn. The monument was erected in 1910 and funded by the local Daughters of the Confederacy chapter. A ballot proposal in 2020 to remove the monument was defeated by a large margin of Union County voters.

Among the Confederate generals from Arkansas was Albert Rust of Union County. The Virginia native arrived in the area in 1837 at age 19. In the 1850s, Rust served in the state legislature and in Congress. Rust, a vocal supporter of secession, organized the Arkansas Third Infantry and fought at the Battle of Cheat Mountain in Virginia. Promoted to brigadier general, he saw action in several states. After the war, he resumed his law practice in El Dorado; he died in 1870. (Courtesy of SAHPS.)

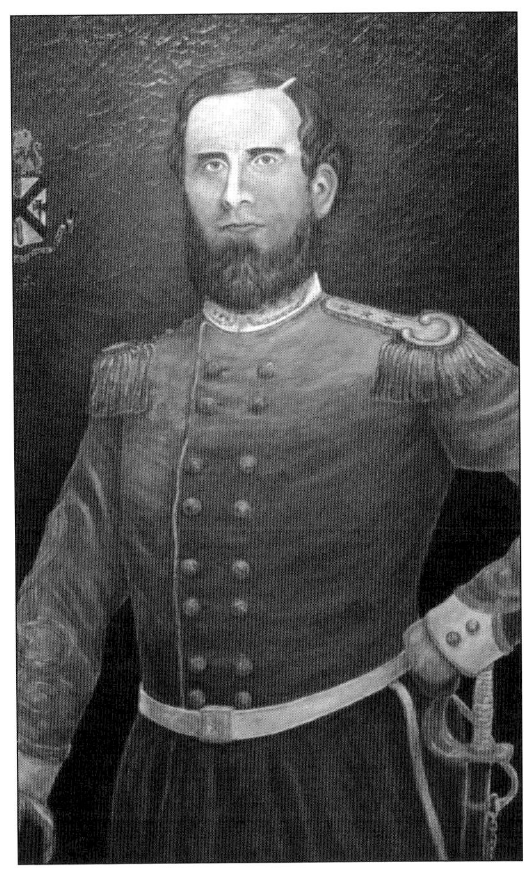

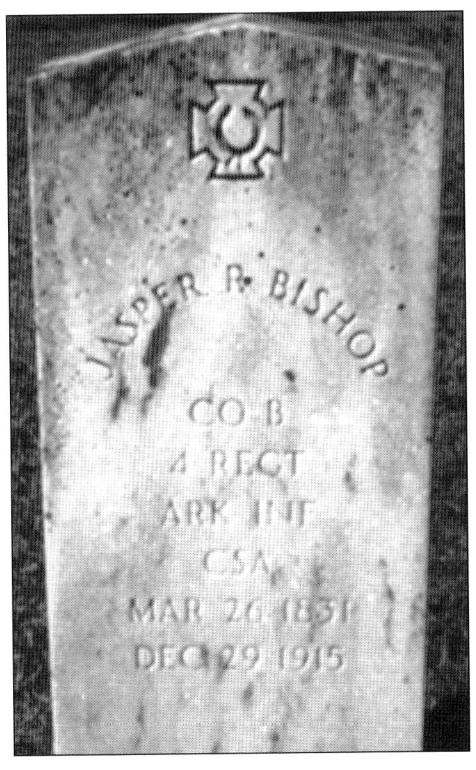

Confederate soldiers are buried across Union County. One of these, Jasper Runch Bishop, lies in the Roselawn Cemetery in Junction City, where he had enlisted at the start of the war. Among his battles had been Pea Ridge and conflicts at Camden, Arkansas. When he died in 1915 at age 84, he had been a member of the Masonic Lodge since 1857, and he also served as a justice of the peace for 50 years. (Photograph by Ray Hanley.)

One of the more storied Confederate soldiers from Union County was Col. John Crowell Wright, who was born in Georgia in 1835 and had moved with his family to Union County in 1843. At the outbreak of the Civil War, Wright joined the Confederate army. Holding the rank of colonel, he was captured at the Battle of Fort Donelson but later escaped to rejoin the Confederates. He fought in the Battle of Poison Springs and at Camden in south Arkansas. He died in 1915. (Courtesy of SAHPS.)

"Tell me all the news and especially about infantile paralysis. . . . My hands are too full to write, Amos had a spell of tonsillitis and Elizabeth has the measles." This tale of woe was penned on a postcard of the second Union County Courthouse, which was erected in 1881. The county's population was 30,000 in 1911 when the card was mailed, up from only 13,000 when the courthouse had been built.

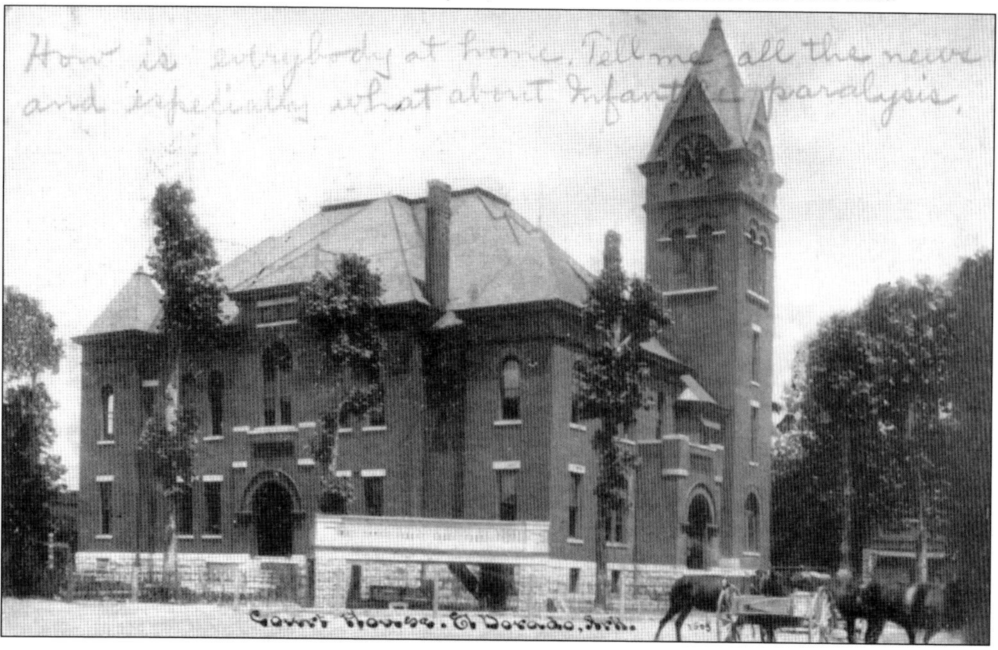

The deadliest happenings in peacetime Arkansas took place on the El Dorado town square in the summer of 1902. Town marshal Guy B. Tucker was at the center of a deadly feud that lasted three years; the Tucker-Parnell feud reportedly saw at least a dozen killed by the time it ended in 1905. Marshal Tucker is pictured here; his arm is missing, from being ambushed and shot several times after the start of the feud. The marshal was the grandfather of Jim Guy Tucker, governor of Arkansas in the 1990s. (Courtesy of SAHPS.)

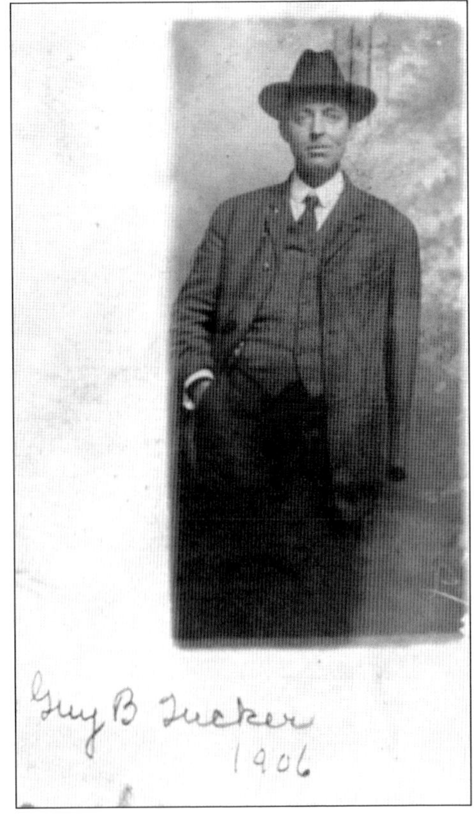

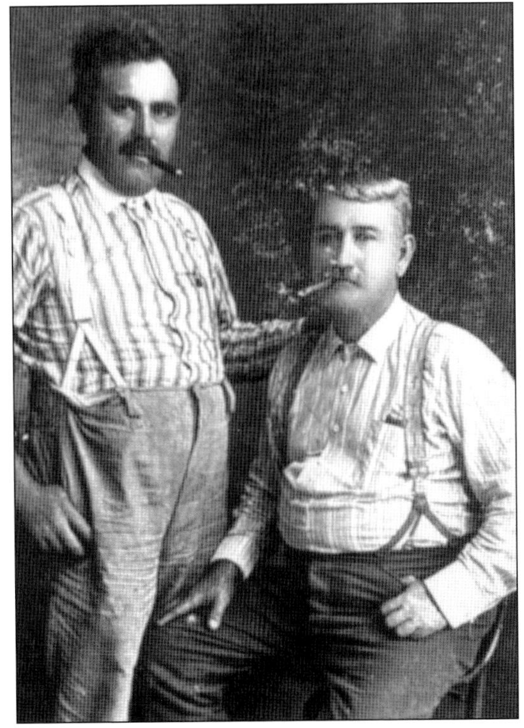

Before Marshal Tucker got into a gun battle, the genesis of conflict was a fight over a woman. William Puckett arrived from Texarkana intent on marrying Jessie Stephenson, who worked in the photography studio of Bob Mullens. The photographer (who had his own romantic designs on the young lady) confronted Puckett and ordered him to leave El Dorado. Bob Mullens is pictured to the left, posed with his friend Tom Parnell. (Courtesy of SAHPS.)

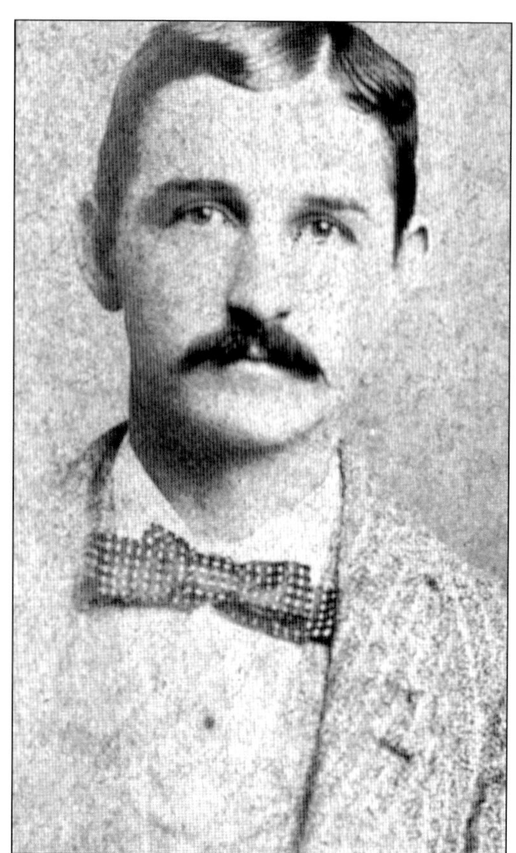

Pictured here, Harrison Dearing was a town constable who had arrested Bob Mullens over the altercation with William Puckett. After Mullens was released from jail, he accosted Constable Dearing on the street, slapping him on the face. Dearing immediately pulled his pistol and shot Mullens dead. (Courtesy of SAHPS.)

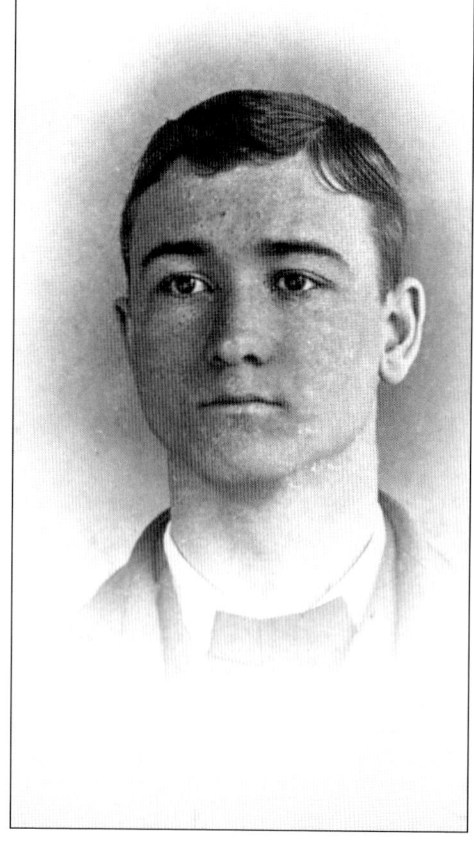

In a fury over the death of their friend Bob Mullens, Tom Parnell's family sought revenge. On October 9, 1902, heated words were exchanged with both Marshal Tucker and Constable Dearing. Marshal Tucker approached the Parnells with gun drawn, and when the smoke cleared, three men lay dead: Constable Dearing, Tom Parnell, and his brother Walter (pictured). The wounded included Marshal Tucker, Dr. Robert Hilton, and Matt Parnell. (Courtesy of SAHPS.)

At age 31, Irene Dearing became a widow when her husband, Constable Harrison Dearing, age 40, died in the shoot-out on the El Dorado square. Irene outlived her husband by 11 years, dying in 1913. (Courtesy of SAHPS.)

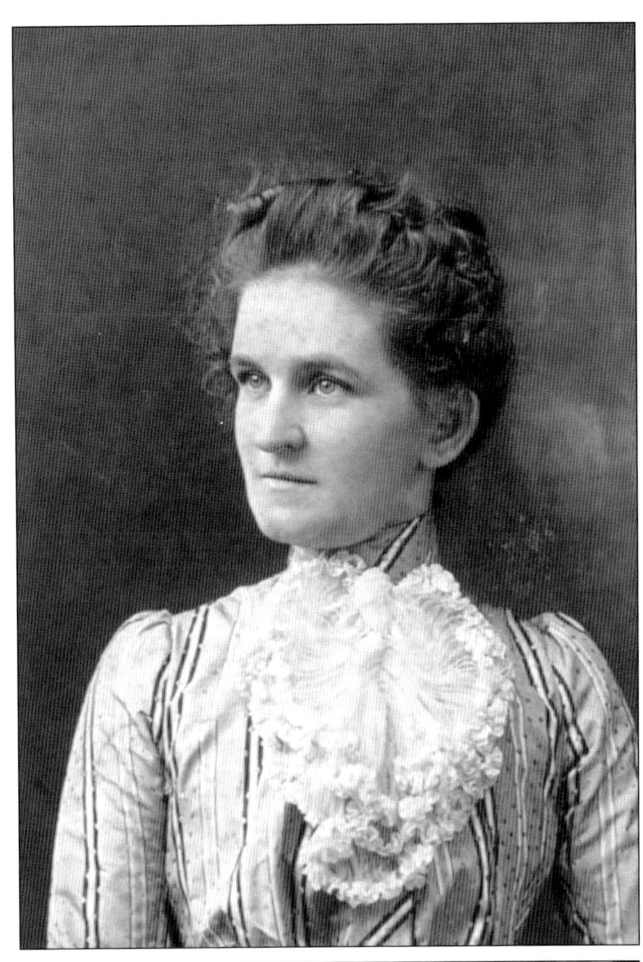

The Tucker-Parnell feud carried over into 1903, with attacks visited upon supporters of each side. In August, someone sent Marshal Guy Tucker a jug of strychnine-laced whiskey, and the Parnells were suspected. Five days later, Tucker confronted John Parnell (pictured) on the courthouse square, in part over a letter Parnell sent the local newspaper attacking Tucker. The marshal pulled his pistol and shot John Parnell dead. Tucker survived all his wounds and died of a heart attack in 1924. (Courtesy of SAHPS.)

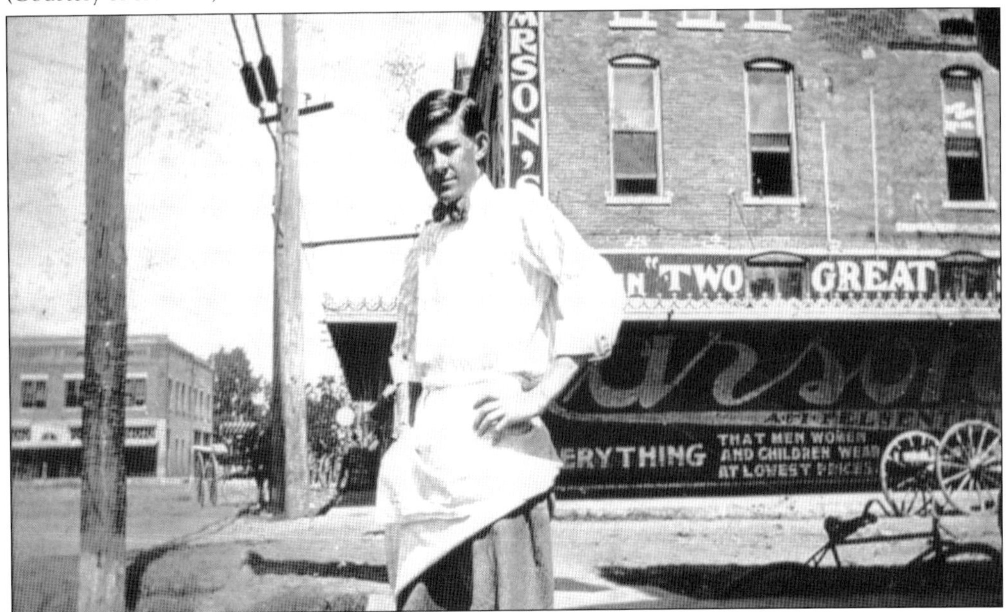

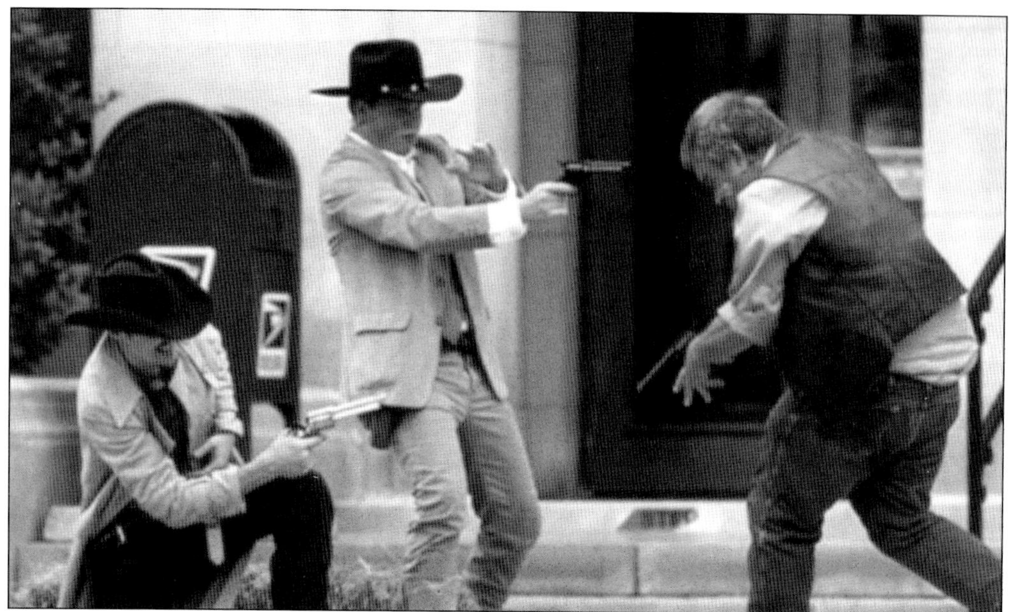

In recent years, El Dorado has reenacted the shoot-out on the square, to the delight of residents and visitors alike as they come to see the living history. "Shootout at Sundown" has long been a Saturday evening event during the summer in El Dorado. It was declared by the American Bus Association a "Top 100 Event to Attend." (Courtesy of SAHPS.)

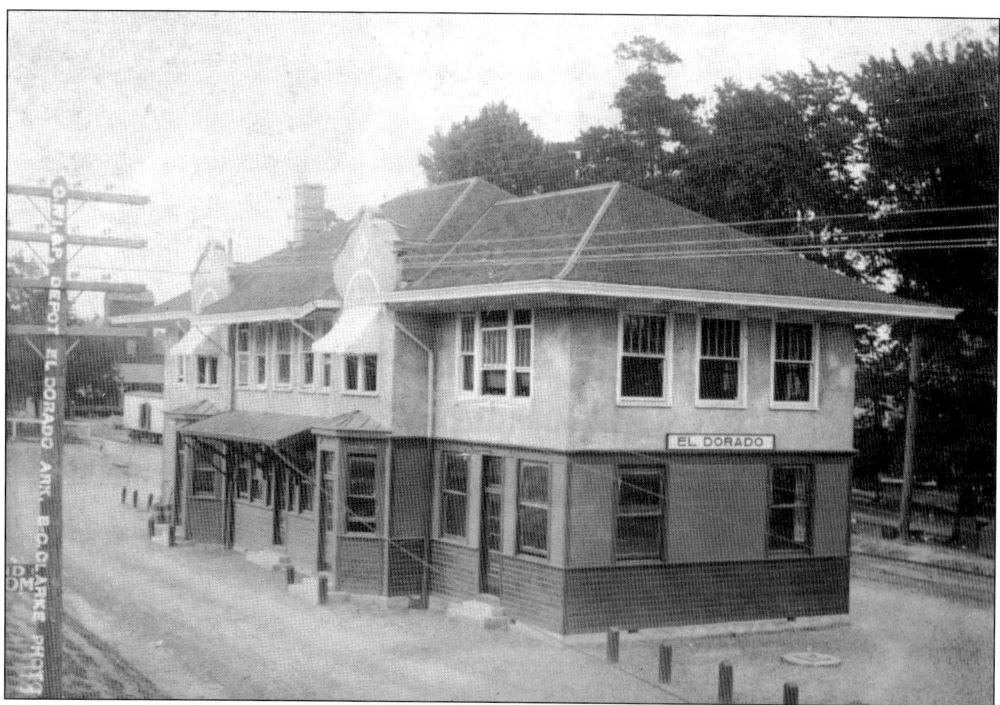

A two-story train depot was built in El Dorado in the 1900s to serve the Chicago, Rock Island & Pacific Railroad. It was a hub for the shipping of lumber and cotton, and it later served the oil boom. Sadly, it was razed decades ago.

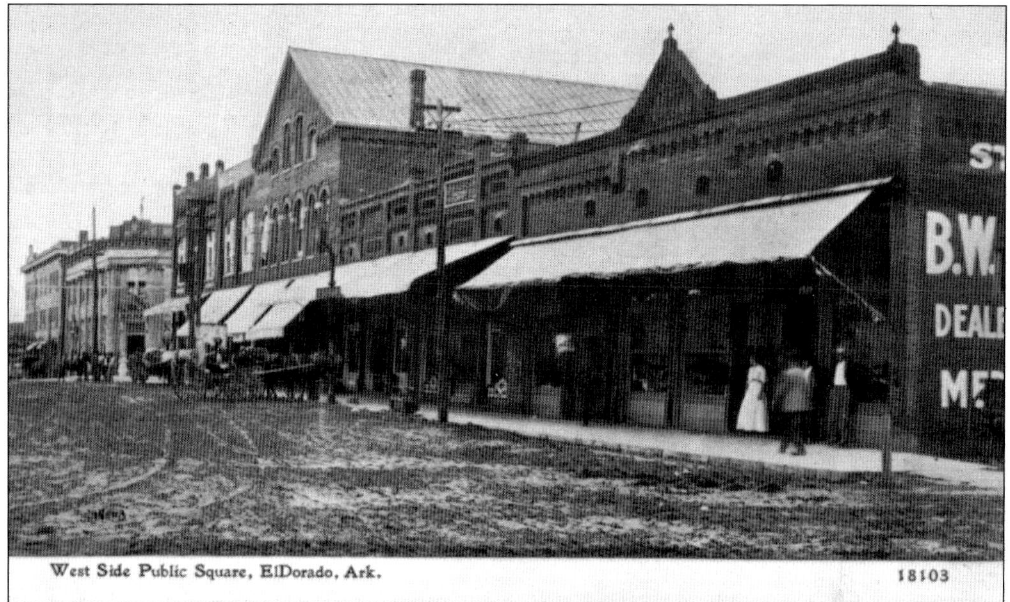

West Side Public Square, ElDorado, Ark. 18103

The 1910 census put the population of El Dorado at 4,200, but the town was growing along its dirt streets of brick buildings that clustered around the courthouse square. Many of the residents of Union County shopped at B.W. Reeves's department store, labeled on its side as seen in the above view of the west side of the square. Blewmer White "B.W." Reeves was born in 1848 in El Dorado, where he lived and prospered, eventually owning a large farm outside of town that supported his family of seven children. Reeves was drawn back into town to found a department store that made him perhaps the best-known merchant in south Arkansas. He even served as the town's mayor for a time. He built this handsome home on Washington Avenue (below), though it was razed some years back. Reeves died in 1924, but his family kept the business going for decades more.

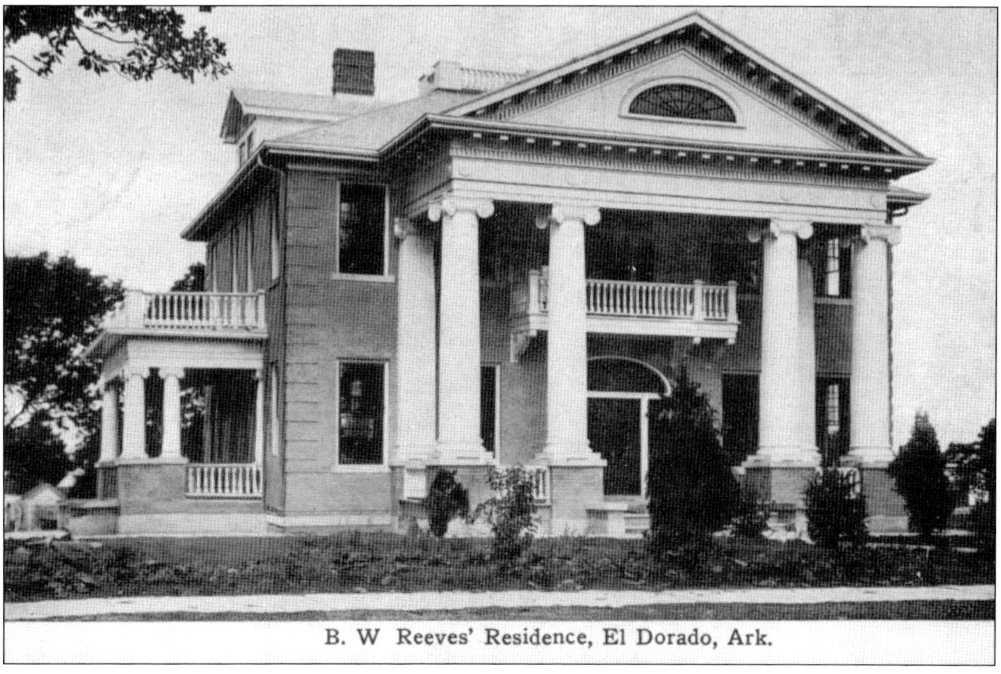

B. W Reeves' Residence, El Dorado, Ark.

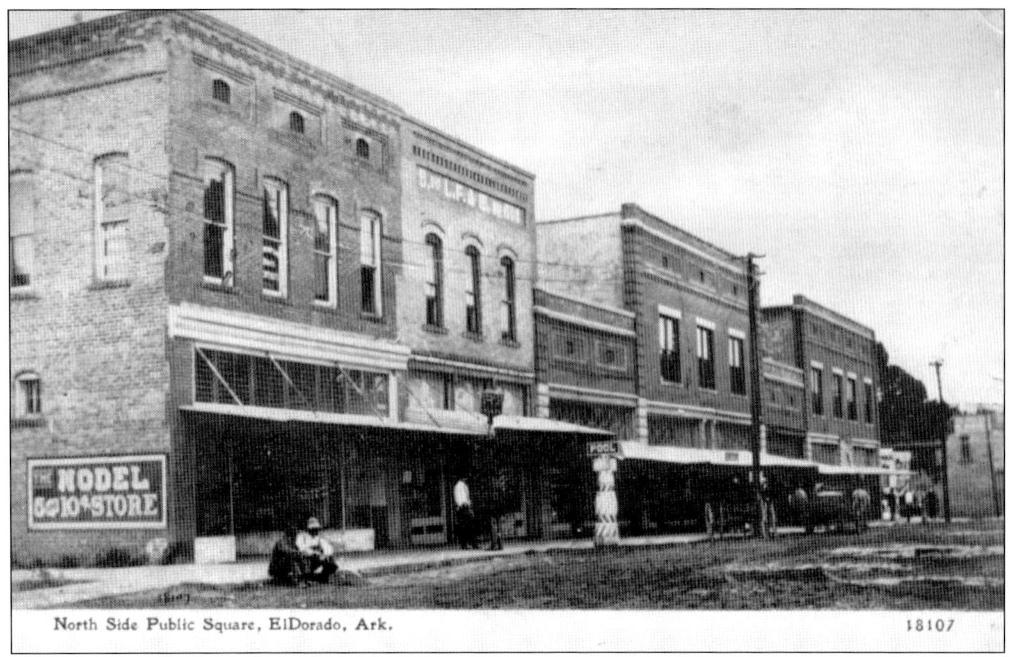

Postcard photographs taken around the square of the then small town of El Dorado were sent far and wide. This view of the north side of the square was captured around 1908. The Model 5&10¢ Store occupied the end of the block, with a pool hall in the middle. The 2024 photograph below reflects the remarkable revival of downtown El Dorado over the past couple of decades, with the entire block seemingly intact, restored, and repurposed. (Below, photograph by Ray Hanley.)

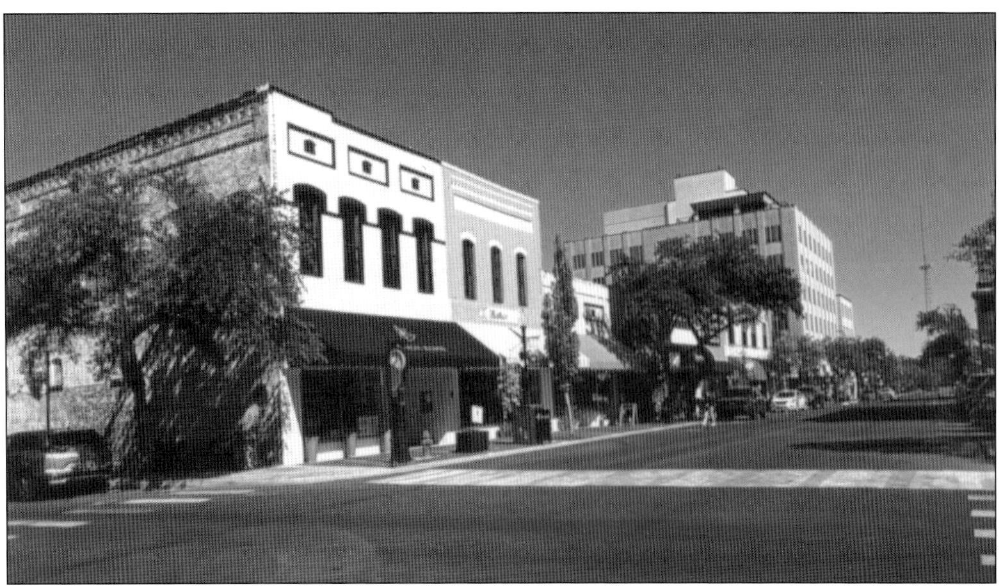

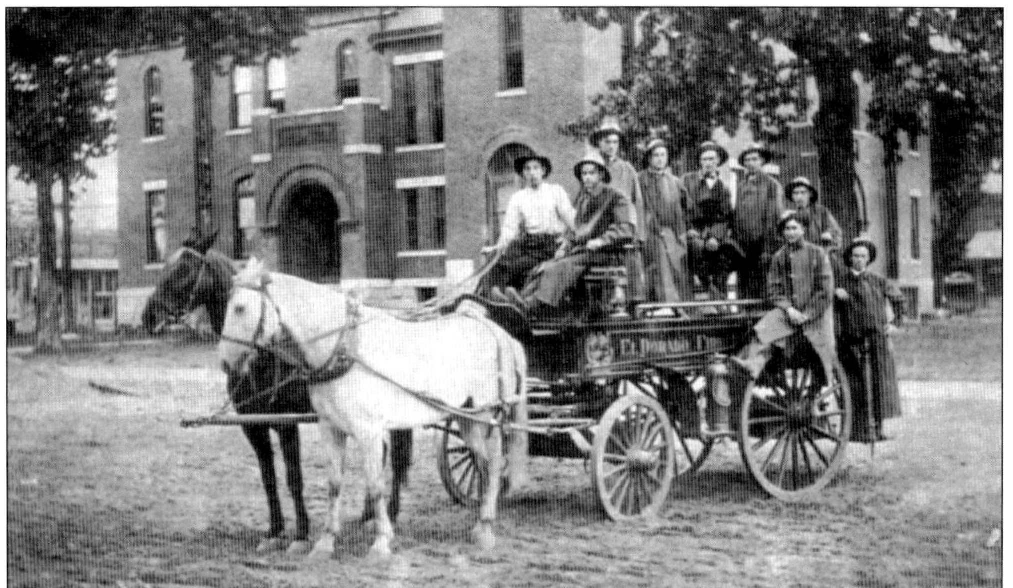

As El Dorado grew in the early 1900s, fire was a threat, even to the expanding number of brick buildings. The town's fire protection, seen here around 1905, consisted of the horse-drawn fire wagon posed on the courthouse lawn. The first motor-powered fire trucks rolled out within a few short years. (Courtesy of SAHPS.)

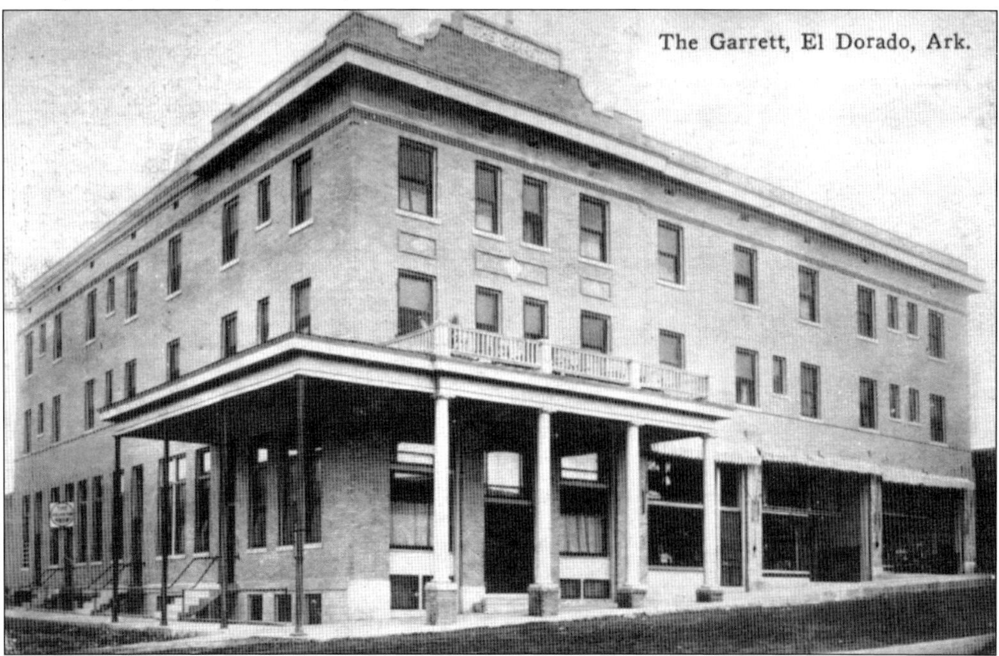

Rufus Napoleon Garrett was born of humble means in 1858 in Clark County. By the time he arrived in Union County, he had started the South Arkansas Lumber Company and the Arkansas Southern Railroad. Garrett started the First National Bank and served as its president for 14 years. In 1910, at a cost of $18,000, he opened the Garrett Hotel, which, for years, offered the finest accommodations in town. The Garrett was eventually razed; the site today is occupied by the Haywood Hotel.

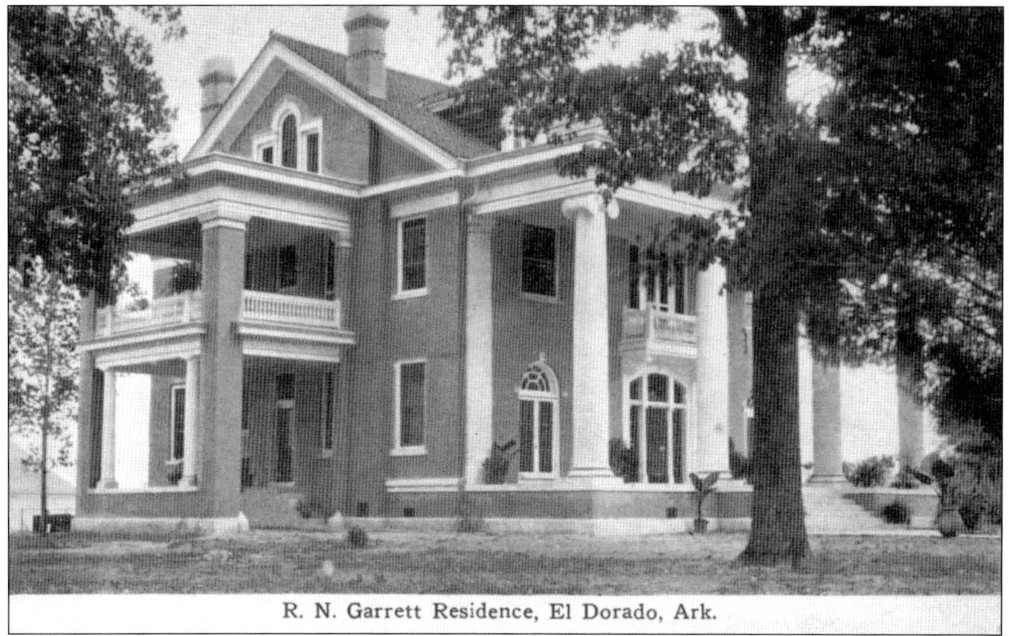

R. N. Garrett Residence, El Dorado, Ark.

R.N. Garrett built a fine home on the corner of Peach Street and Jefferson Avenue. Garrett died in 1943, by which time his son Napoleon Garrett Jr. was in the US Army fighting in Europe. The young man was killed on D-Day in 1944 on the beaches of Normandy. The Garrett family home was razed years ago.

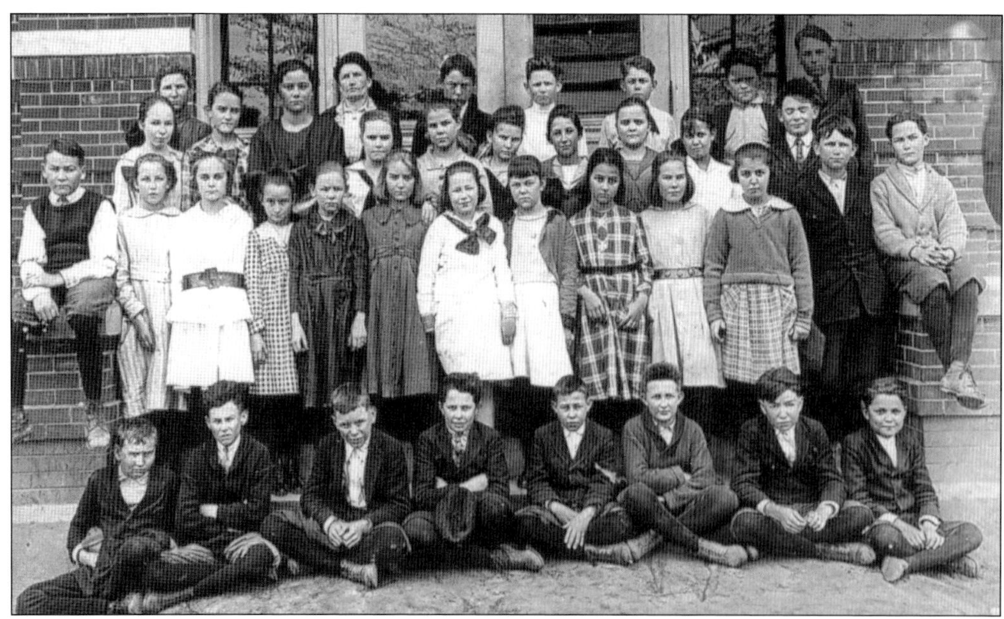

Yocum Public School in El Dorado posed a group of its students around 1910. At the time, Arkansas supplied $12 per student per year to school districts, in an era when the average teacher's salary was less than $300 a year. More than a century later, Yocum School still operates, though serving only kindergarten-fourth grade. (Courtesy of SAHPS.)

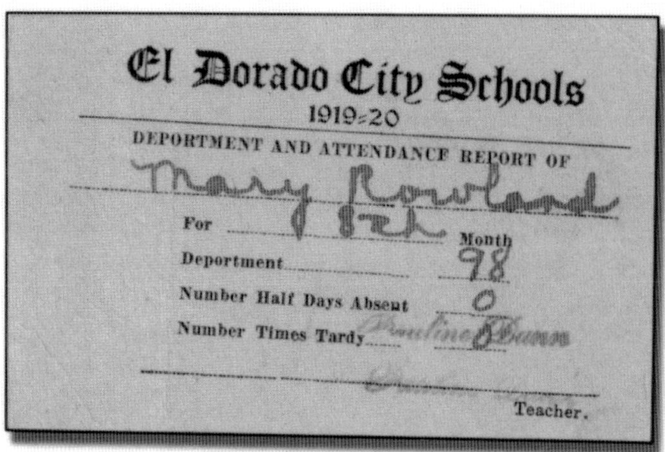

El Dorado City Schools
1919-20

DEPORTMENT AND ATTENDANCE REPORT OF Mary Rowland

For 8th Month

Deportment 98

Number Half Days Absent 0

Number Times Tardy 0

Pauline Bunn

Teacher.

TO THE PARENT OR GUARDIAN:

Please examine, sign, and have this card returned as soon as possible for registration.

A WHITE card indicates EXCELLENCE
A GREEN card indicates GOOD WORK
A BLUE card indicates AVERAGE WORK
A RED card indicates INFERIOR WORK
A YELLOW card indicates NON-ACCREDITED WORK

Supt.

J A Rowland
Parent's Own Signature

TO THE PARENT OR GUARDIAN:

Our school desires to emphasize the importance of regularity and punctuality in attendance, and the best deportment. May we not co-operate in securing this end?

DONALD MACQUEEN
Supt.

J A Rowland
Parent's Own Signature

The report card system was structured for discipline in 1919–1920. Mary Rowland's report card of her studies in the eighth grade showed that she did well, based on the color of her card. The cards were color-coordinated, based on performance; Rowland's card was white for excellent. The parents had to sign a bit of a contract on the card, pledging to instill "regularity and punctuality" in attendance.

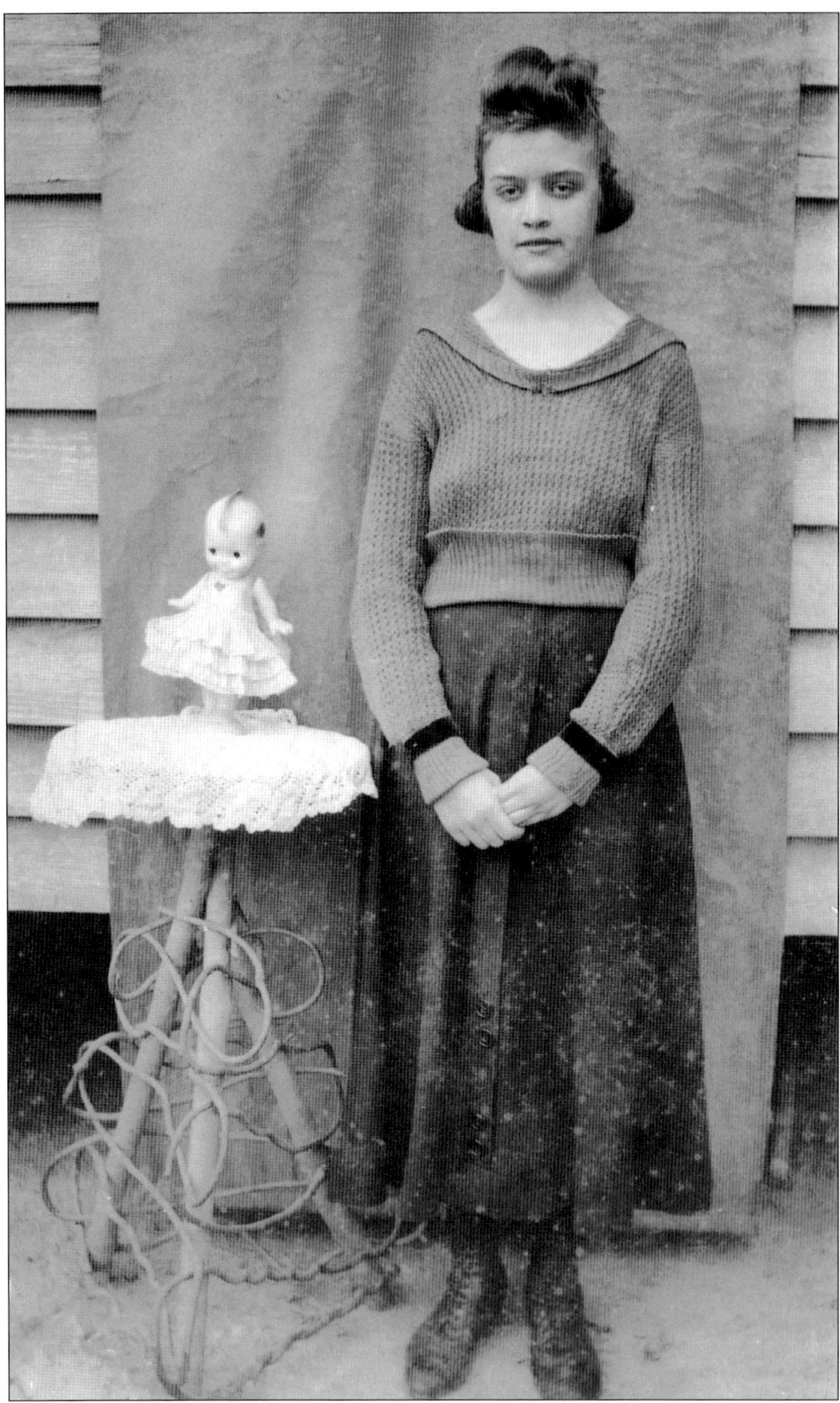

Around 1915, one of the students in El Dorado was a young lady named Annie Martin, who looked to be perhaps 12 or 13 years old in this photograph. Martin posed in the yard of her home with a Kewpie doll displayed on a wicker table. The average school year in Arkansas at the time was about 110 days.

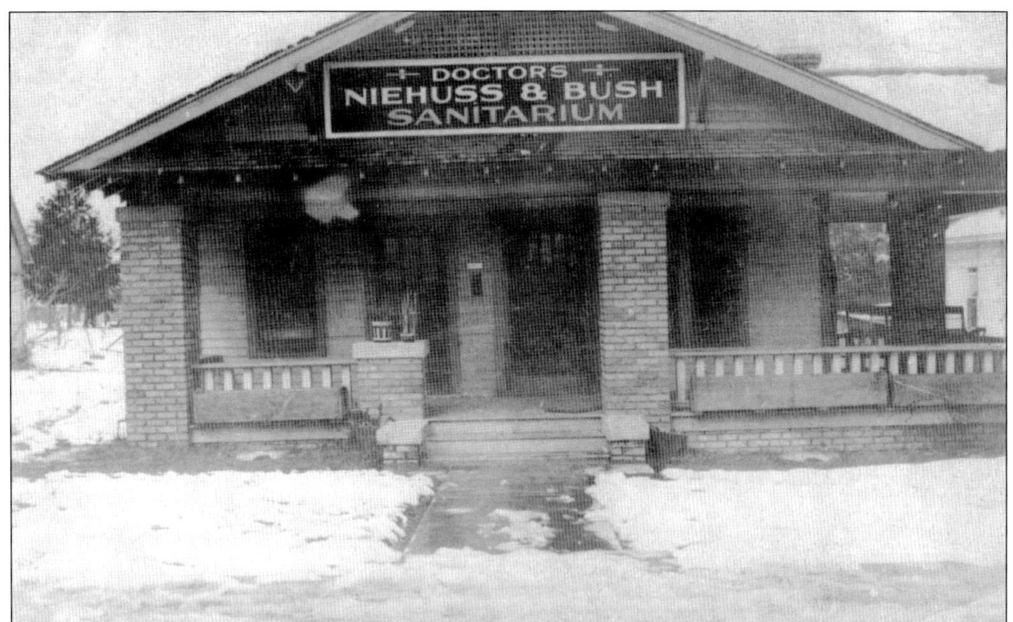

Drs. Henry Niehuss and Thomas Bush opened their sanitarium on College Avenue in 1923. Essentially, the converted house was a clinic with a few hospital beds added. Dr. Niehuss supported his adopted city in a variety of ways, including being a charter member and president of the El Dorado Rotary Club. He died in 1961 in Texas.

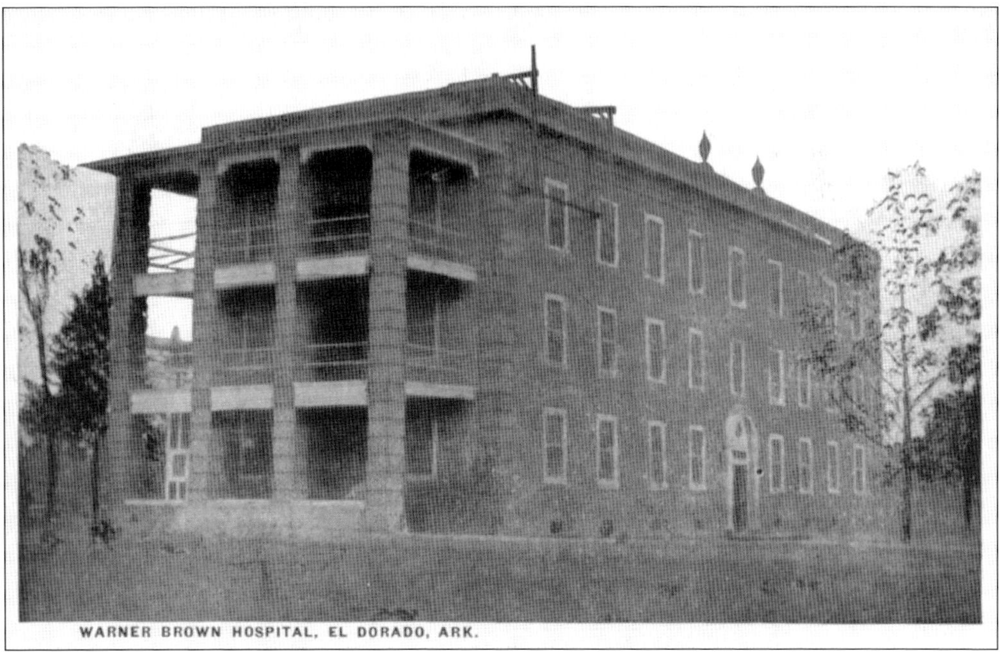

The growing city of El Dorado needed a proper hospital, and in 1919, work began on the Warner Brown Hospital. The facility was funded by local businessman Paul Brown, who named it after his father who had died in 1858. The doors opened in 1921 with 68 beds and a staff of 10. The Sisters of Mercy took over the hospital in 1927, and in 1954, a large modern annex was built. The buildings still stand today, while the city has a more modern hospital in another location.

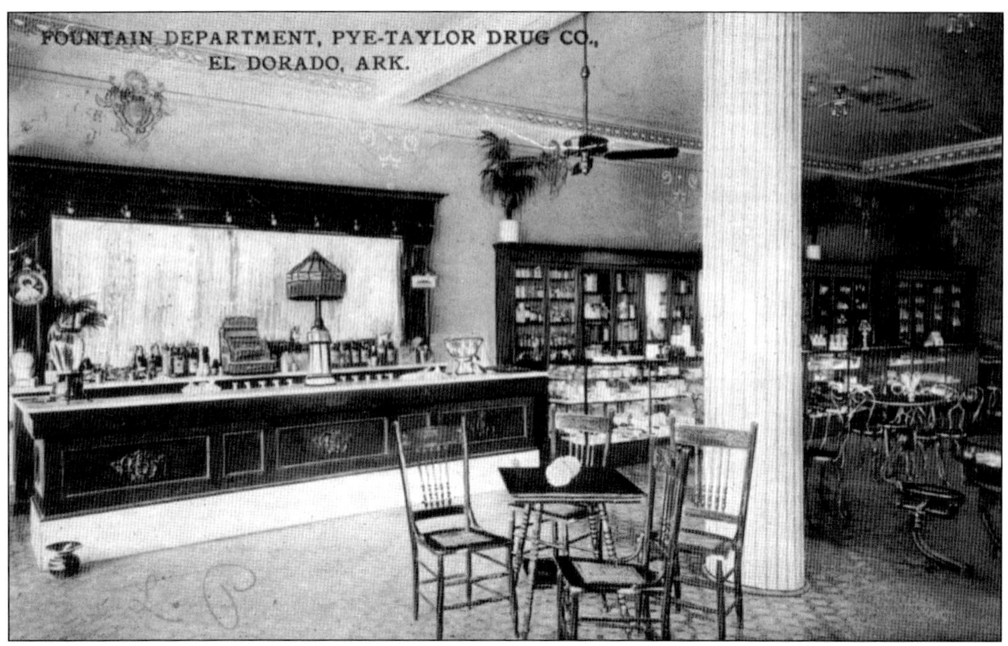

People in need of a prescription medicine compounded by a pharmacist might have visited the Pye-Talyor Drug Company on the courthouse square. Ice cream sodas were another option available at the store's soda fountain, as seen here. Tobacco chewers would have used the spittoon seen to the left. The store is gone today but the actual soda fountain, in storage for now, belongs to the South Arkansas Historic Preservation Society.

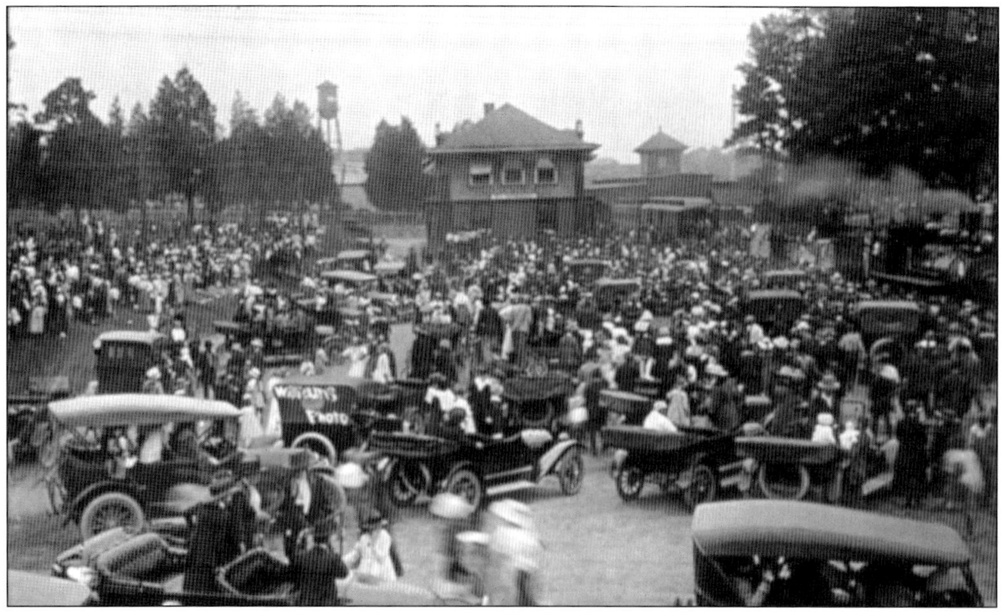

El Dorado had sent its share of young men, both enlisted and draftees, off to fight in World War I. Most would make it back home, and in 1919, the town turned out at the Rock Island depot to meet the returning troop trains. One local man died in battle; Roy Kinard's name appears on the war memorial to the lost, which stands on the courthouse lawn. (Courtesy of SAHPS.)

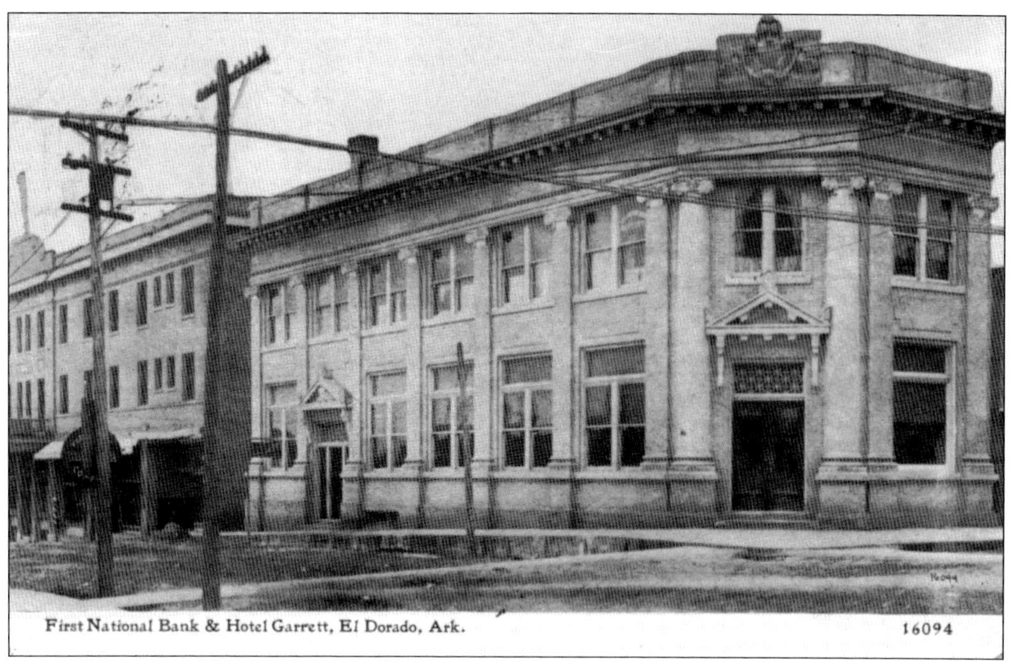

Rufus Garrett owned the Garrett Hotel (at left, above), but he was also president of the stately First National Bank (at right, above) that he had helped organize. As seen below, a long line of marble-fronted teller windows ran the length of the building. Each window provided tobacco-chewing customers with a spittoon on the floor, which presumably an employee had to empty and clean each day. Like the hotel, the bank building is gone today.

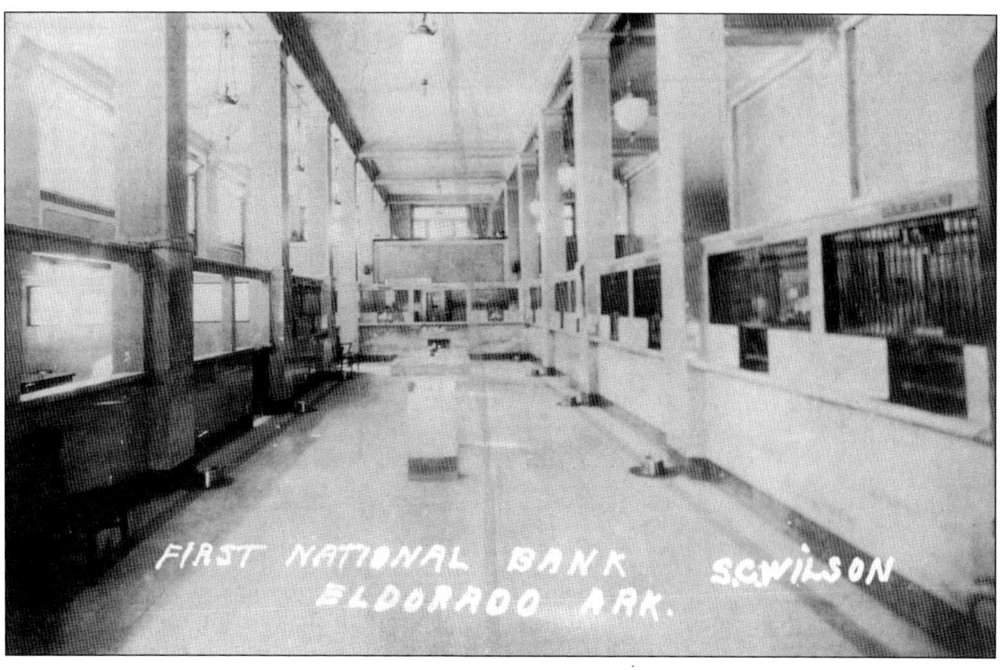

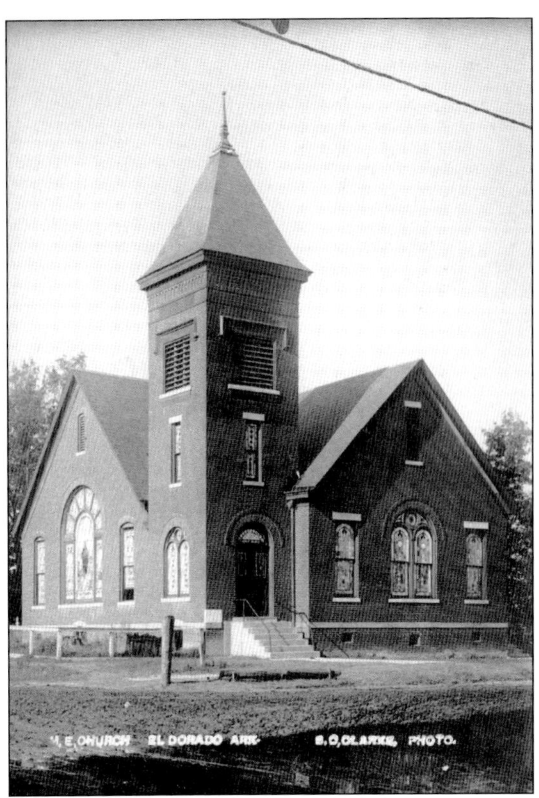

The establishment of churches in El Dorado came early, constructed by those families immigrating to Union County. The first Methodist church was a log structure; the pictured brick building was built in 1901 on South Hillsboro Street. It provided adequate space for its congregation until the oil boom of 1921.

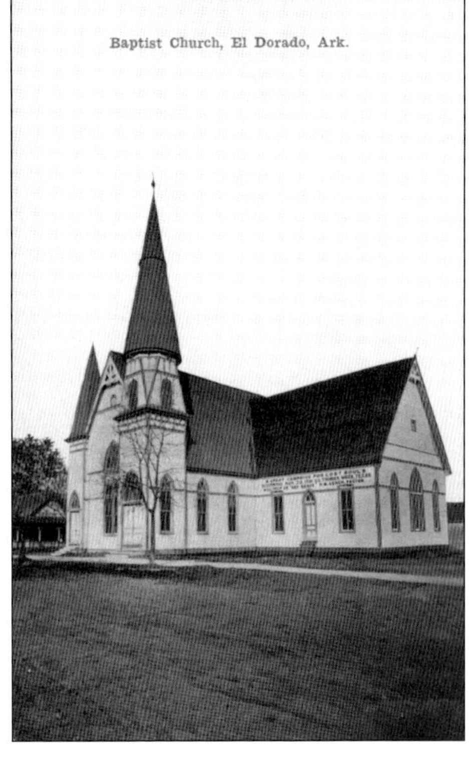

In small-town Arkansas, wherever there was a Methodist church, there always seemed to also be at least one church of the Baptist faith. The town's first Baptist church went up in 1845, served by itinerant preachers. In 1894, the congregation acquired property along East Main Street and built this 50-by-80-foot building complete with stained-glass windows, factory-made pews, and a pedal organ. The church was replaced in the 1920s.

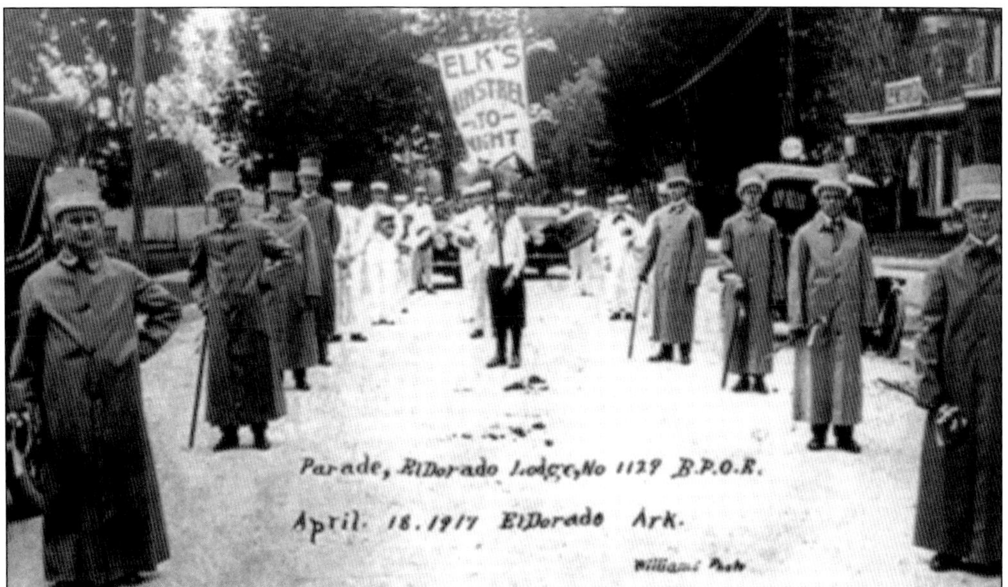

The Benevolent and Protective Order of the Elks was a fraternal organization formed in New York in 1868. Chapters of the Elks soon spread nationwide, including to El Dorado. The pictured parade was to promote a minstrel show set for that evening; such shows sometimes involved White men performing in blackface.

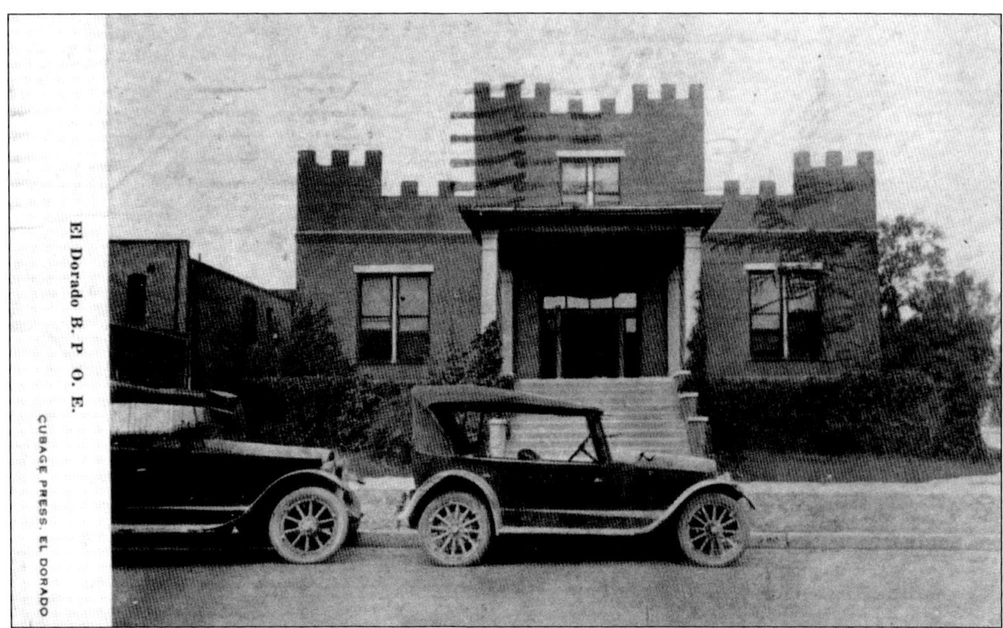

When the Elks were not parading, they might have been found in their local lodge, as seen here. The pictured lodge with its striking roofline has been gone for decades, though the fraternal group has carried on. Its headquarters is situated on East Nineteenth Street today.

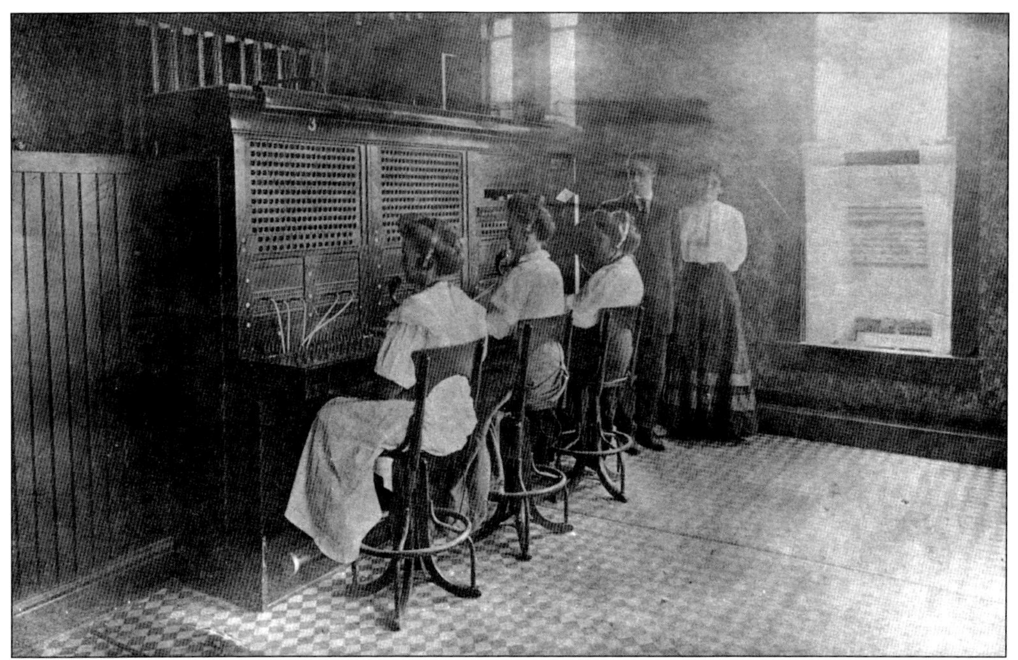

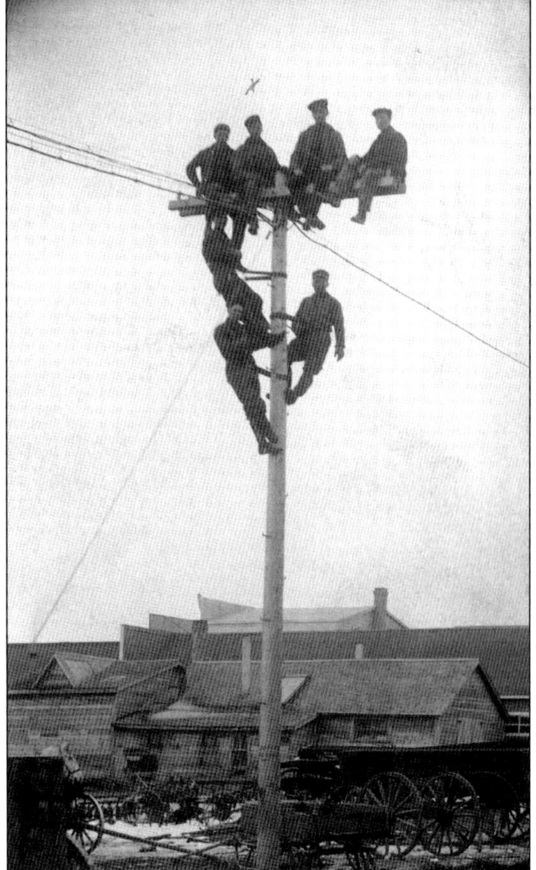

By 1912, the little town of El Dorado had telephone service, staffed by a cadre of ladies who operated the switchboards. The message penned on the back of this postcard sent to Little Rock reads, "Hello Leah. I am the 'boss' of this little out-fit. How do you like it? Bama."

El Dorado's phone service was made possible by the line crews who worked out in the weather, putting up poles and stringing wire. A lot of people outside the city did not yet have telephones, but the work of linemen, like the ones shown here around 1910, gradually pushed the reach of instant communication out into rural Union County.

Two

Black Gold Changes El Dorado Forever

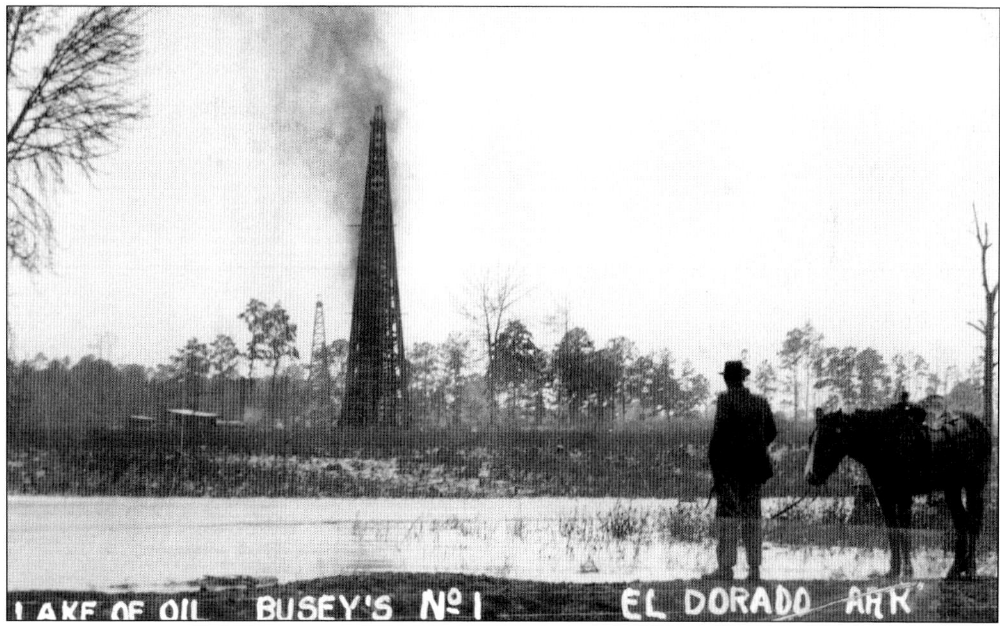

By 1921, years of frustration had taken their toll on the hopes and fortunes of Arkansas wildcatters, as oil was often struck in neighboring Louisiana and Texas. With the exception of gas discoveries and a few small oil wells, only dry holes appeared across Union County. Dr. Samuel Busey, who was neither a physician nor the geologist he claimed to be, sought to capitalize on this opportunity. For a 51 percent take of other people's money, Busey paid to finish a well outside El Dorado that had halted at 900 feet. On January 10, 1921, at a depth of 2,223 feet, the ground shook, and a gusher of black gold shot into the air. Within six months, there were more than 100 active wells in the area, changing Union County for the next century and beyond.

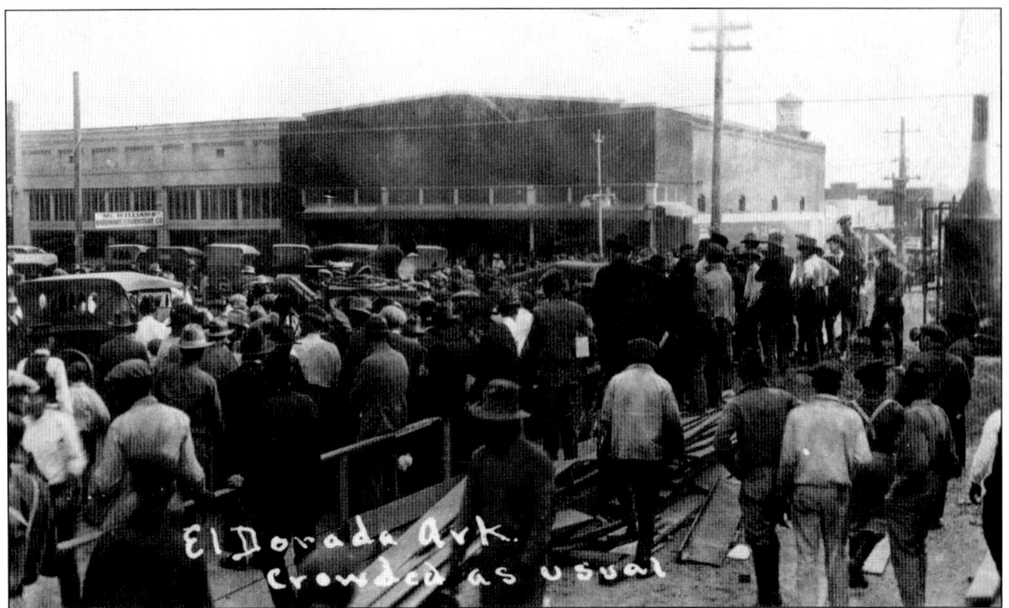

"This is the way the streets are here all the time and nearly impossible to get a place to stay." The notation on this postcard, sent after the 1921 oil boom began, tells the story. In a few short weeks, El Dorado had jumped from a population of 4,000 to an estimated 15,000, and more were pouring in daily with every train. At the height of the oil boom, some 40,000 people were in the area seeking their fortunes.

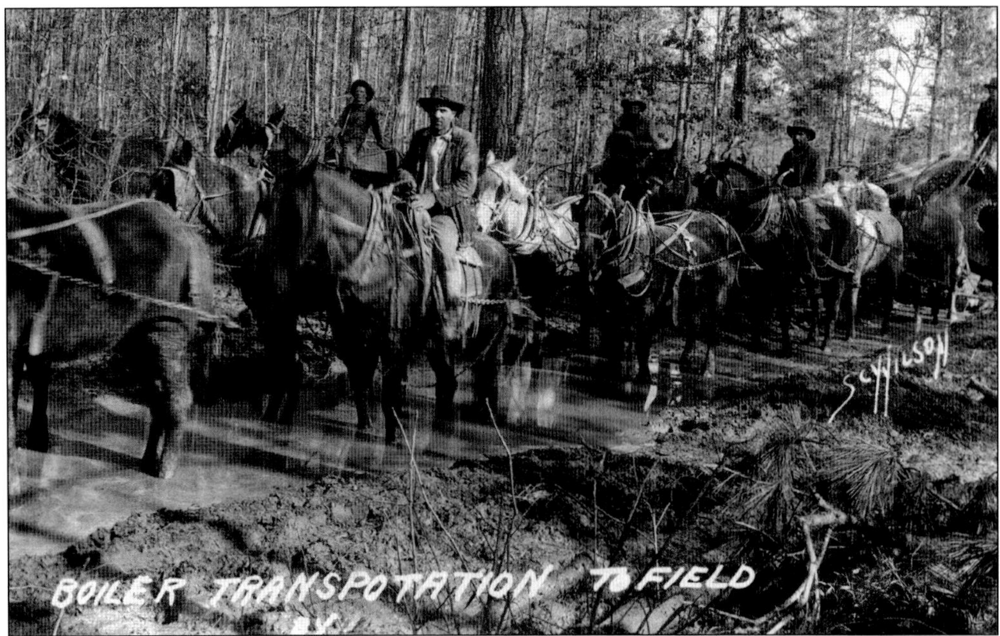

The roads around El Dorado were only rutted dirt wagon paths, far from ready to handle the flood of traffic hauling equipment for the oil fields. Hundreds of mules and oxen were brought in to navigate the muddy roads and fields, pulling freight wagons little different than those used on the American frontier in the prior century.

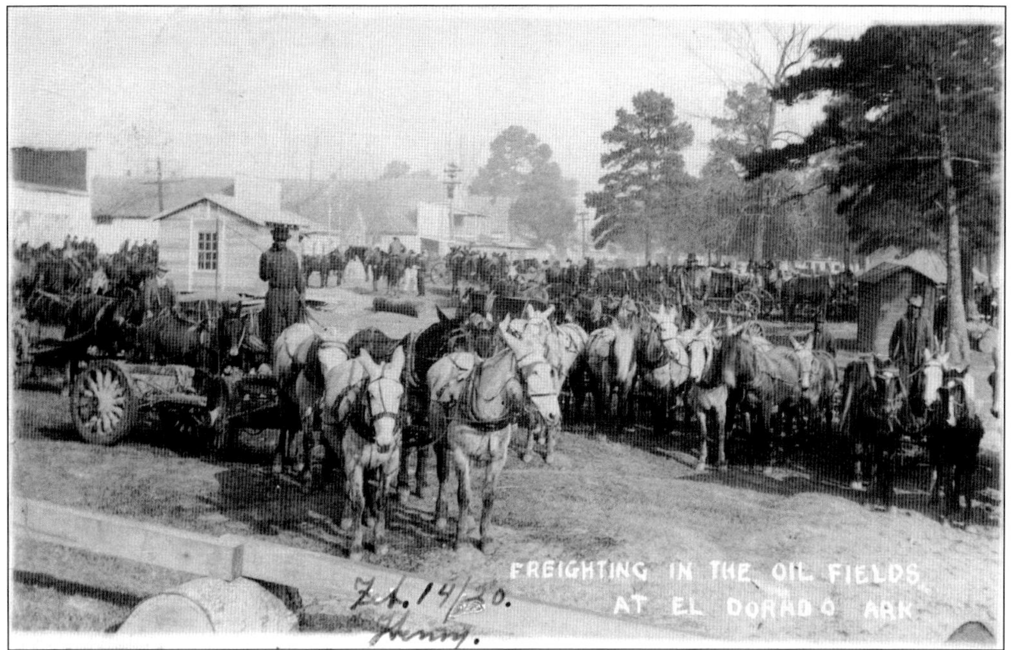

"Freighting in the oil fields" labeled a postcard mailed in 1921, which gave a look out over a sea of mules. It took hundreds of strong teamsters to manage and drive the mules, horses, and oxen that pulled the heavy equipment from the train depot to the oil fields.

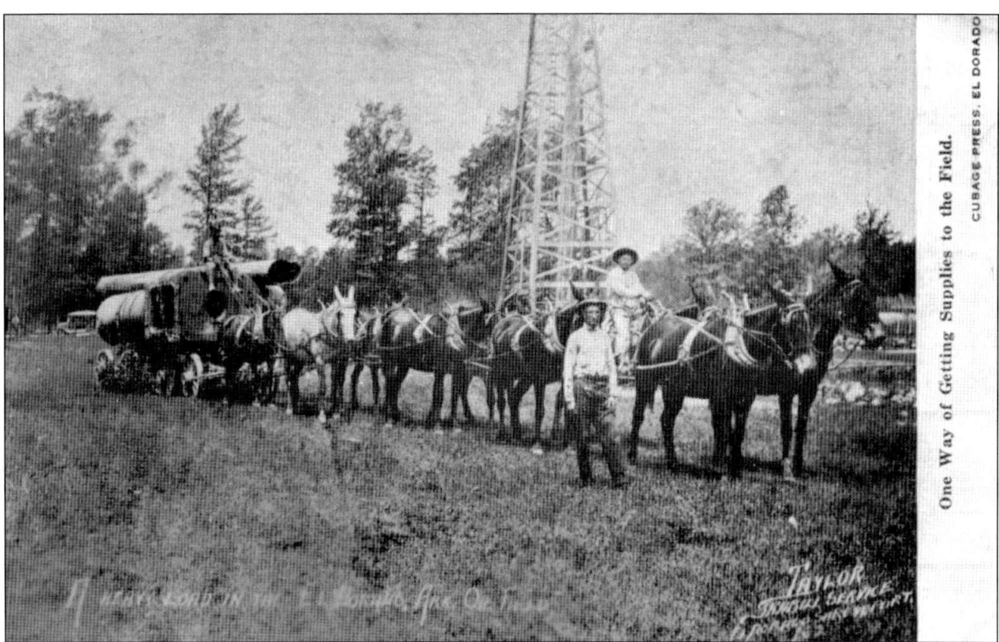

"One way of getting supplies to the field," read the card. It took a team of 10 powerful mules to pull the pipes and other supplies to the drill sites in the woods and fields that surrounded El Dorado.

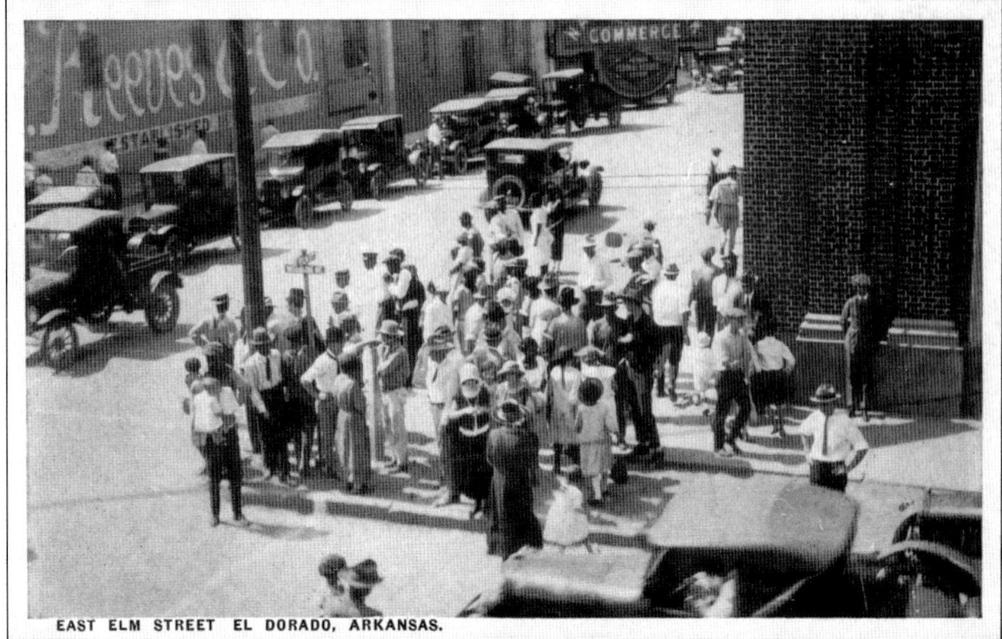

In the early 1920s, not only the streets were crowded with an influx of automobiles, but the sidewalks were full as well. Above, on the corner of Elm Street and Washington Avenue, around 40 pedestrians were preparing to cross the intersection, as a long line of mostly Model T cars moved slowly past.

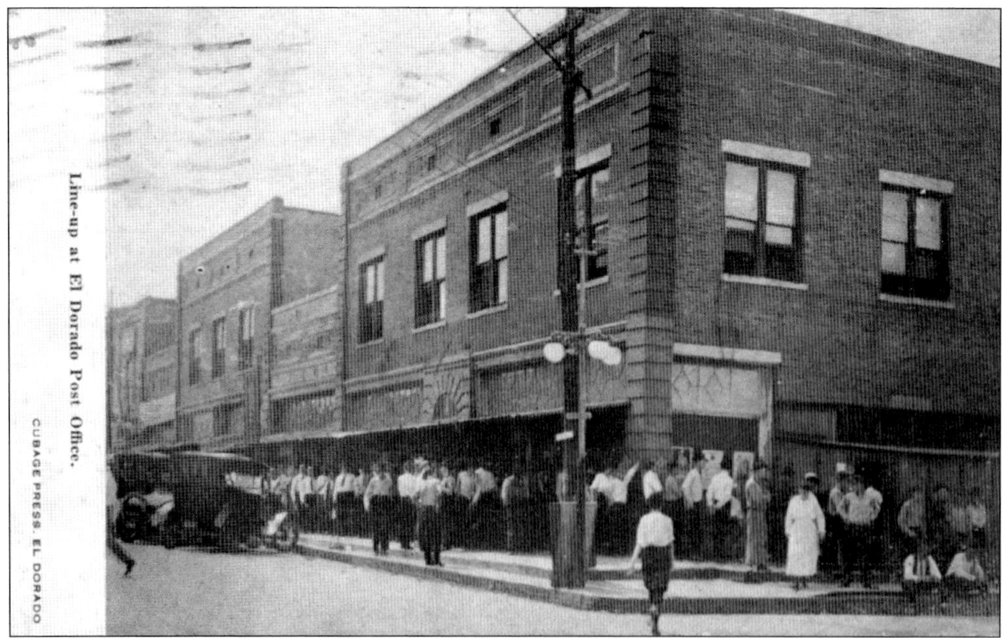

"My darling little wife, we got here last eve, went out to Smackover, there is a lot of work here." J.M. Chumley wrote this note to his wife in Bivins, Texas. The postcard view captured the crowd lined up to get into the post office, which had not been built or staffed to handle the thousands of postal patrons who had flooded into town.

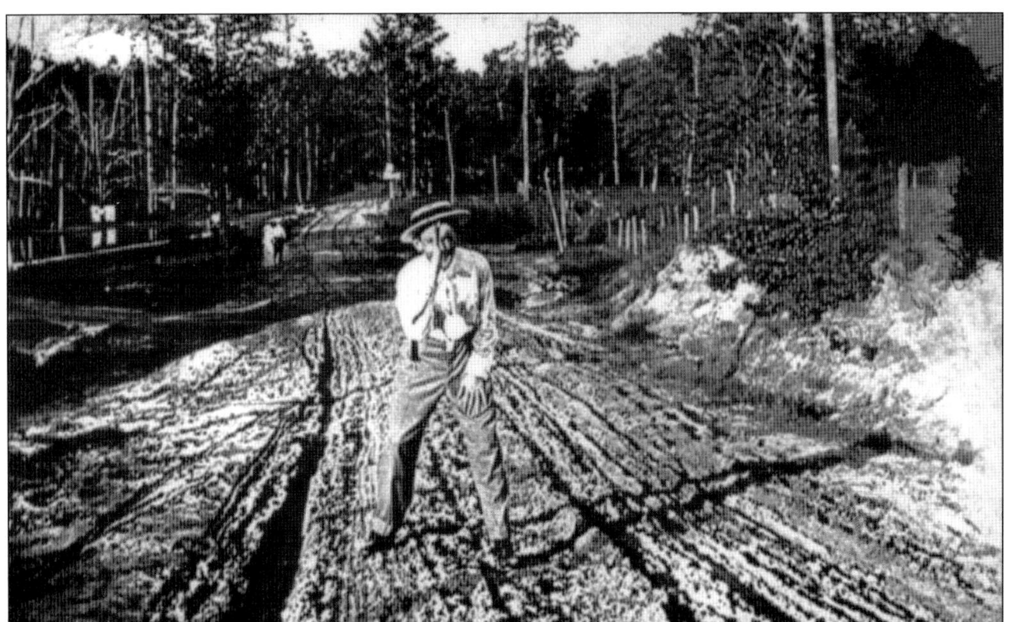

Even where roads existed, as seen here, those roads became a quagmire after every rain. This young man was apparently trying to help someone find the best path in the muddy rutted lane. (Courtesy of SAHPS.)

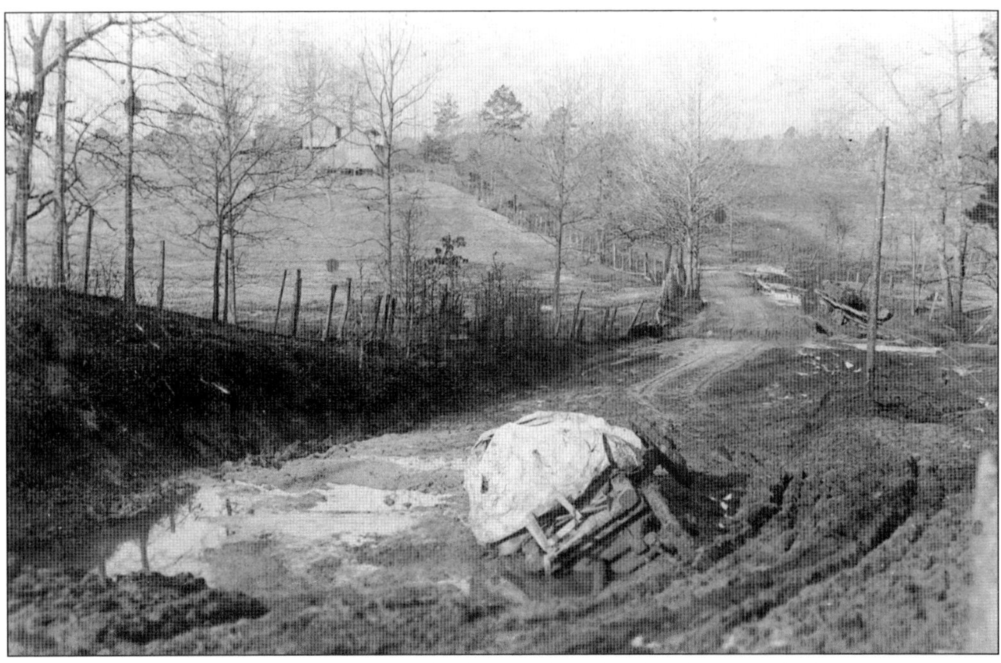

Sometimes wagons and equipment, hopelessly mired, had to be abandoned where they stopped. As seen here, tracks had been made to skirt around a wreckage, as other wagons had passed seeking a firmer path. Mules sometimes died in their harness from the effort of trying to pull a wagon free, and their carcasses were left in the mud, creating health hazards for all.

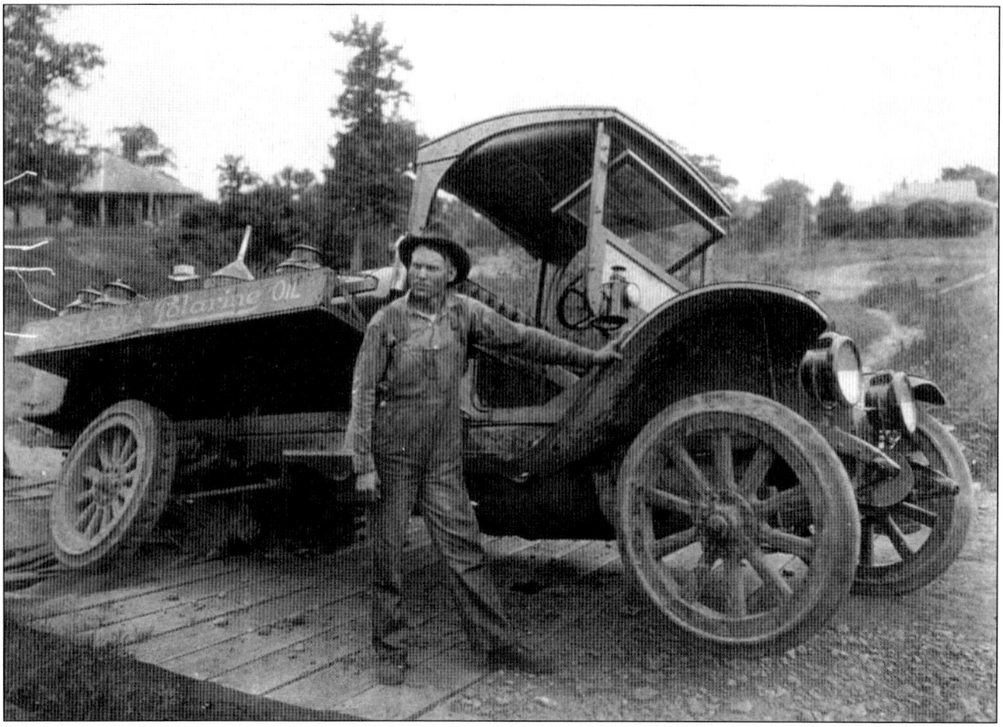

Even motorized trucks had challenges in the muddy reaches of oil boom Union County. This truck belonged to the Stancola Polarine Oil Company; it seems to have fallen through a plank bridge on its way to the oil fields.

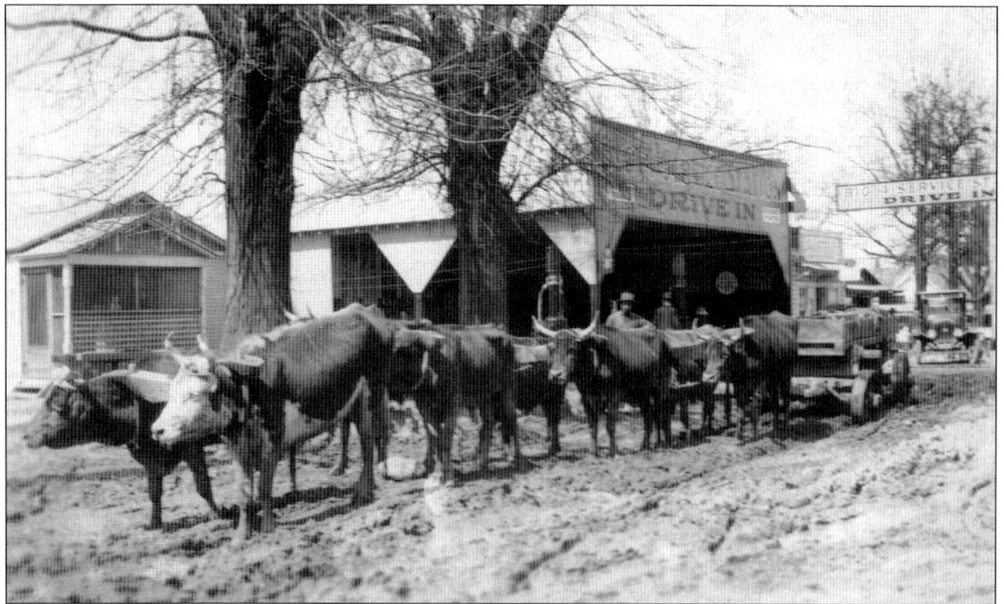

It was not only the outlying roads that were unprepared for the crush of arrivals; the city streets of El Dorado were also sadly overworked. Businesses were often hastily thrown together, like the Big 4 Service Station shown here. The long team of oxen passing by is hauling a piece of oil equipment; it took many strong oxen to get such machinery through the mud.

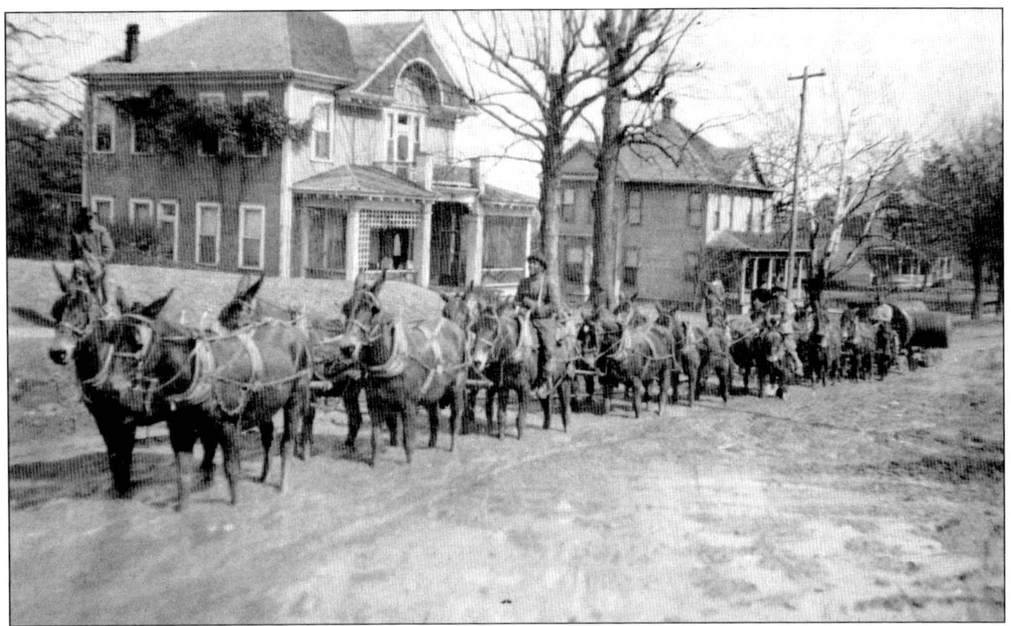

The owners of fine large homes in El Dorado also endured the affliction of the roads at their doors. Each thoroughfare became a muddy morass when it rained, and in dry weather, clouds of dust rose from the passing wagons.

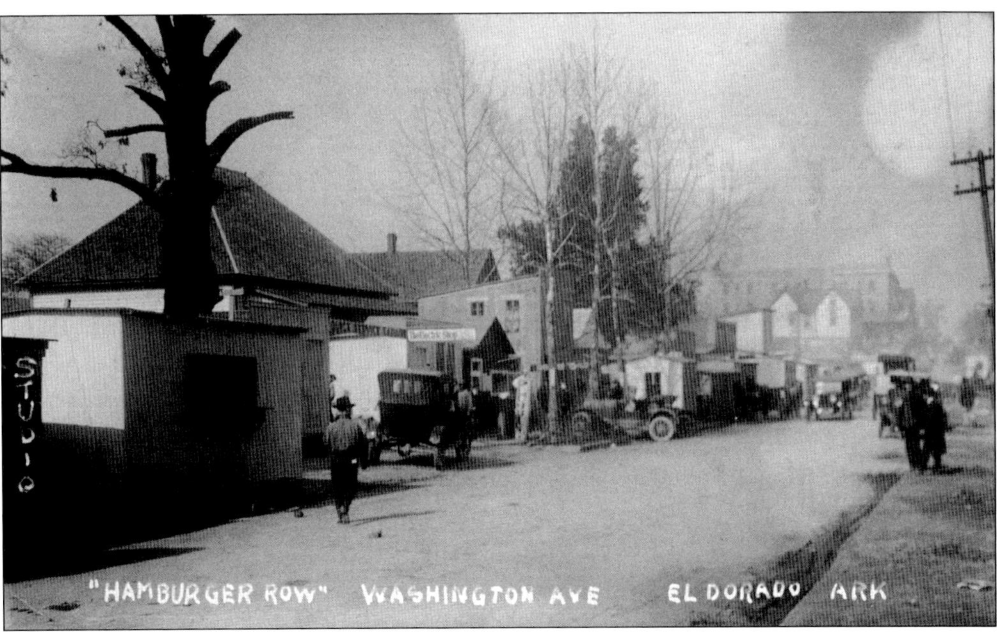

Food was soon in short supply, as thousands of workers crowded into El Dorado. Even with money in their pockets, men found few options for food or places to sleep. Mayor Frank H. Smith, with city council support, ordered that the city sidewalks be rented out for eating and sleeping spaces. Called "Hamburger Row," this area along Washington Avenue became three blocks of chaotic activity. Laws were violated with abandon. One madam, a woman known as "Two Shot Blondie," delivered not only prostitutes on Hamburger Row but moonshine as well.

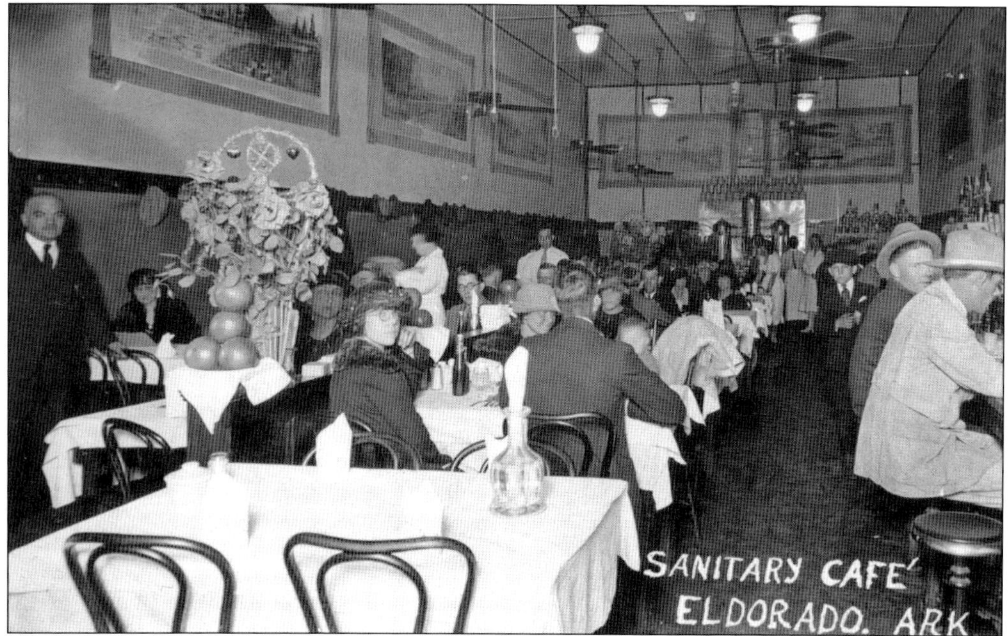

If a patron had the money and the luck to get a table, they might have dined at the Sanitary Café. This establishment opened on the El Dorado courthouse square to feed some of the businessmen who flooded into town.

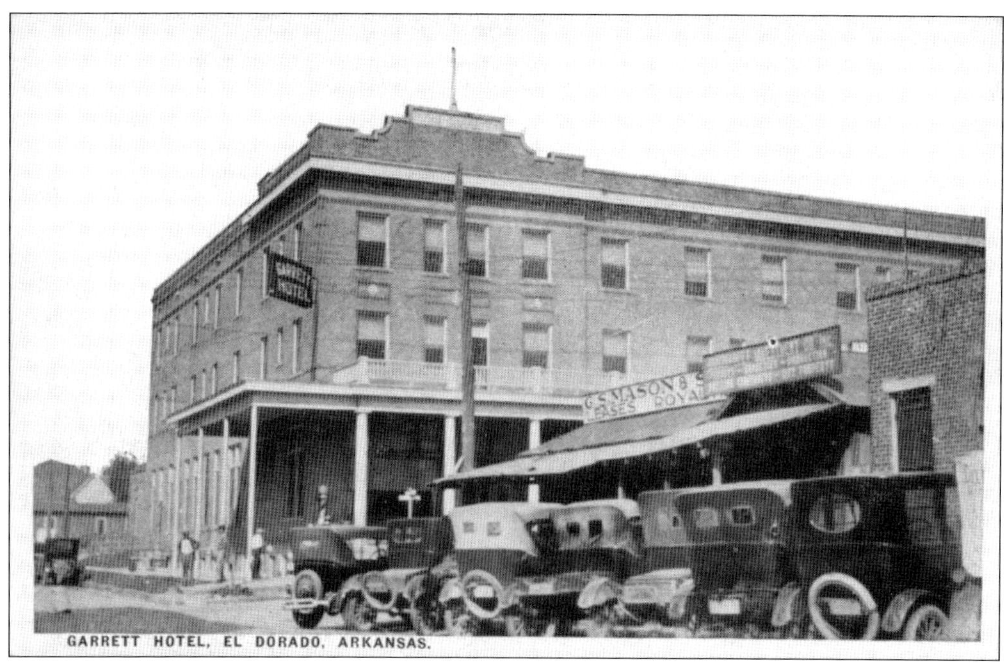

The Garrett Hotel put cots in its hallways and even converted chairs in the lobby for places to sleep. Another 50 men were allowed to sleep inside the courthouse. Barbershops rented chairs for $2 a night as places to sleep. Tents went up all over town, filled with cots. Homeowners rented out beds for $1 or $2 a night.

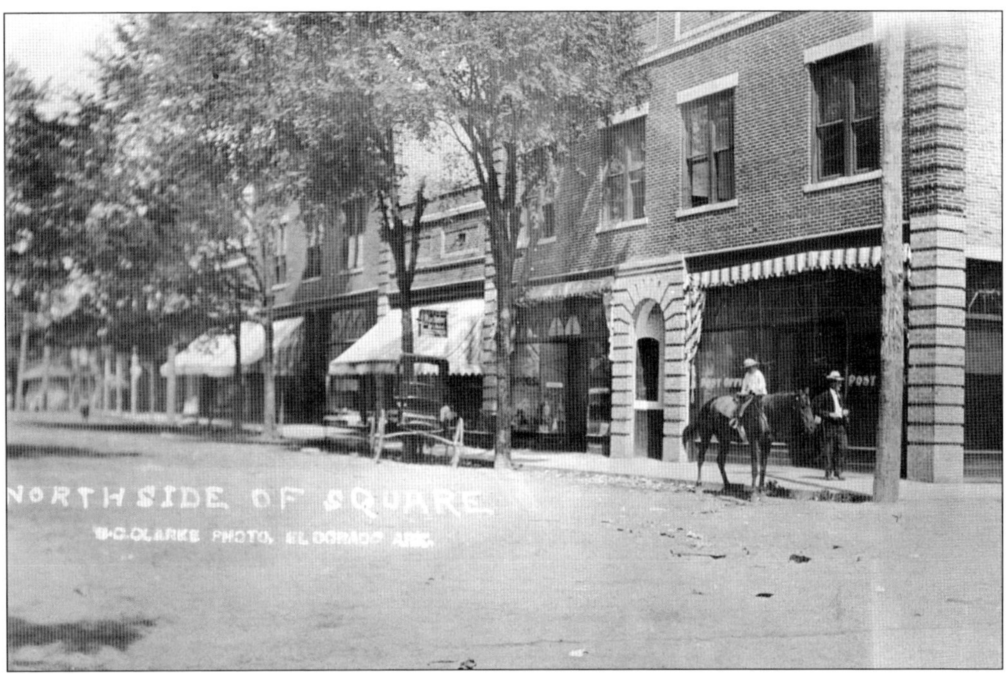

In a visual depicting "before and after oil," the block on the north side of the courthouse square is seen in 1908 (above) and again in the early 1920s (below). The intricate brickwork in the arched doorway is seen in both views. Wagons, horses, and trees in the 1908 photograph contrast with the packed automobiles along the same block a few years later. With the prosperity of the oil boom, the trees were removed to allow parking for more cars. This block, along with the same arched brick doorway, is intact and nicely restored today.

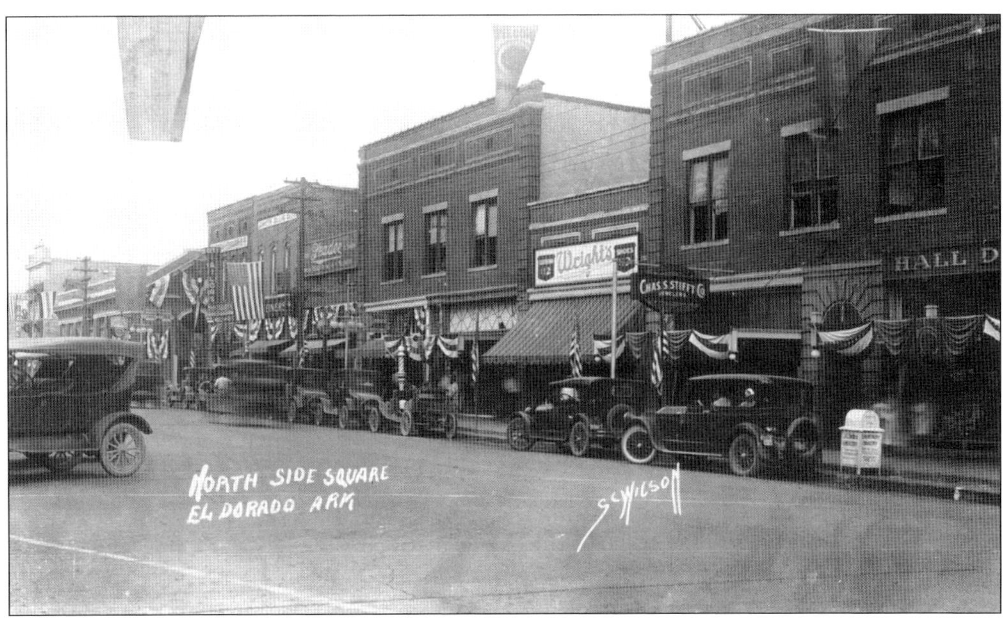

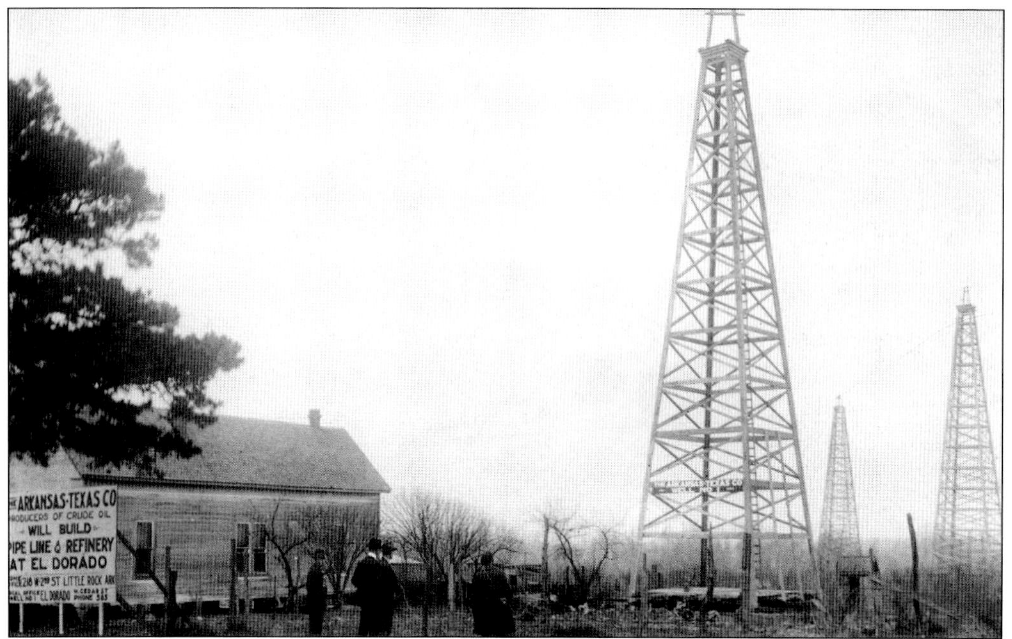

Oil derricks were visible from rooftops in downtown El Dorado. Here, the Arkansas-Texas Co. (with offices in Little Rock, per the sign) had visiting men in suits looking out to wooden derricks marching toward the horizon. By 1923, a total of at least 59 oil companies existed in El Dorado.

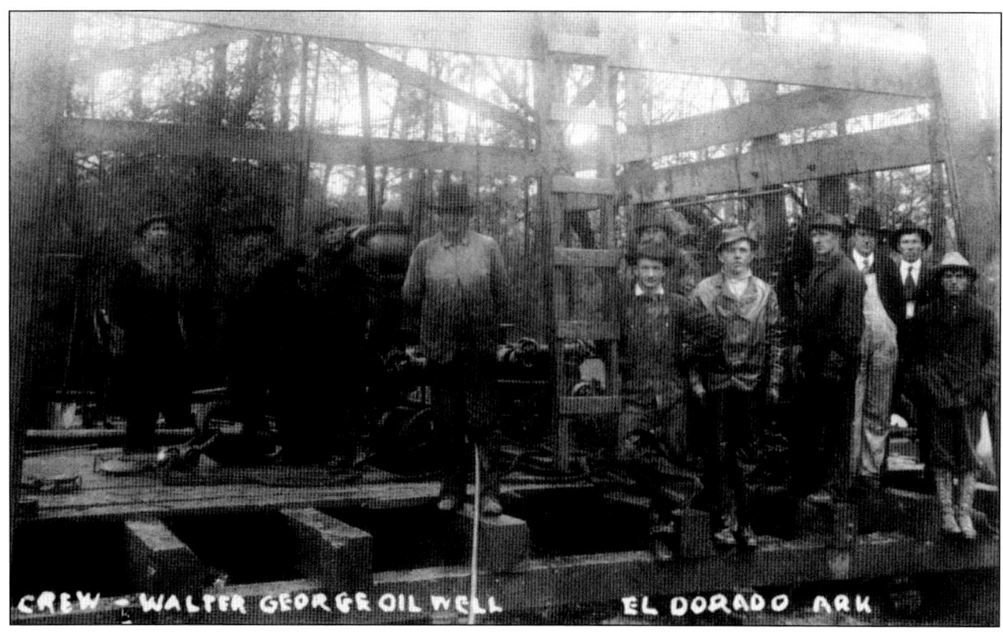

By the summer of 1921, a mere six months after Busey's first strike, there were reported to be 275 oil wells operating around El Dorado. The crew on a well belonging to the Walter George Company took time to pose at the bottom of a derrick. The crude oil pulled up by the well was selling for about 70¢ a barrel at that time.

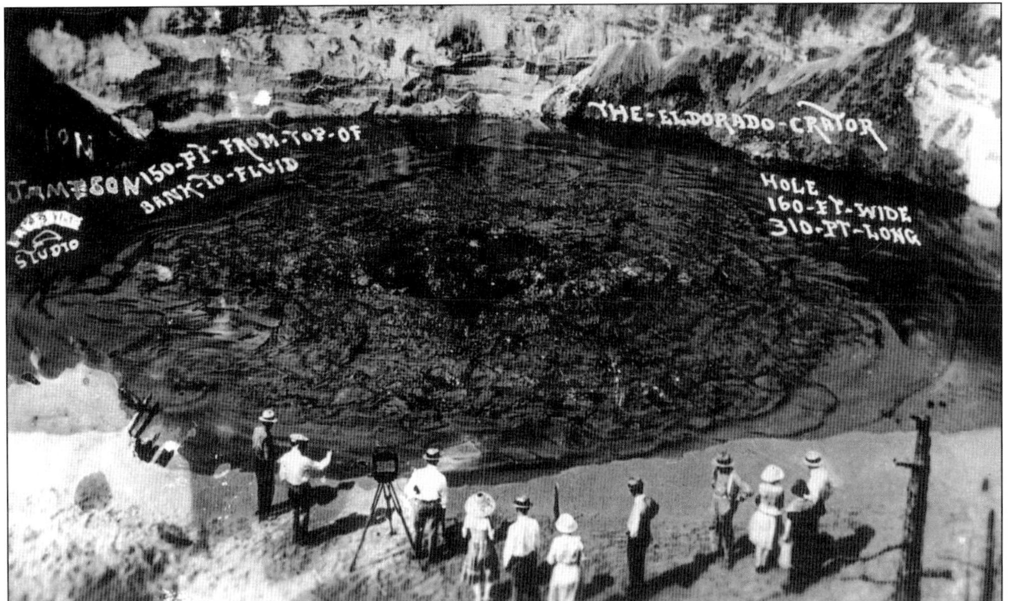

Not all the wells went as planned, and "cratering" was a risk. In the case of "the El Dorado Crater," a buildup of gas had erupted so violently that the derricks and equipment disappeared into a boiling cauldron. By the time the activity settled down, the crater was 150 feet deep, 160 feet wide, and 310 feet long. In the foreground, a movie camera is set on a tripod to capture the scene.

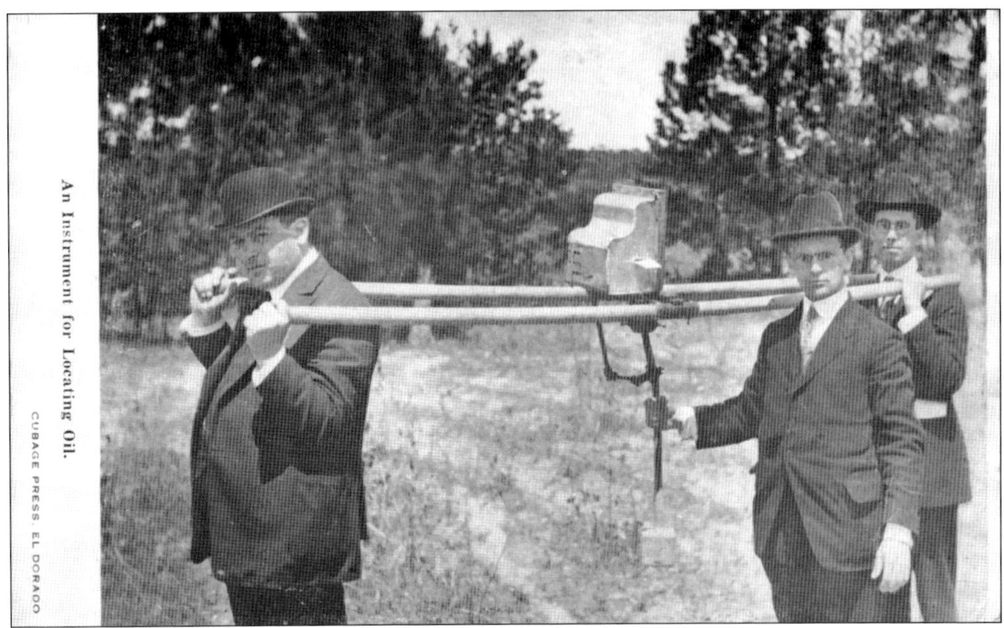

Some sought to make their money not by drilling for oil but by selling devices they promoted to give the oil seekers an advantage. Such was this "divining" type of device displayed by well-dressed salesmen; it supposedly would point to where oil was under the ground. That the device actually worked seems quite improbable.

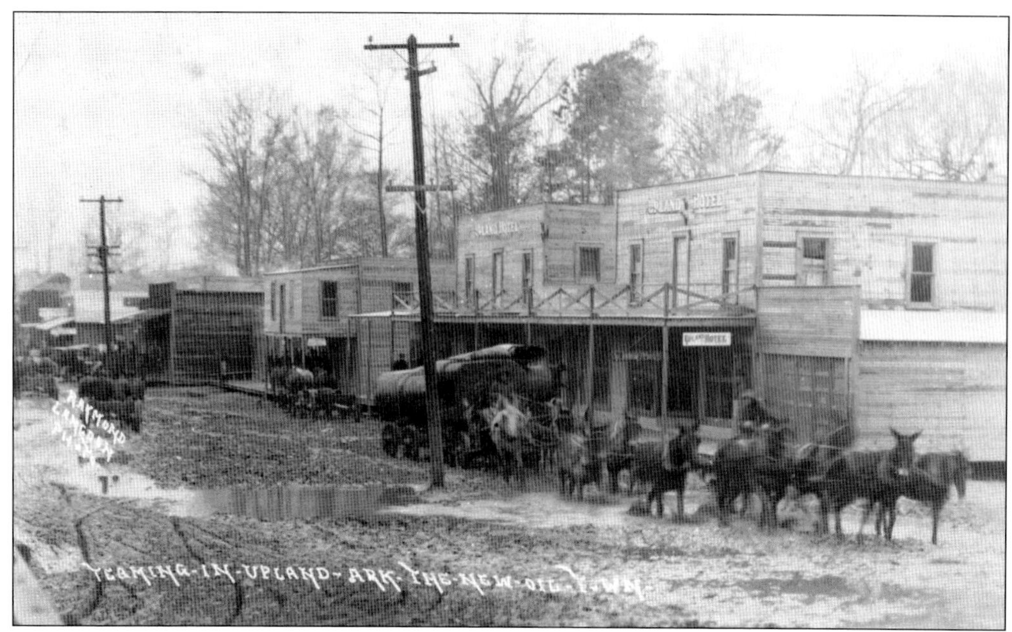

Seven miles south of El Dorado was the rough little town of Upland, noted to be "the New Oil Town" in this 1922 postcard. It was also known to be filled with gambling dens and brothels. The owner of the Upland Hotel was upbeat, noting, "My rooms are bringing in $50 per night, we are putting in about 20 more." The Upland Hotel sign is seen hanging over the plank walk, with a team of mules parked in the muddy street.

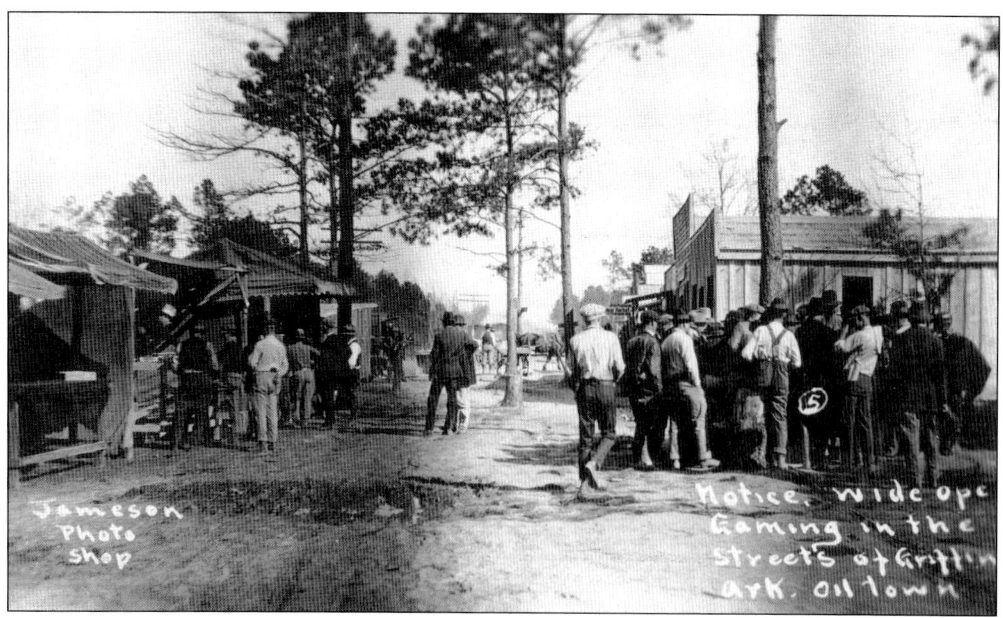

A few miles to the southwest of El Dorado was the town of Griffin, which was, like Upland, a rough and rowdy place. The postcard says, "Notice, wide open gaming in the streets of Griffin Ark. oil town." Apparently, a card or dice game was underway where the men are gathered to the right.

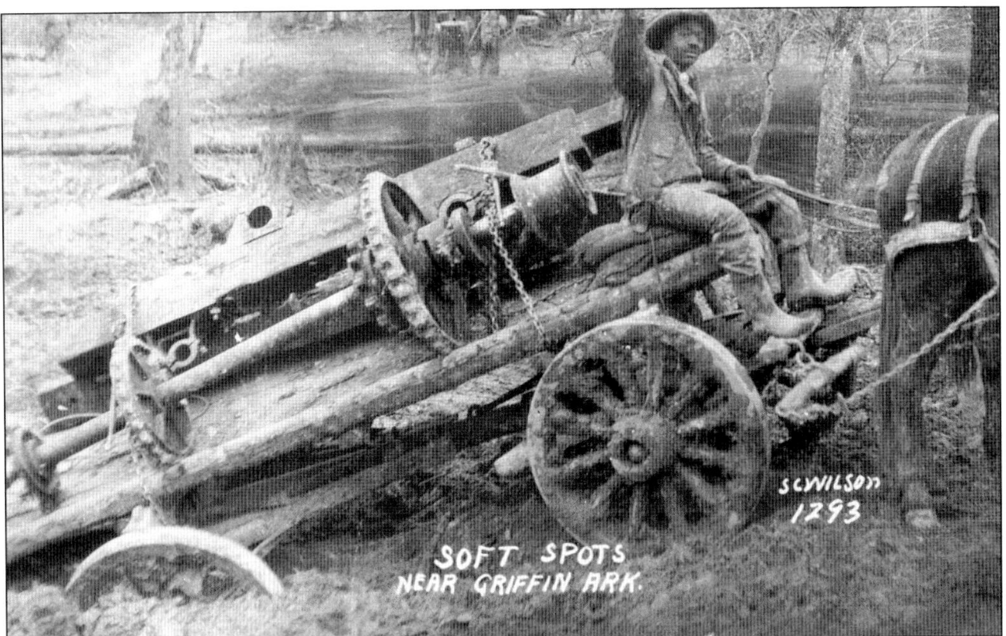

The oil fields outside the town of Griffin were just as bogged down by mud as were others in Union County. "Soft spots," reads the card showing an equipment wagon sunk over its rear axle, mired in the thick mud as the driver waves with a bemused expression.

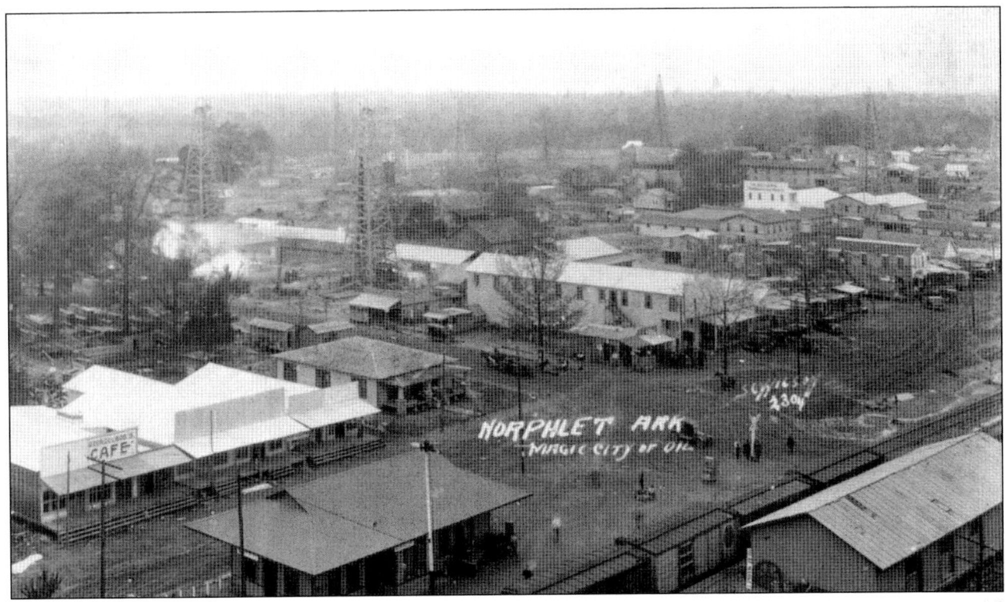

A few miles north of El Dorado, the settlement of Norphlet boomed as the "Magic City of Oil." Photographed from atop an oil derrick, the town had gained a railroad depot with daily service from El Dorado. "This is a picture of our fair city before the fire took nearly all of what [you] can see," was the writer's message to his mother in New York. Indeed, a fire wiped out all the town's wooden buildings in 1927.

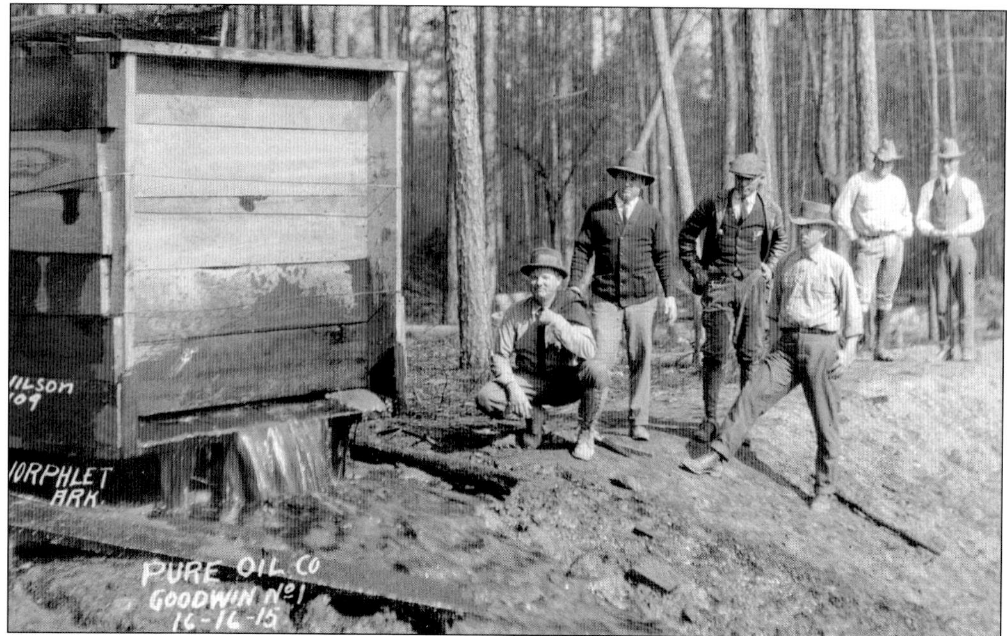

The Pure Oil Company had a producing well at Norphlet, and storing the extracted oil was a problem there as elsewhere. Here, what may be oil is seen pouring out of a wooden structure, as the men pose for the camera.

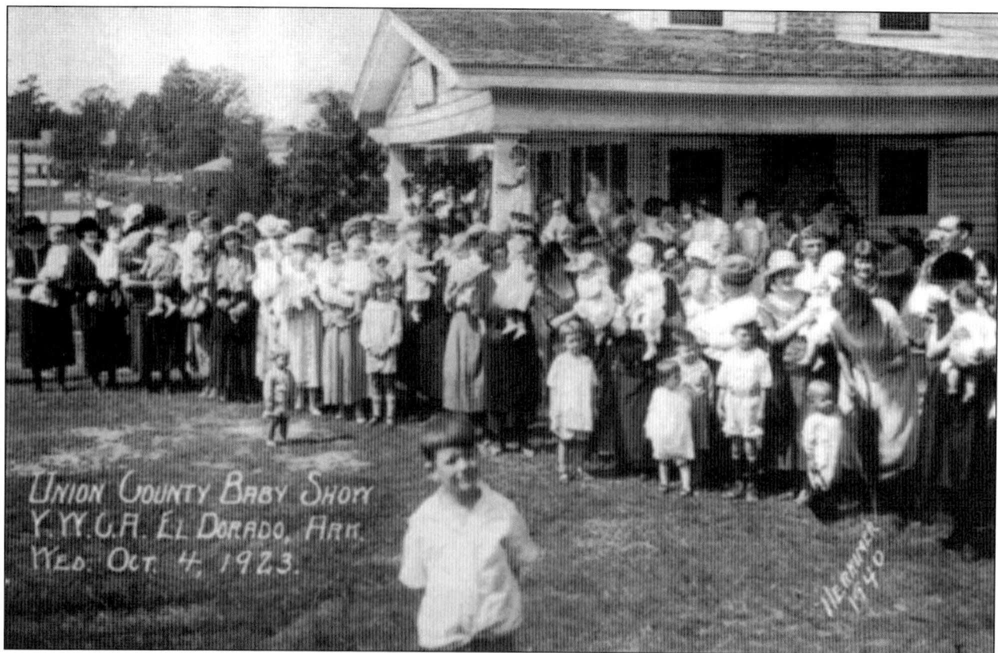

By 1923, El Dorado was changing from a wild boomtown to a more settled community. Oil companies opened their headquarters, and refineries were built, creating diverse jobs. Employees began to relocate their families to the city, and many children were enrolled in the El Dorado schools. In October of that year, the Union County Baby Show was held at the YWCA. (Courtesy of SAHPS.)

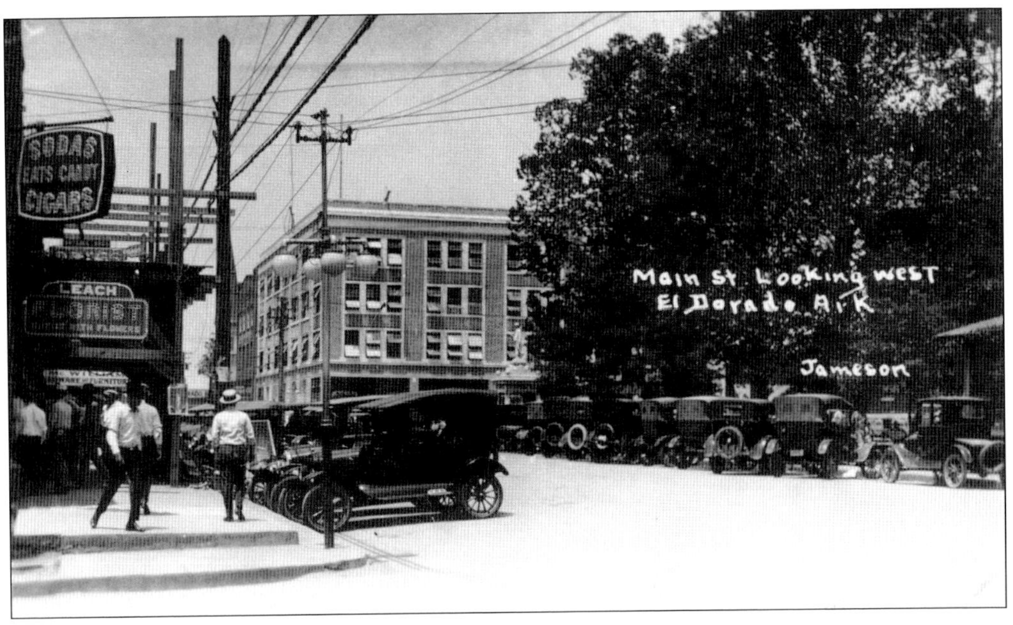

By the early 1920s, the city streets that a decade earlier had seen mostly horse-drawn wagons and buggies were now jammed with automobiles, mostly Ford Model Ts. Parking spaces were at a premium, as seen above on Main Street. Businesses in this view include Brooke Bros. Drugs, M.C. William Hardware & Furniture, Leach Florist ("Say It with Flowers"), and a corner store selling "Sodas-Eats-Candy-Cigars." Below, the rooftop view looks up Cedar Street, where a line of cars moves along and parked cars stretch as far as the camera's eye can see.

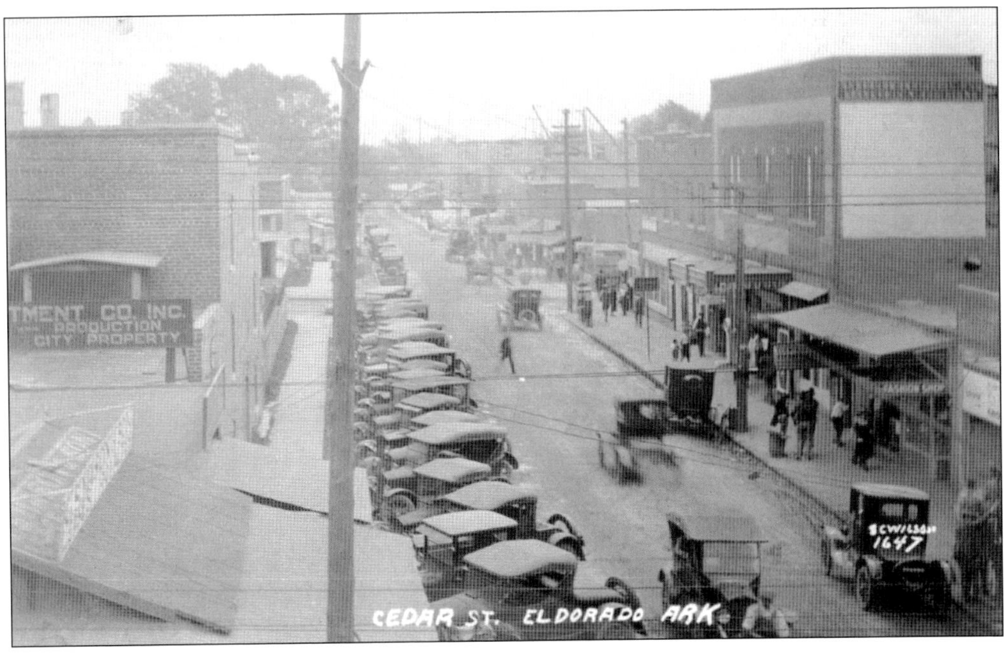

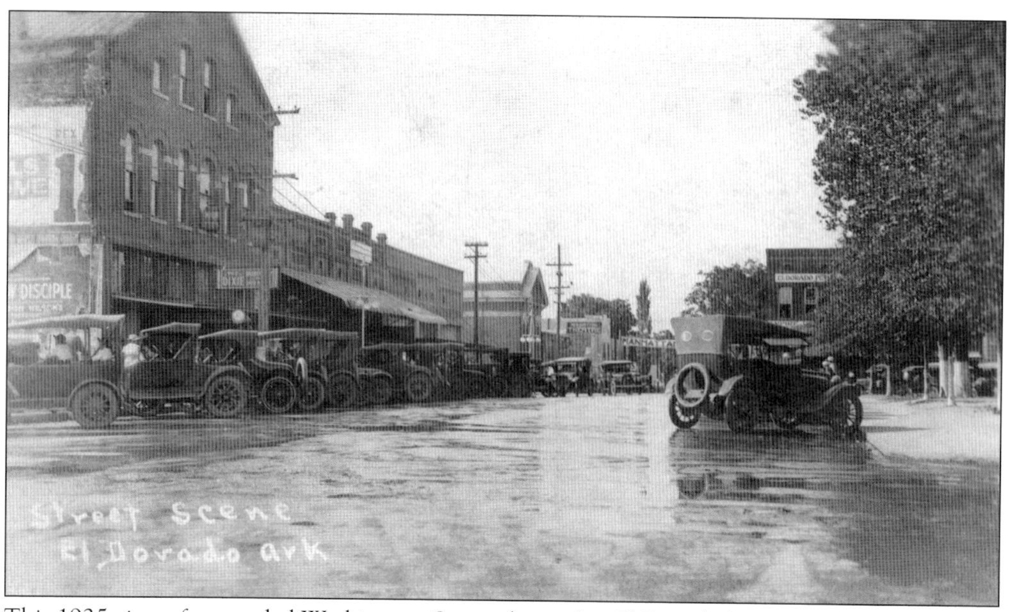

This 1925 view of a crowded Washington Street shows that El Dorado boasted even the Johnston Opera House, the large building to the left. Farther down the street was the Manhattan Theater; the city at one time had 15 movie houses. The opera house is gone today, and the site is a vacant lot. All but one of the theaters are gone today.

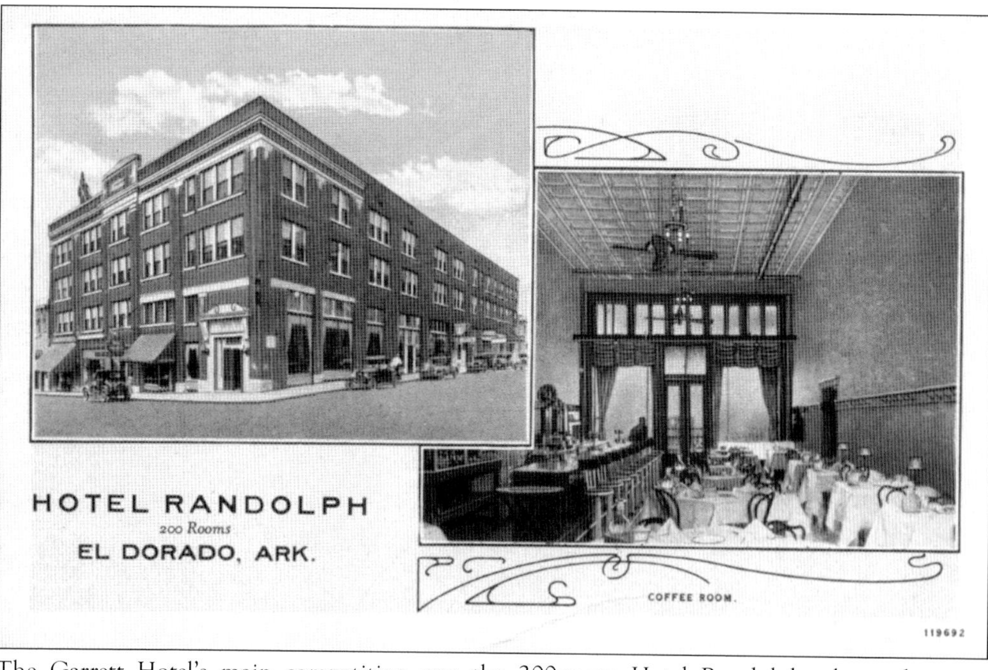

The Garrett Hotel's main competition was the 200-room Hotel Randolph, shown here on a postcard featuring its "coffee room" at the corner of Washington Avenue and Cedar Street. The hotel was also home to the Petroleum Club and a banquet room. In 2024, the "El Dorado Haunted Tour" operator told groups that tunnels once ran from the Randolph to the courthouse and to the Rialto Theater and that supposedly six bodies remain underground from a cave-in. The hotel was razed in the 1960s.

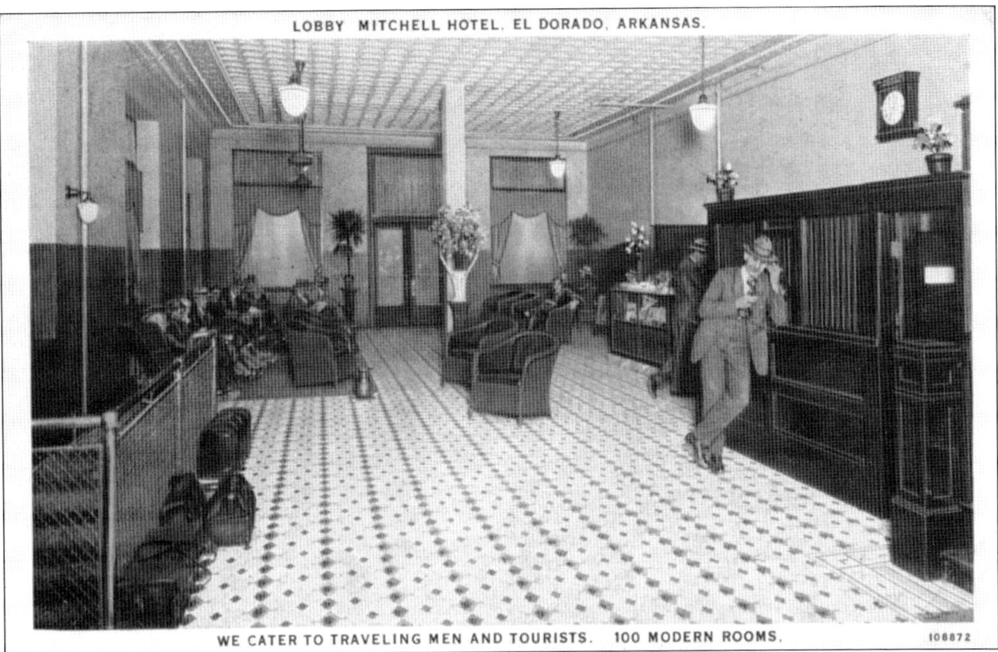

While the Garrett Hotel remained the town's finest accommodation, other smaller hotels opened up to meet the demand for lodging. One was the Mitchell Hotel, which had a lobby with tiled floors, wicker chairs, and fresh flowers; one guest is seen at the right, using a candlestick phone. The card boasts, "100 rooms–60 baths–Hot and cold running water in all rooms–Steam heat–European plan–Every mattress a Sealy."

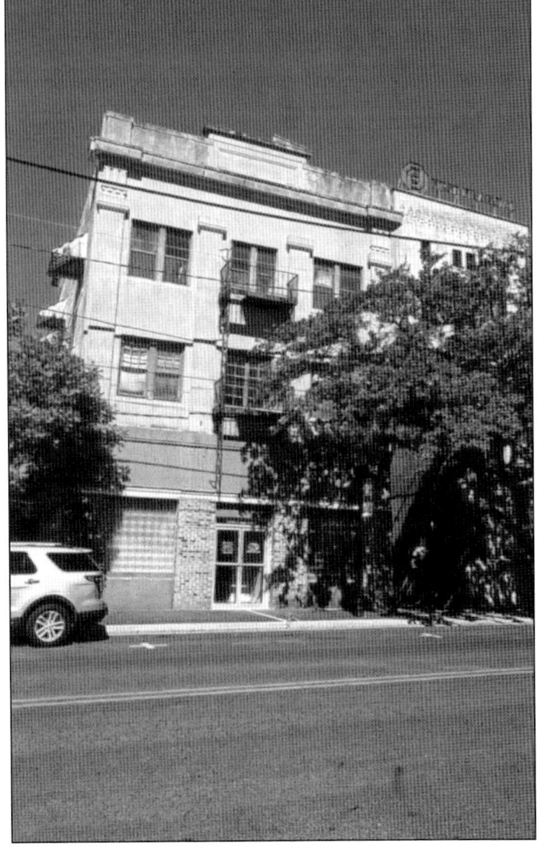

The Mitchell Hotel went out of business many years ago, but unlike most other defunct hotels of the era, its building survived. Today used as an office building, it has the original hotel's fire escape still leading down from the top floor, as seen in this 2024 photograph.

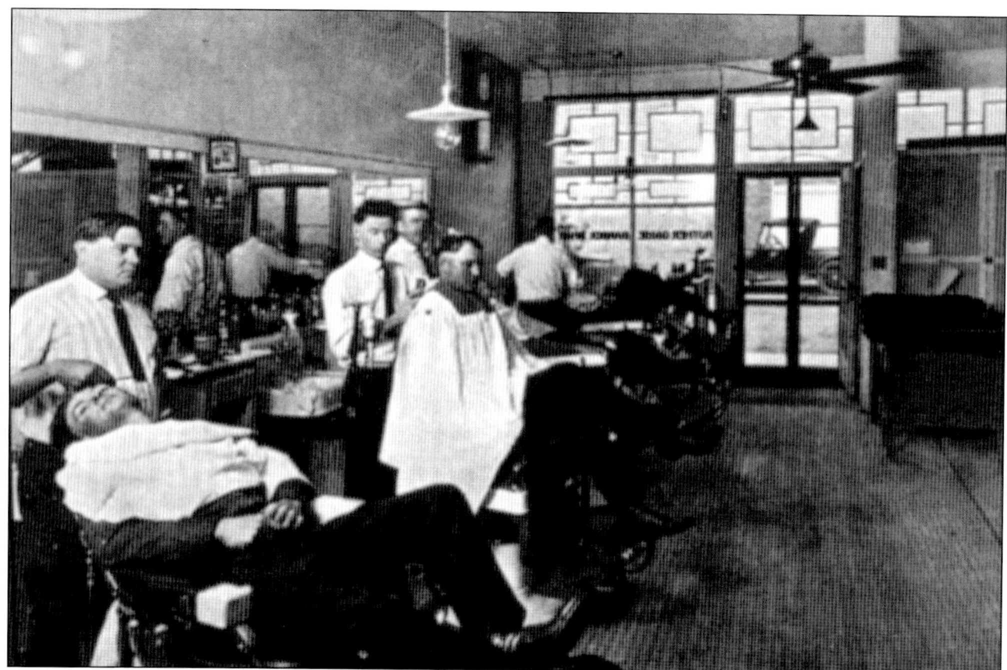

The Esquire Barber Shop opened inside the Arcadia Hotel in 1920 and was well-positioned to do a major business during the oil boom. When the Arcadia was torn down, the barbershop relocated to the Murphy Oil Building; it still operates today as an "old-time" barbershop. (Courtesy of SAHPS.)

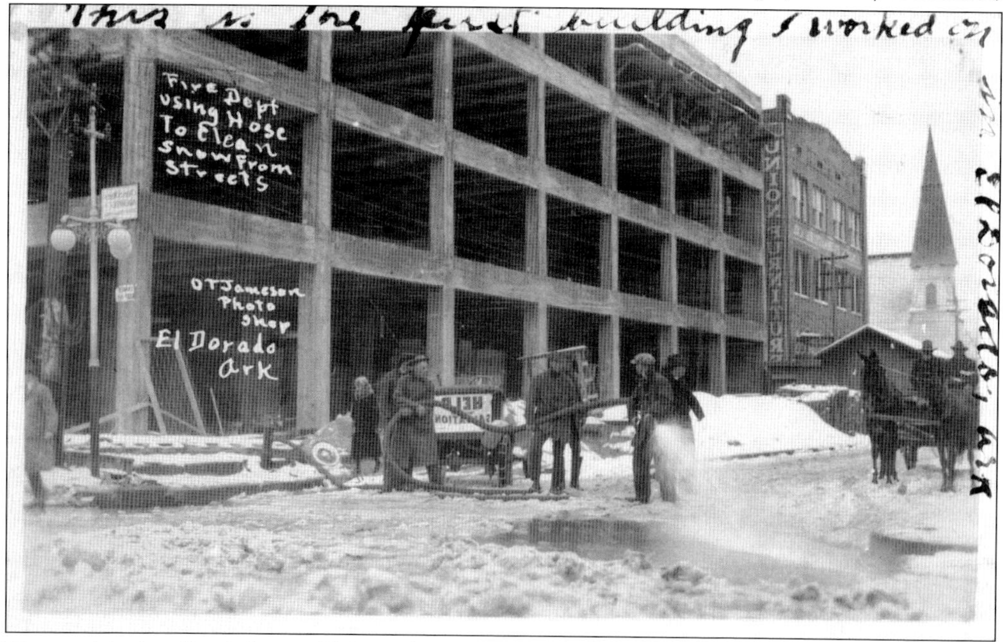

The wealth that flooded into El Dorado in the first few years after oil was struck generated a flurry of building activity in the downtown area. Above, the fire department was washing away the remains of a rare south Arkansas snowfall. Behind the firemen is the framework of the new Armstrong Building under construction. In June 1923, J.M. Chumley wrote to his wife in Bivins, Texas, "This is the first building I worked on in El Dorado, Ark."

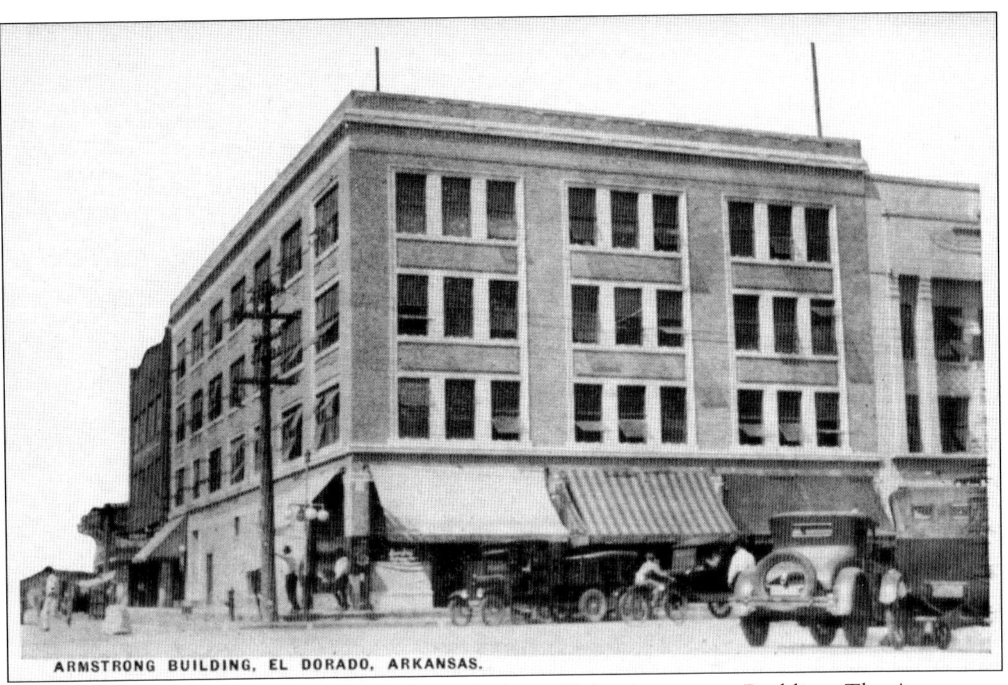

The structure seen here was known as the Charles J. Hoke Armstrong Building. The Armstrong family owned the farmland upon which Dr. Busey struck oil, setting off the boom that brought in people and money to support such a large office building. The historic building still provides office space in downtown El Dorado today.

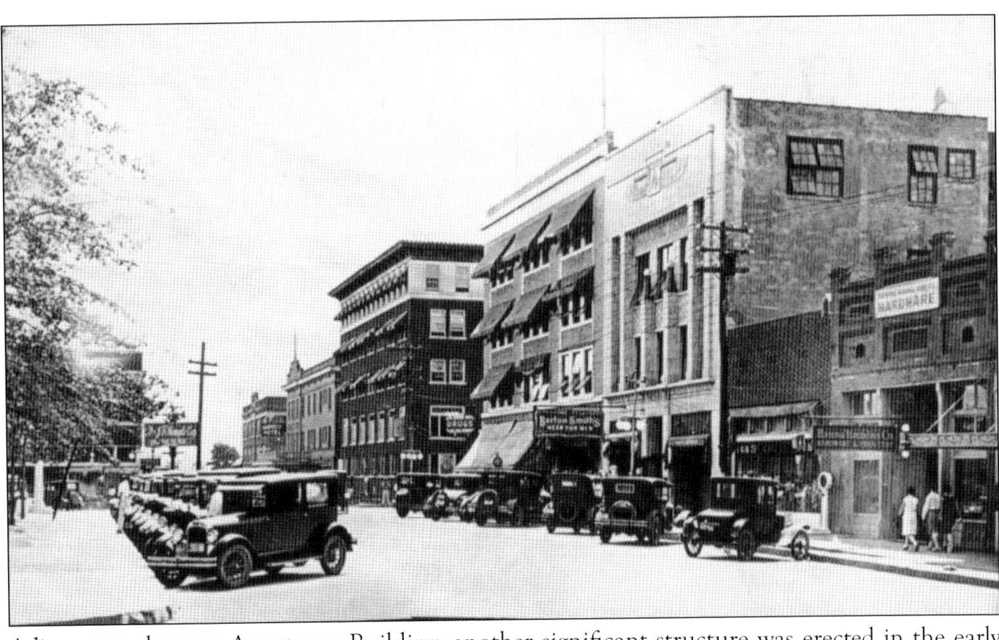

Adjacent to the new Armstrong Building, another significant structure was erected in the early 1920s. The Masonic Building to the right is one of the best examples of Art Deco styling in Arkansas. It still stands today, across from the courthouse within El Dorado's historic district.

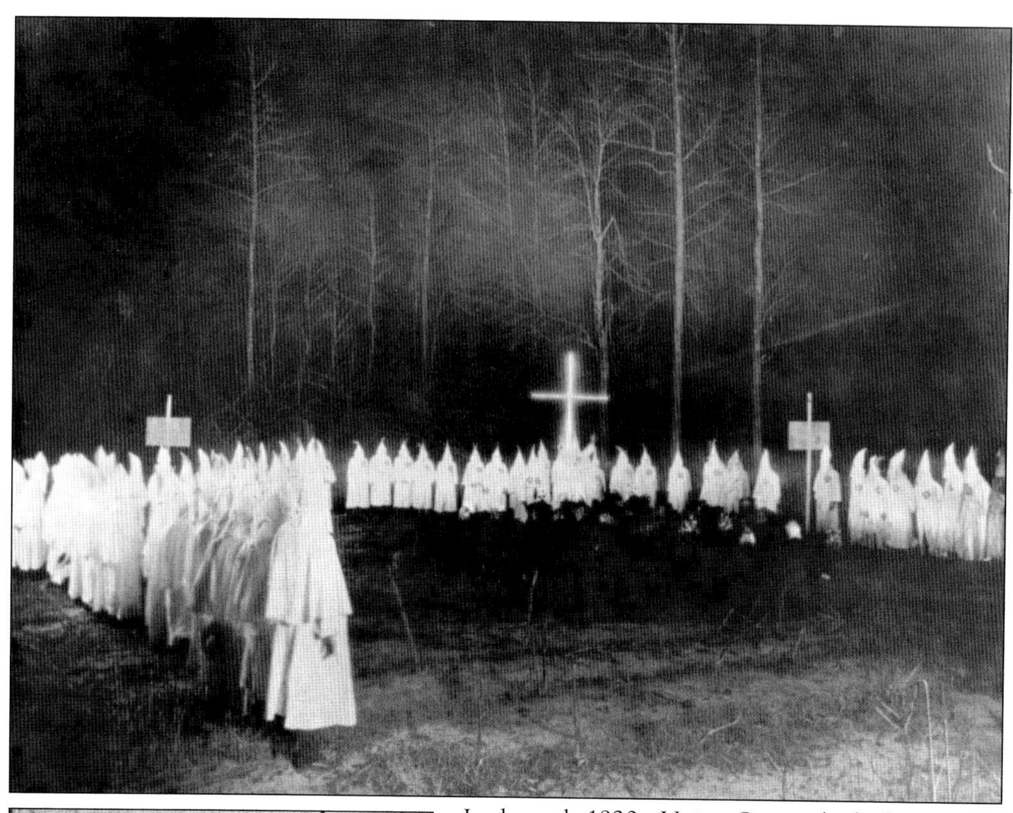

In the early 1920s, Union County had a large active chapter of the Ku Klux Klan, which thrust itself into the sometimes-lawless situations that overwhelmed law enforcement during the oil boom. The *Arkansas Traveler*, a weekly KKK newspaper, was published in El Dorado at the time. The gathering pictured here outside of town represents the Klan at its peak in Union County. The group's ill intentions were directed not so much at Black workers but rather toward the gamblers and other purveyors of vice in the boomtowns. (Courtesy of the Butler Center, Little Rock.)

NEGRO IS LYNCHED IN UNION COUNTY

Five Men Arrested Following Death of Teamster Near Norphlet.

Special to the Gazette.

El Dorado, Aug. 11. — Five men are in the Union county jail, charged with being members of a mob that lynched Ed. Brock, a negro teamster, at Murphyville, six miles northeast of Norphlet, at 2 o'clock Friday afternoon, details of which just reached El Dorado tonight. The men, who were arrested by Deputies Son Robinson and William Robinson and are being held without bond pending hearing, are: W. C. Ran-[illegible], J. A. Sasrer, I. J. McNeil, J. S. [illegible]right and Thomas Clack, all of whom are workers in the oil fields.

Information gathered by the officers is that the negro insulted Mrs. W. C.

Union County was not immune from the racial strife of the 1920s seen across the nation. The most notorious incident was the lynching of a young African American teamster, Edward Brock, for allegedly insulting a White woman near Norphlet. A mob of oil workers seized the Black man, hung him from a tree limb, and riddled his body with bullets. Five oil field workers were arrested for the actions, but no record exists to show if they were tried or punished. Brock was one of four Black men lynched in Union County between 1883 and 1923. (Courtesy of SAHPS.)

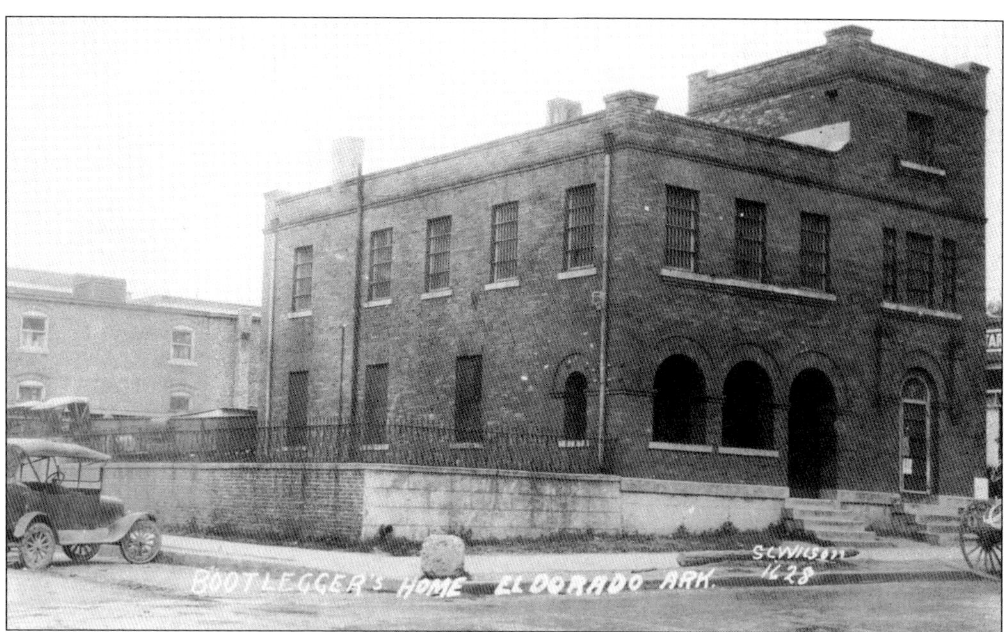

The influx of thousands of oil seekers, many being rough men not always well-behaved, gave the Union County Jail a lot of business. Prohibition had been the law in Arkansas for several years at the time the oil boom hit Union County, to the dismay of many thirsty oil field workers with money in their pockets. Hence, this postcard in 1923 called the jail the "Bootleggers home." The jail was torn down in 1930, and the cells were relocated to the county courthouse until a new jail was built outside the city in the 1980s.

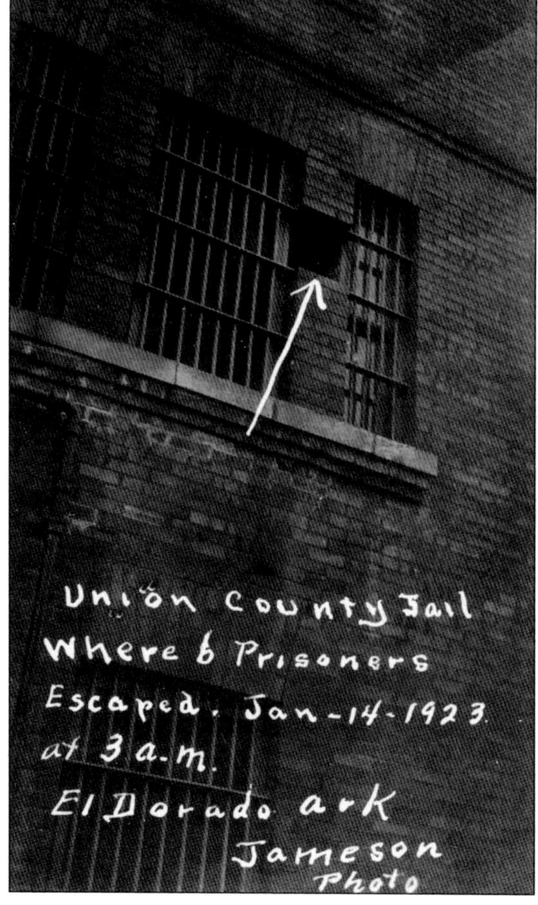

On a cold January night in 1923, five prisoners broke out of the Union County jail by breaching the bars on a second-floor window. Cyle Alexander had been in jail for shooting up an oil workers' camp, J.C. Jones was in for robbery, and J. Walker was there for stealing a car. They lowered themselves to the ground on a rope; the auto thief Jones was caught as he reached the ground, though the others escaped, at least for a time.

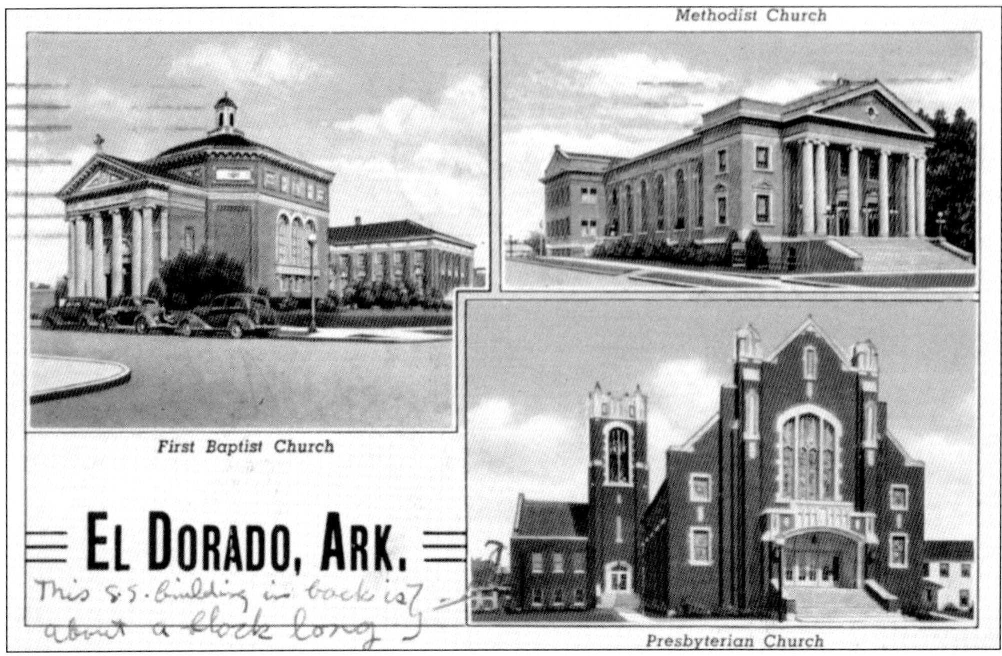

The modest Baptist and Methodist churches were seen previously on page 26 in images from around 1910. Like so many things in El Dorado, the small churches lacked the capacity to serve the worshipers who were among the thousands of people who poured into the area. First Baptist erected this striking building over the winter of 1921–1922, and the Methodist and Presbyterian churches followed; all three still serve today.

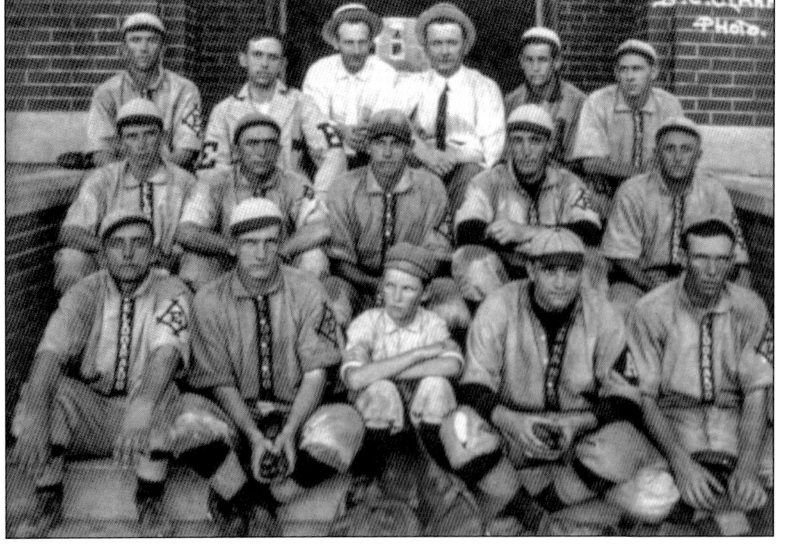

By the early 1920s, a professional baseball team, the Oilers, had formed in El Dorado. The town's name was on the front center of their uniforms. The managers are seen in the third row in this photograph, with the batboy in the first row. (Courtesy of SAHPS.)

Three

The Smackover Oil Strike

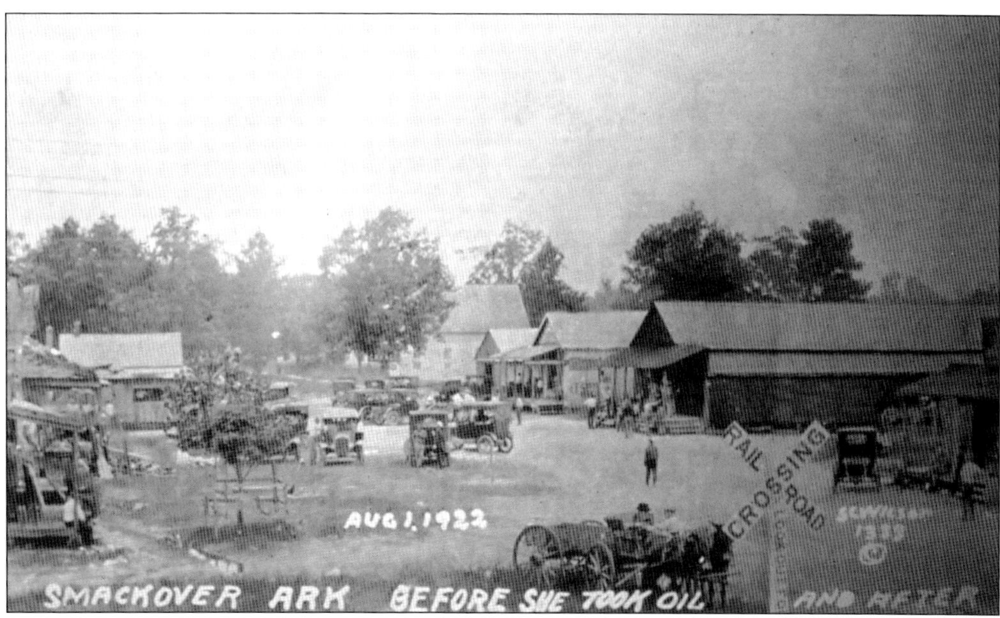

The unincorporated hamlet of Smackover, a dozen miles north of El Dorado, had been relatively quiet during the oil strike frenzy in 1921. The community's name was apparently a variation on "sumac," a bush that grew in the area. Nobody could have foreseen what the once sleepy crossroads would look like by year's end. An enterprising local photographer, S.C. Wilson, took a series of photographs of the oil boom days. Above, he captured a view of the town in August 1922, when it was little more than a small village of about 60 residents, formed to support surrounding timber operations.

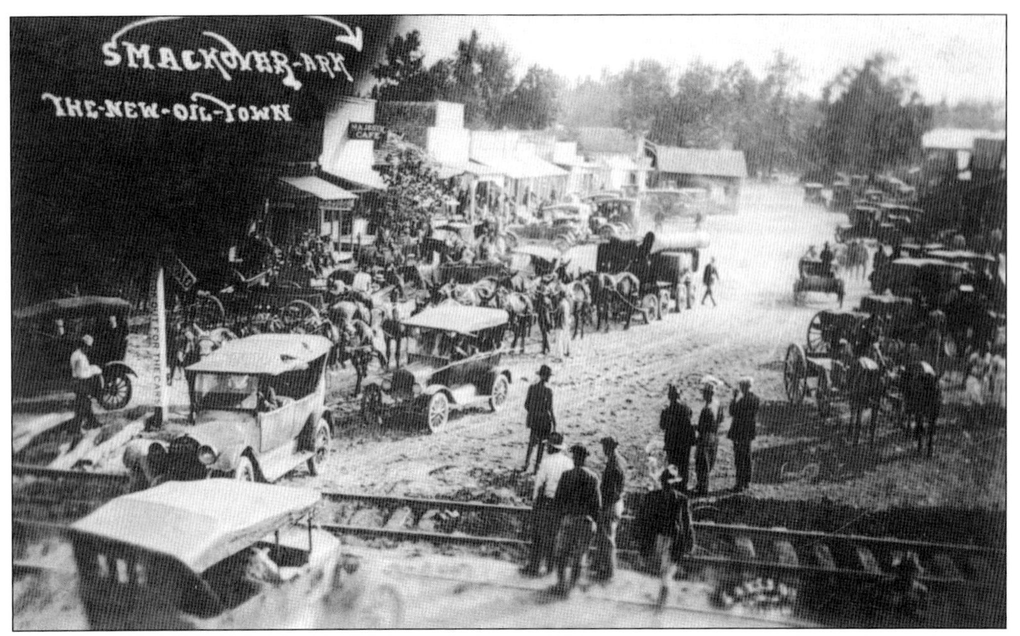

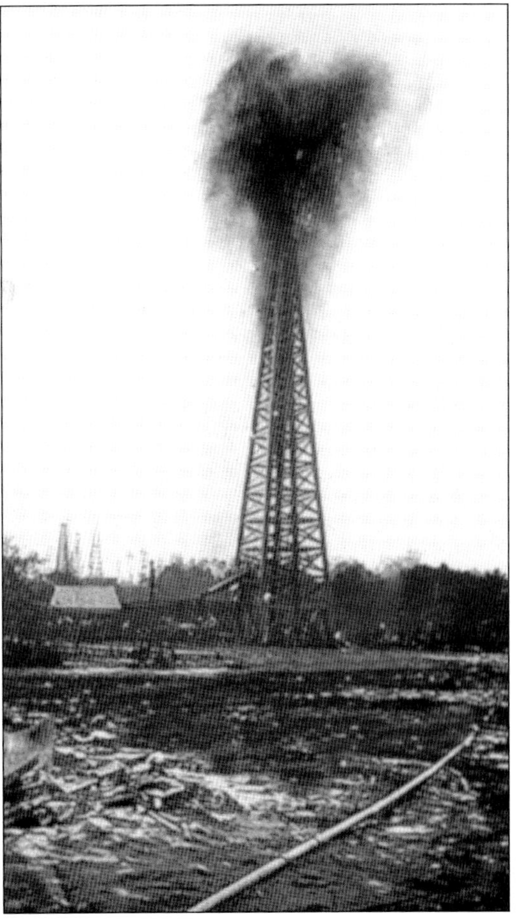

Sidney Umstead operated a sawmill two miles north of town, but he believed oil lay beneath the ground where he harvested timber. He very quietly bought up and leased land in the area. On July 1, 1922, his wildcat well hit a massive pool of oil at 2,066 feet. An oil boom was soon underway, exceeding the one in El Dorado the year before.

Witnesses would never forget their amazement at watching an oil well come in and shoot crude high into the sky over the wooden derricks. Tiny Smackover would become the center of the oil world for a time.

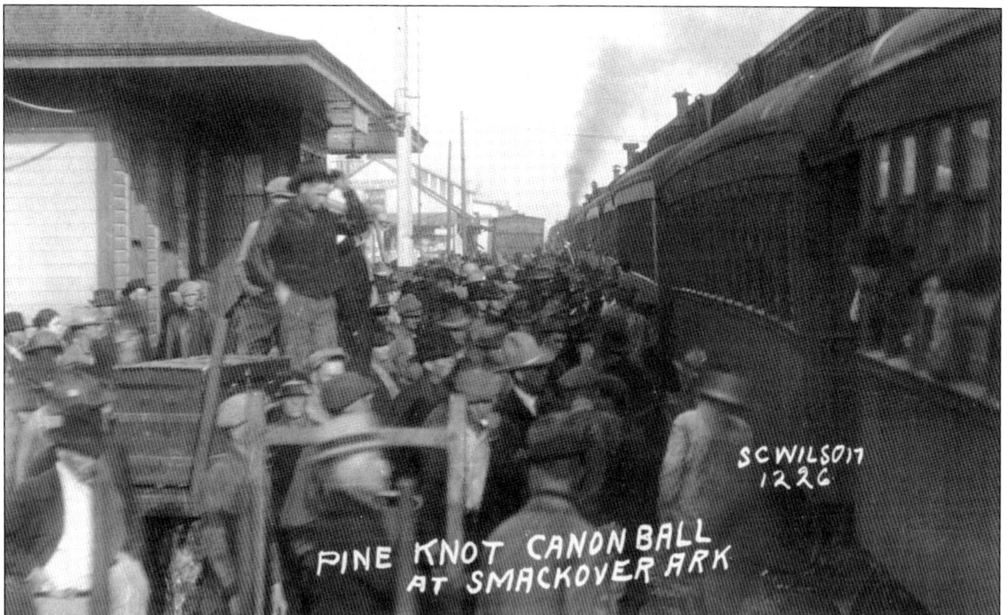

Within six months, a thousand wells had been drilled around Smackover, with a reported success rate of 92 percent; dry holes were rare. The local train depot was a frenzy of arriving people seeking wealth, along with tons of equipment needed on the drilling sites. The train was christened "the Pine Knot Cannonball," for the piney woods that it barreled through.

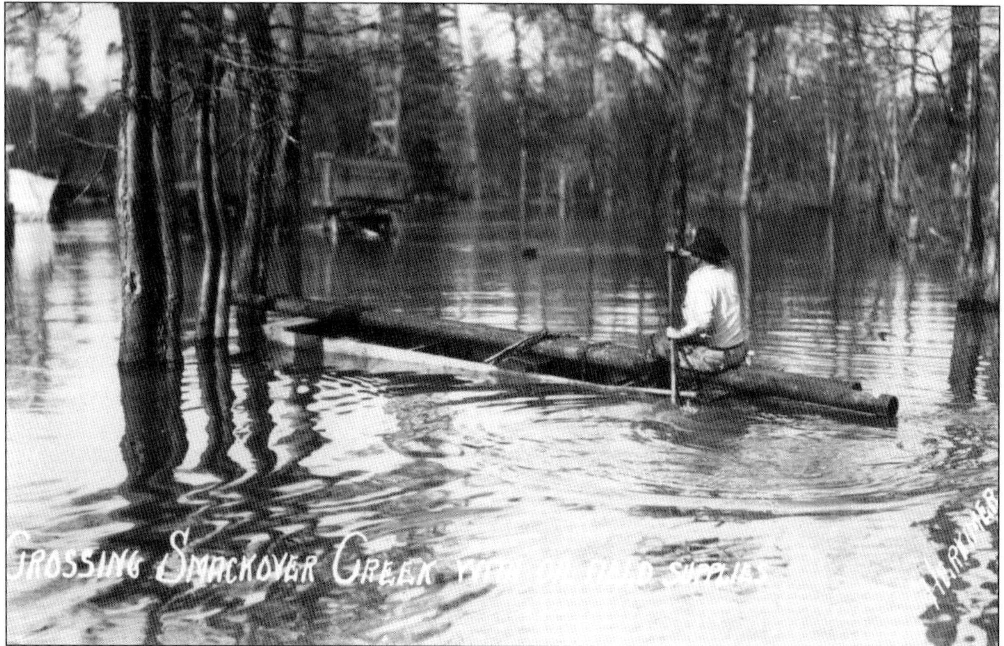

Smackover Creek is pictured here, with a man using a canoe to ferry across sections of oil pipe. Environmental regulations were nonexistent during the oil boom; neither county nor state officials were prepared for the impact. In November 1922, an estimated 100,000 barrels of crude oil leaked into Smackover Creek.

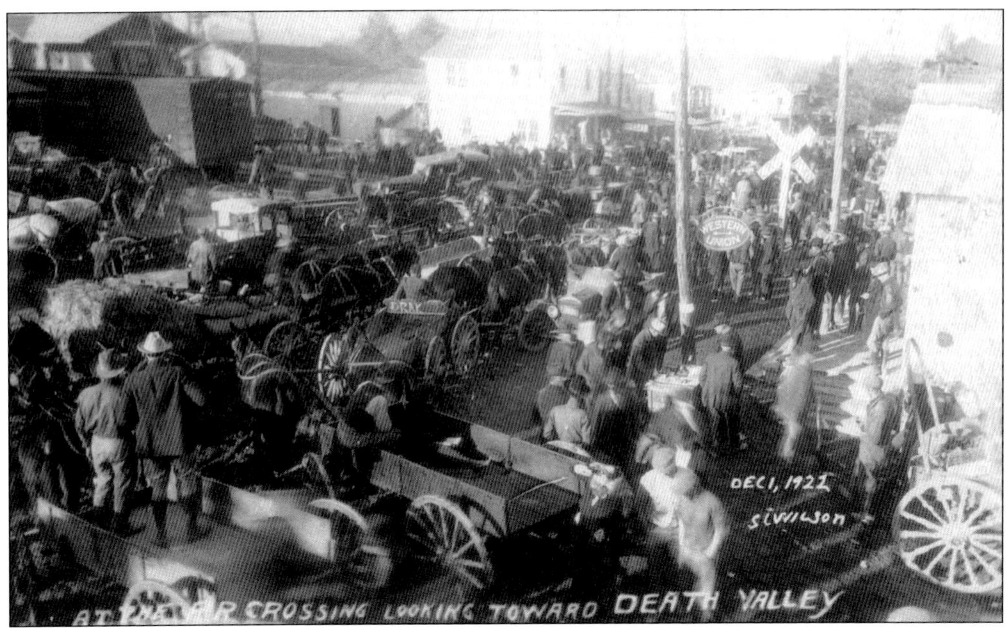

S.C. Wilson labeled this view of Smackover, "At the RR crossing looking toward Death Valley," a name given the roughest, most dangerous part of the boomtown. It consisted of various barrel houses, essentially a collection of drinking, gambling, and prostitution dens. Reportedly, it was not uncommon for four or five people to be killed on any given night. At the start of the boom, the local constable and his two deputies were the extent of local law enforcement.

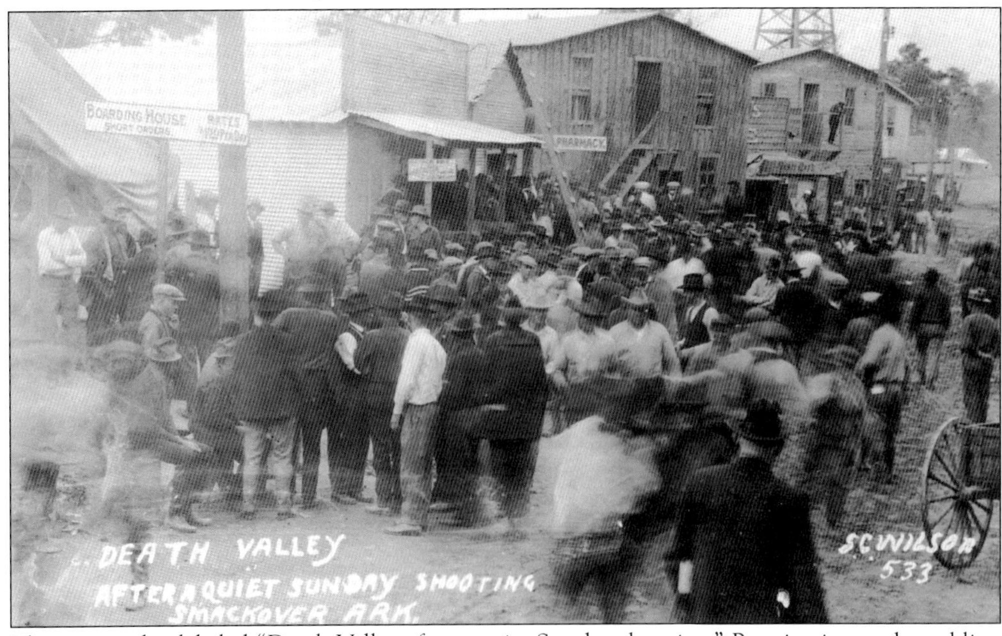

This postcard is labeled "Death Valley after a quiet Sunday shooting." Prostitution and gambling caused frequent violence, with lots of liquor involved even though Prohibition was the law of the land. The "oil field doves," as the prostitutes were called, plied their trade openly by night. During the daytime, the ladies were known to rent horses and visit the outlying drill sites, selling their favors to drilling crews.

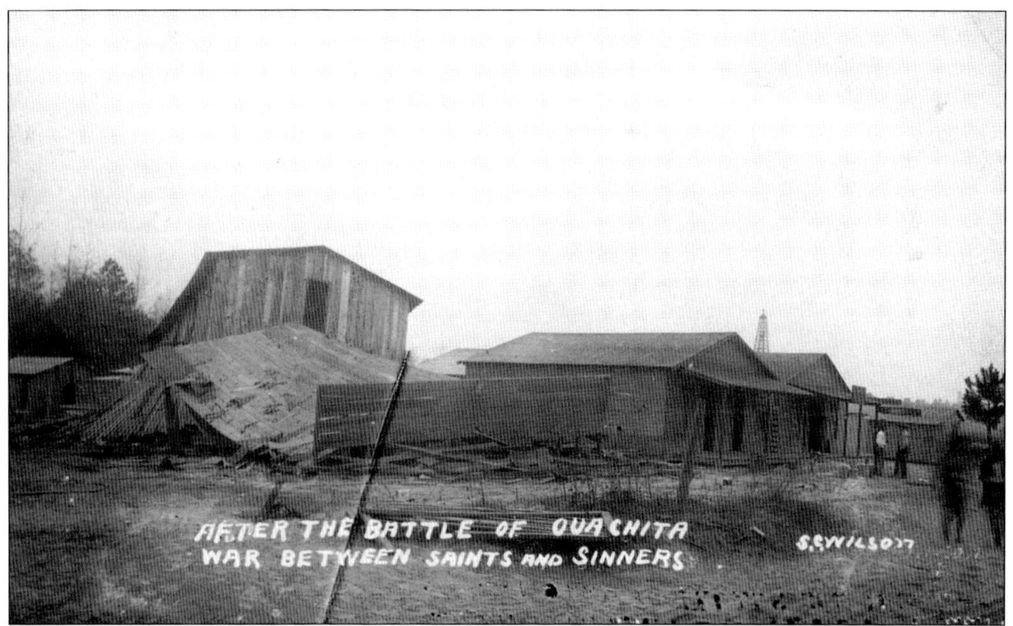

The card's notation reads, "After the battle of Ouachita / War between Saints and Sinners." The collapsed building gives evidence of what had occurred the day before. An armed mob of perhaps 200 men dressed in white robes marched through town, claiming their rally was to protest recent murders. The self-appointed Vigilance Committee, or "Saints," demanded that the lawless elements leave town. One violator was killed, while others were tarred and feathered. The "Saints" were the apparent winners of the altercation.

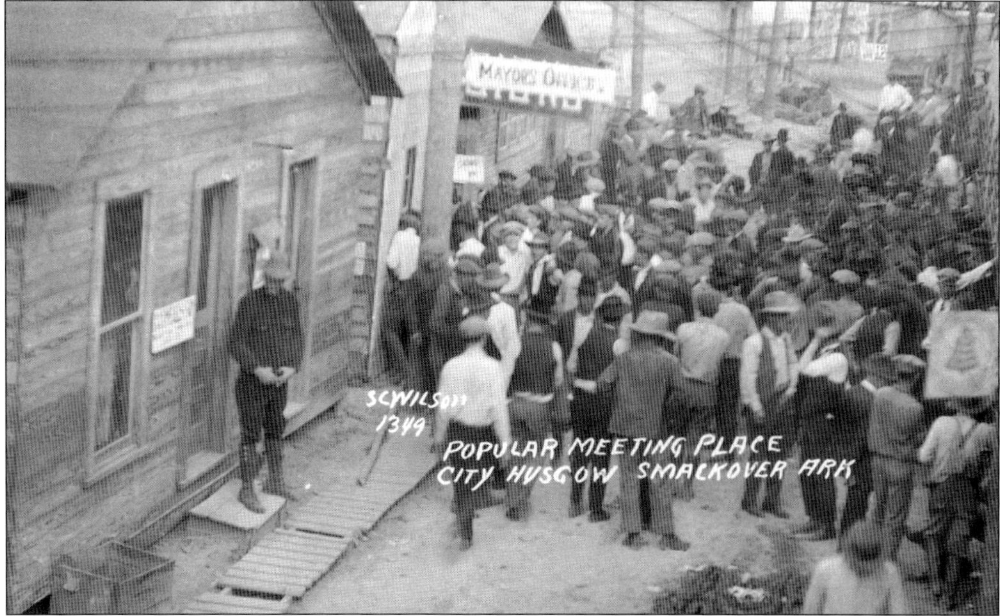

The building shown is noted to be a "Popular Meeting Place/City Husgow." To increase revenue and services like law enforcement, the city of Smackover was quickly incorporated; the populace elected a mayor and added a police force. The shingle for the mayor's office is seen to the right of the jail ("hoosegow") constructed of rough boards.

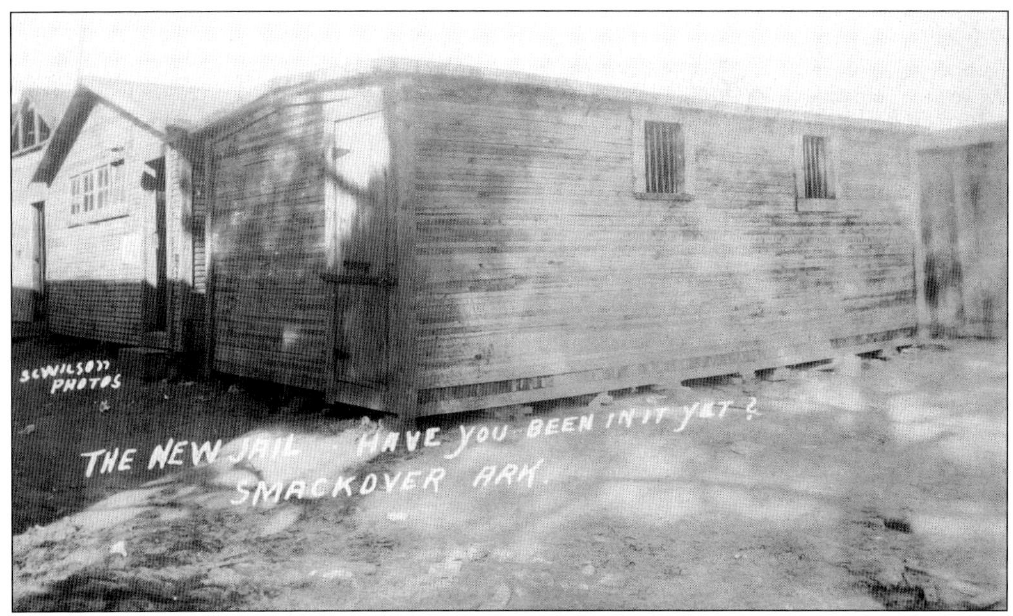

Captioned "The New Jail–Have You Been In It Yet?" by photographer S.C. Wilson, this touch of humor was added to the view of the rough wooden building. Located next to the mayor's office, the jail evidently had two cells with high barred windows; it was perched on pilings of stacked bricks. It is assumed that the jail stayed busy in the rough-and-tumble town of Smackover.

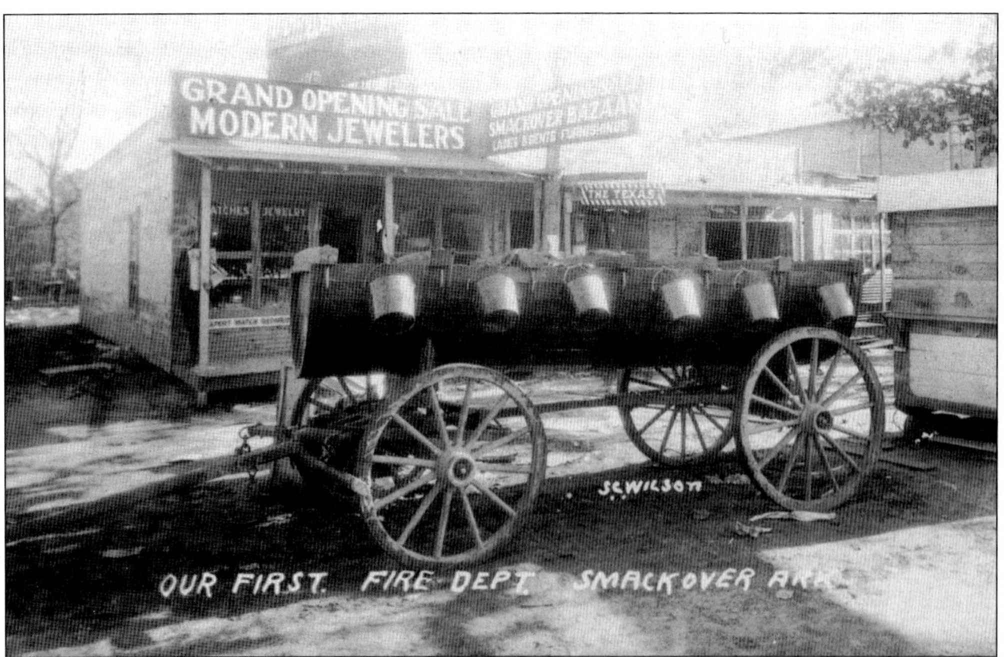

As thin as law enforcement was in the boomtown, Smackover's fire protection was even less. The first fire control effort was this open trough wagon, seen parked in front of a jewelry store that was having its grand opening. The wagon was outfitted with 12 buckets, presumably for use by a "bucket brigade" of citizens.

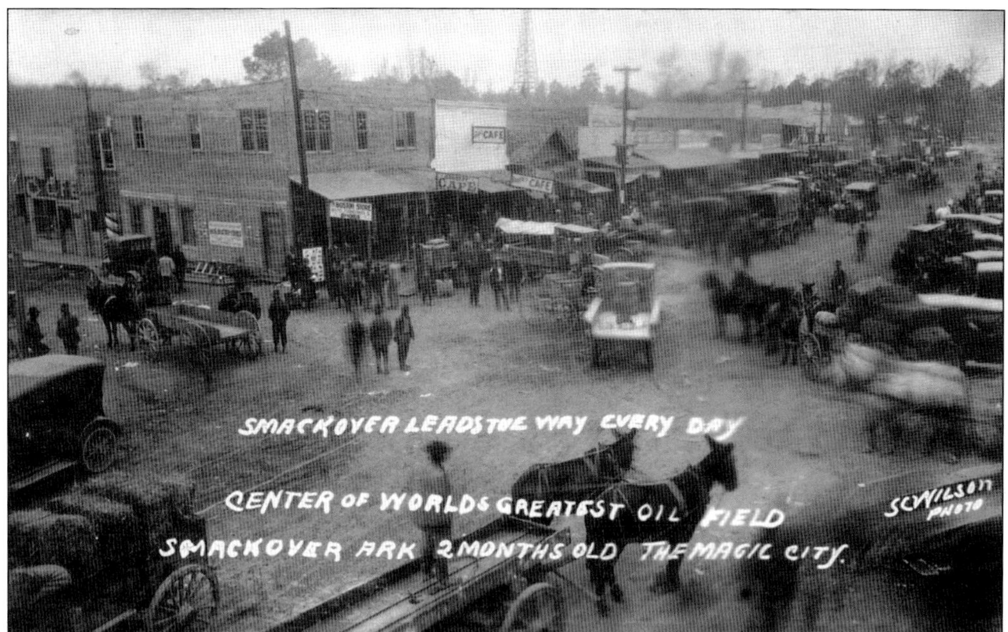

Photographer S.C. Wilson was an early promoter of his town, proclaiming on this card, "Smackover Leads The Way Every Day / Center Of Worlds Greatest Oil Field / Smackover Ark 2 Months Old The Magic City." Wilson perhaps hoped his postcards would be mailed far and wide, attracting more transplants. Before the oil strike in July 1922, Smackover had a population of around 60 persons, but by November 1, only five months later, the census count was at 5,000. Eventually, Smackover peaked at over 25,000 residents.

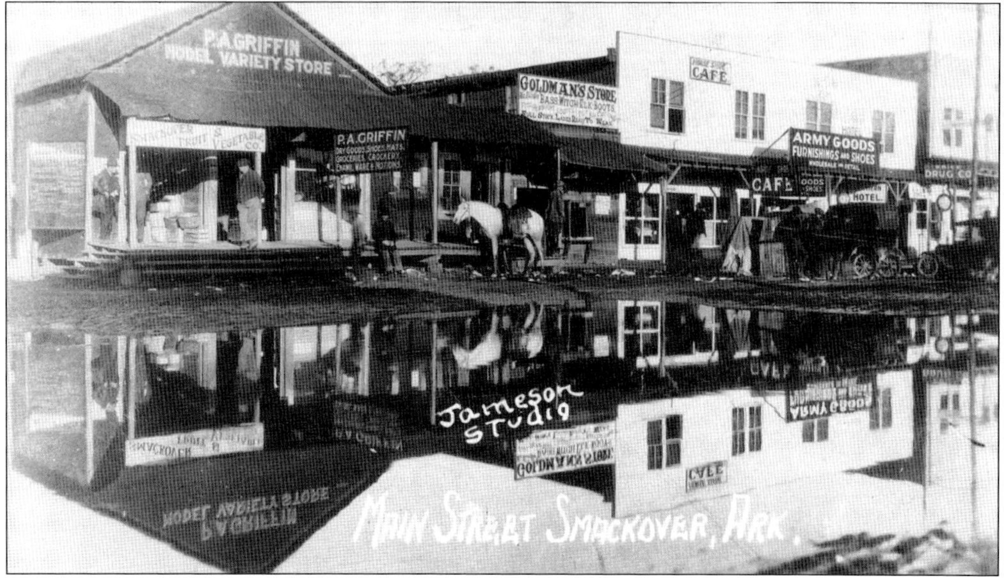

Smackover's main road was Broadway, a rough dirt street that was fine for wagons and horses when the town only had 60 residents. During the oil boom, heavy rains made Broadway a quagmire, with an extensive puddle that reflected buildings like Griffin's Variety Store and the Horseshoe Café. Among the outdoor murals displayed in modern-day Smackover is one that was copied from this postcard photograph.

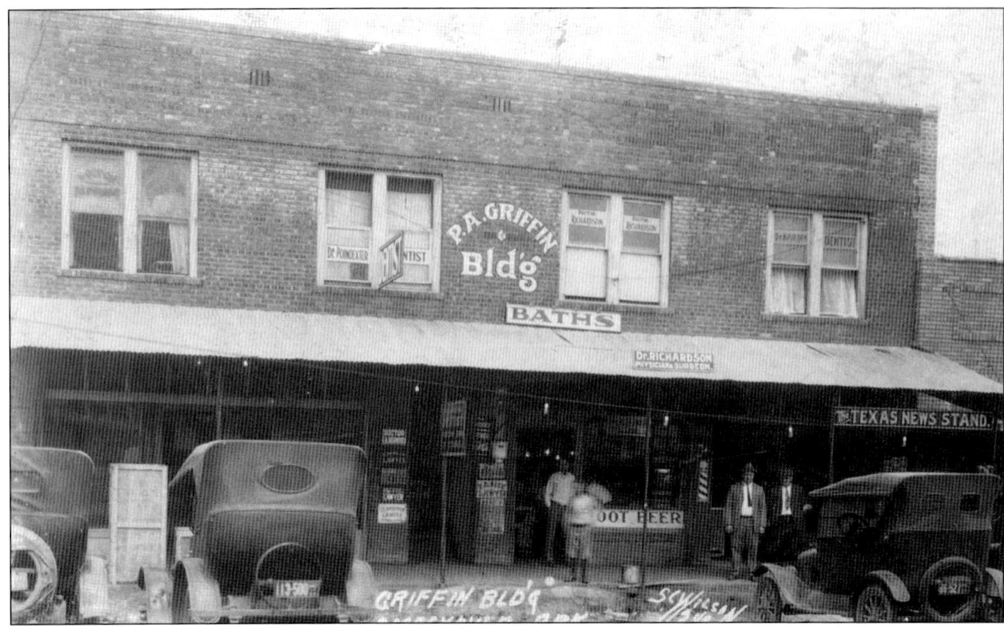

In 1923, a huge fire destroyed all the wooden buildings in Smackover. However, the town would rise from the ashes, erecting mostly brick buildings with divided fire walls. One of these new structures was the P.A. Griffin Building. It held professional offices, a bathhouse, and a store advertising root beer (as alcohol was illegal). At the right is the Texas News Stand, popular with the numerous oil field workers who came from there.

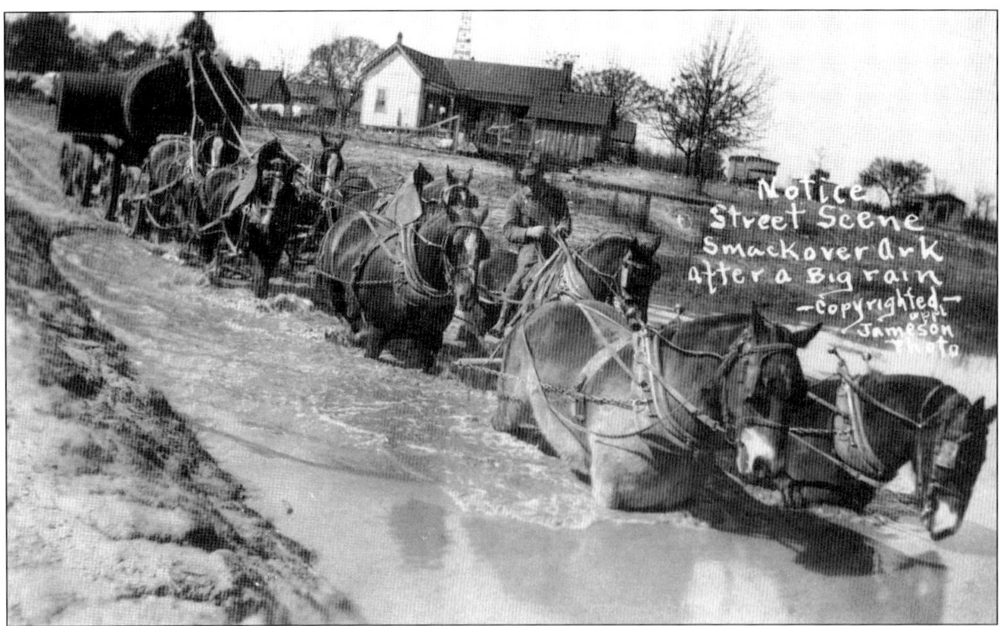

To get huge boilers, pipes, lumber, and other equipment to hundreds of drill sites in the Smackover fields, it took the labor of countless mules and even oxen. The intersection of Hillsboro Street and Washington Avenue in El Dorado, some dozen miles distant from Smackover, became "Mule Skinners Corner." The heavy hauling jobs were negotiated there; a four-mule team rented for $15 a day. Good mules sold for as much as $200–$300 each.

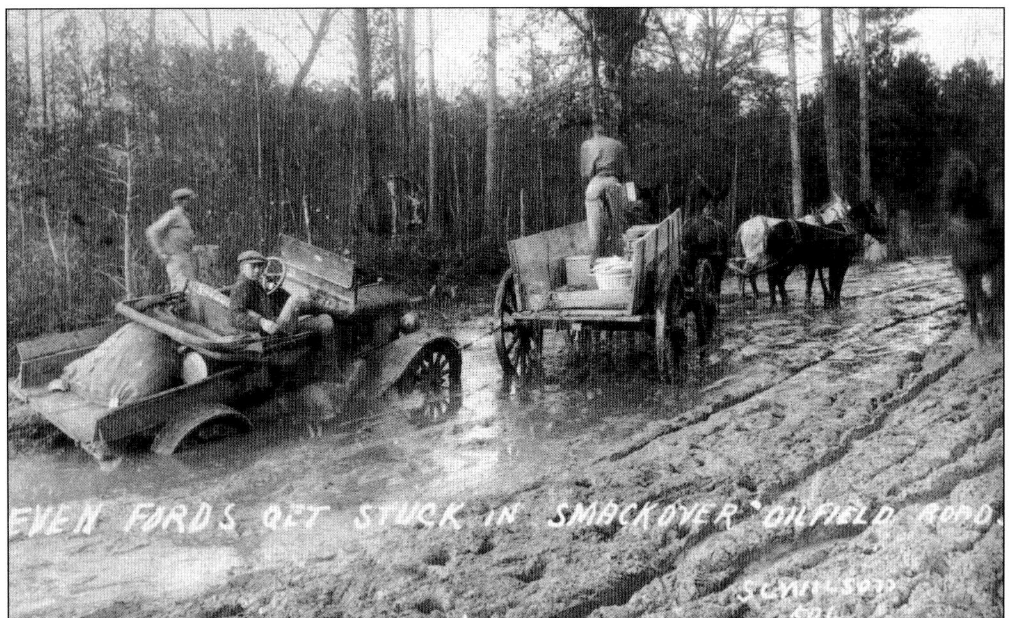

"Even Fords Get Stuck in Smackover Arkansas" was photographer S.C. Wilson's tag on the postcard showing what seemed to have been a Ford truck buried almost to the top of the rear tire. It is likely that a team of mules was needed to extract the stranded vehicle.

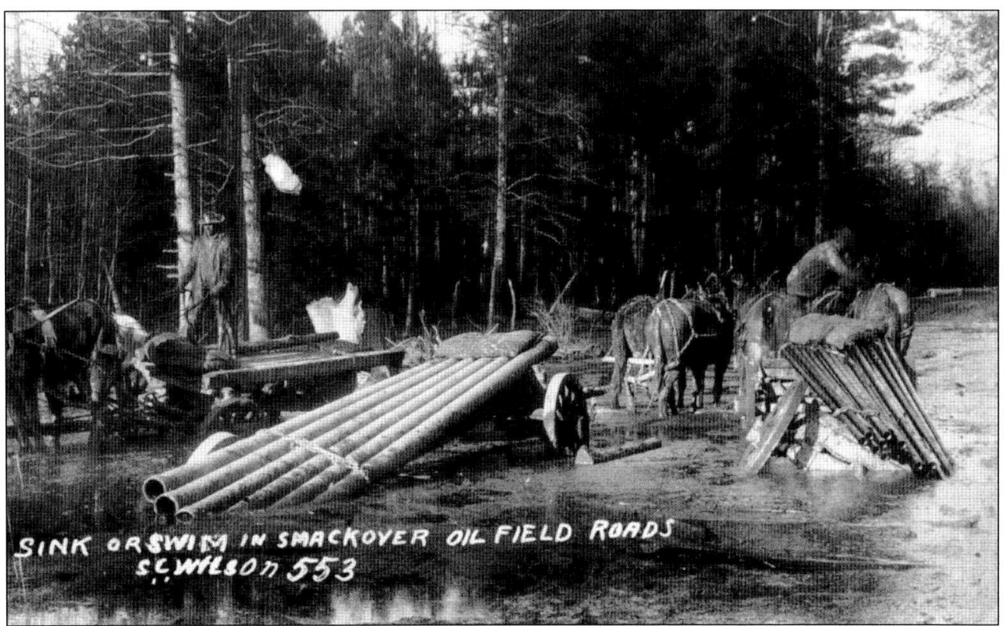

S.C. Wilson noted the two options: "Sink Or Swim In Smackover Oil Field Roads." The effort to transport these oil field pipes ended with the load sinking into the deep mud, while the mules were left standing in their harnesses.

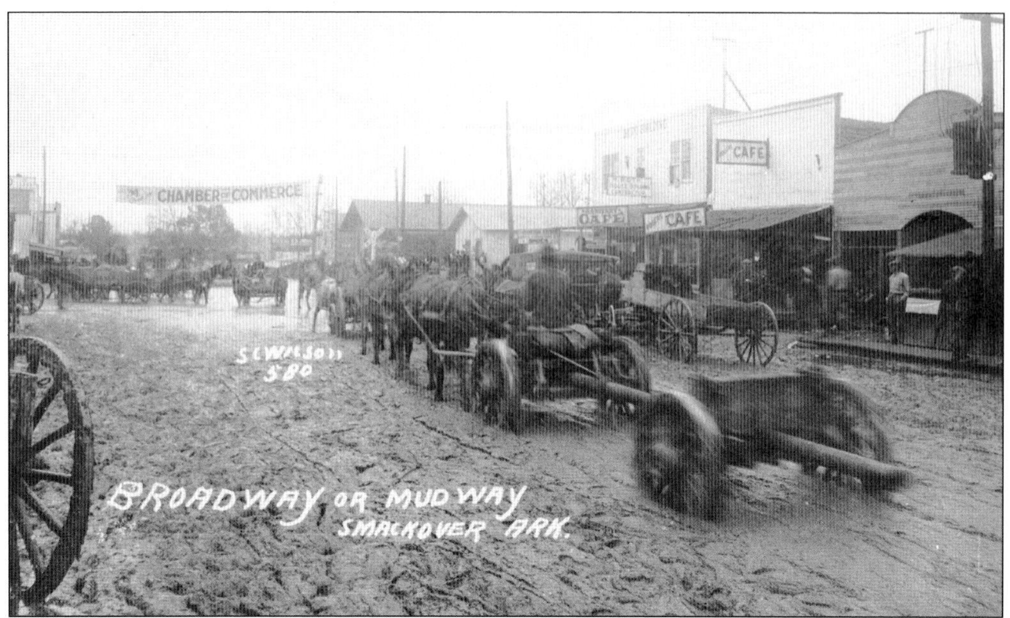

The iron wheels on the wagons cut so deeply into the watery mire that some mules were reported to have fallen in and drowned. The wagons hauling equipment to the wells in the surrounding countryside usually picked up their heavy loads at the train depot, then pulled them down Broadway. After heavy rains, it was "Broadway or Mudway," as the caption notes. The banner over the street in the distance reads, "Chamber of Commerce," and signs for three cafés are seen to the right.

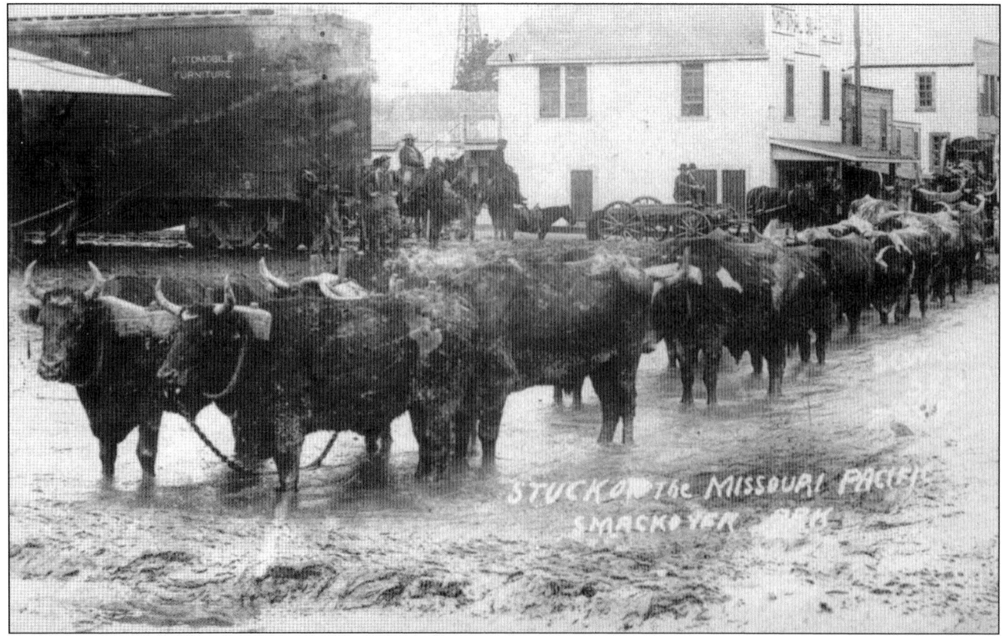

On the day this photograph was taken, a Missouri Pacific train was stopped in its tracks by a long team of oxen pulling equipment down the muddy street. The effort the great beasts expended can only be imagined, all these years later.

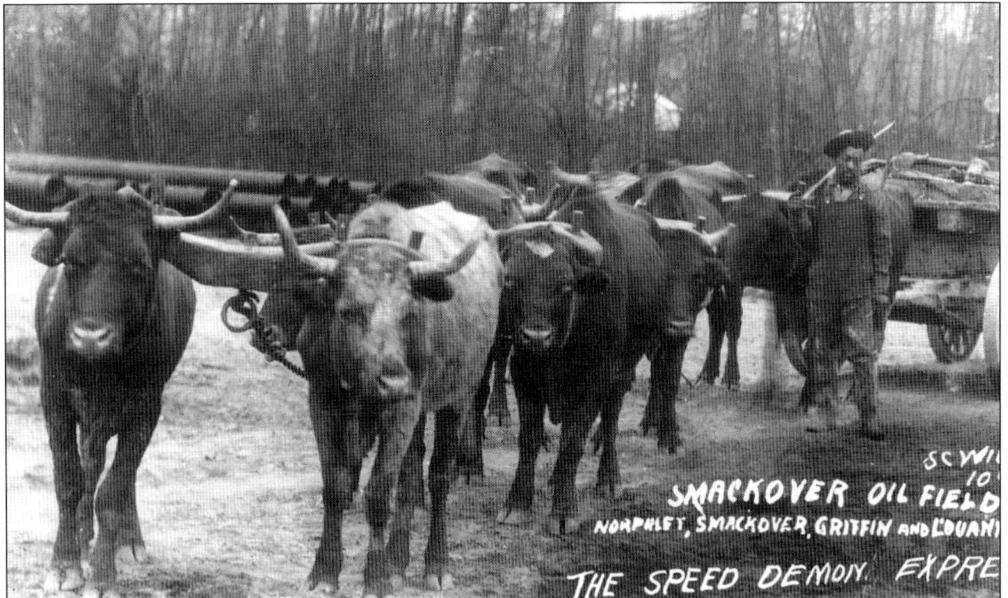

"The Speed Demon Express" was the photographer's wry comment. The huge oxen were anything but speedy, yet often, they were the only hope for moving loads along the muddy tracks between Smackover and the oil fields.

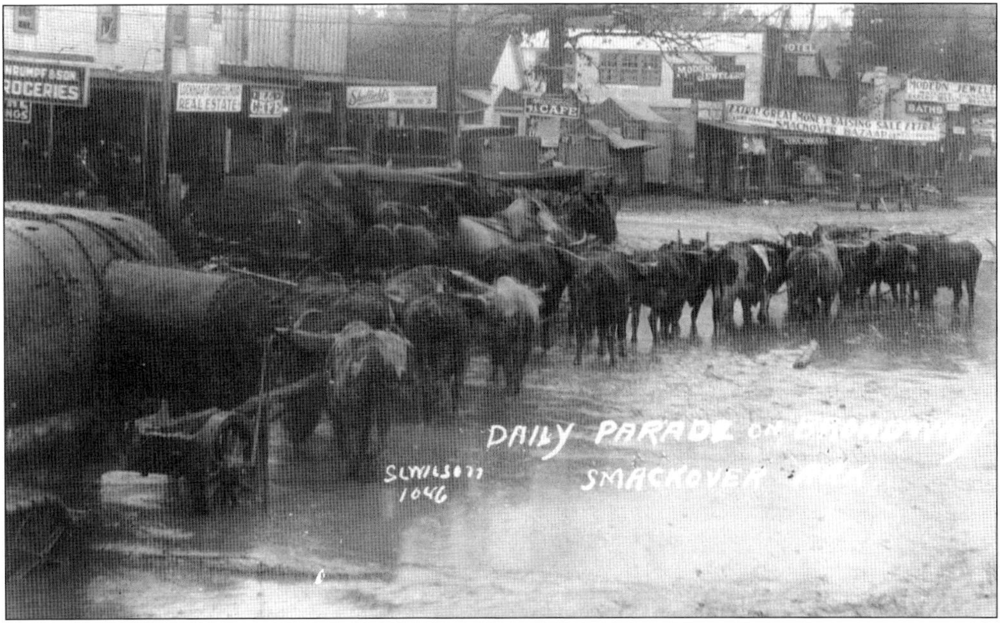

When mud on the roads to the drilling sites became more than mules could manage, teams of powerful oxen were brought in. The beasts are seen here hauling a huge iron boiler. Business signs seen in this view along Broadway include groceries, real estate, cafés, and even two jewelry stores next to a bathhouse. The presence of jewelry stores amid the muddy chaos was indicative of how much money was circulating.

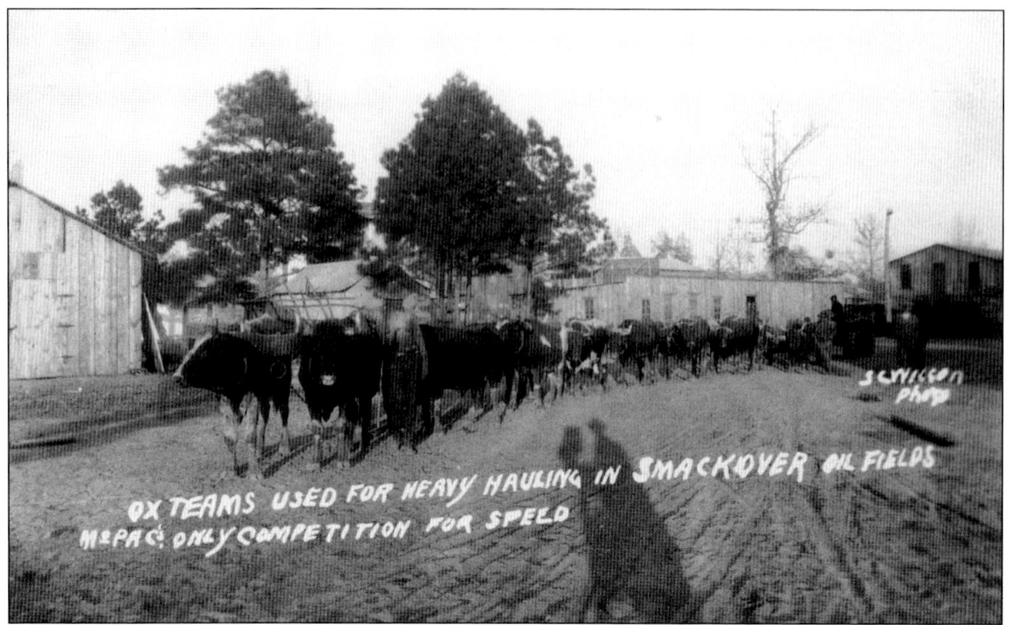

Photographer S.C. Wilson labeled this card, "Ox teams used for heavy hauling–MoPac's only competition for speed." This shot was taken on a sunny day, and the shadow of Wilson with his camera and tripod can be seen in the dirt street.

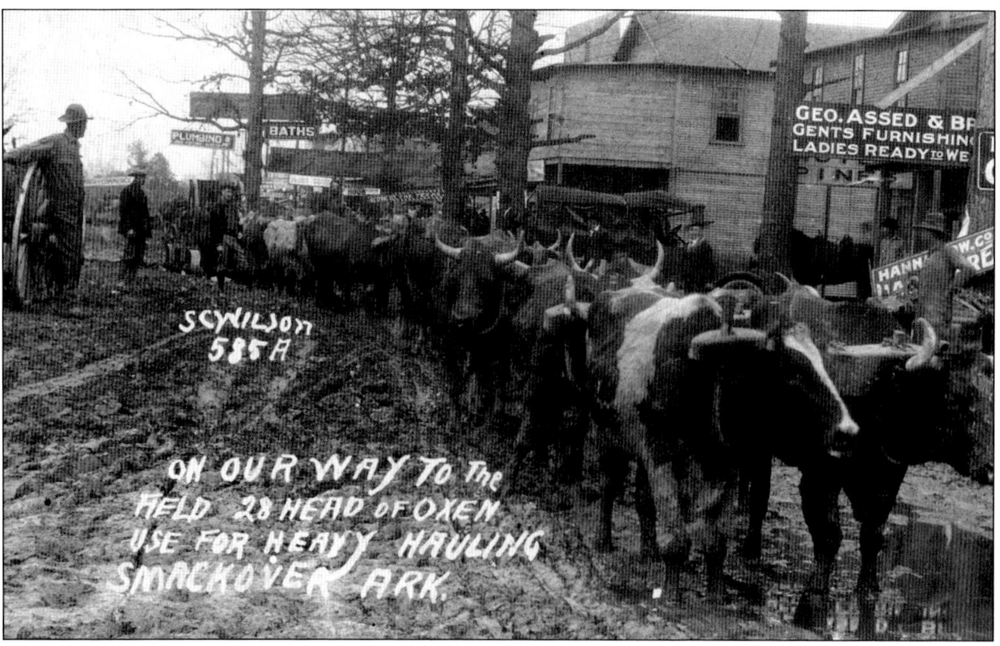

On the front of the card is the caption "On our way to the Field–28 Head of Oxen use for Heavy Hauling." On the back, the sender asked his friend in Maryland, "How do you like our way of transporting heavy machinery to the oil field? I have seen 34 [oxen] to one wagon loaded with [a] boiler." The varied merchant signs in this view implied cleanliness and civility, standing in contrast to the muddy street and struggling beasts.

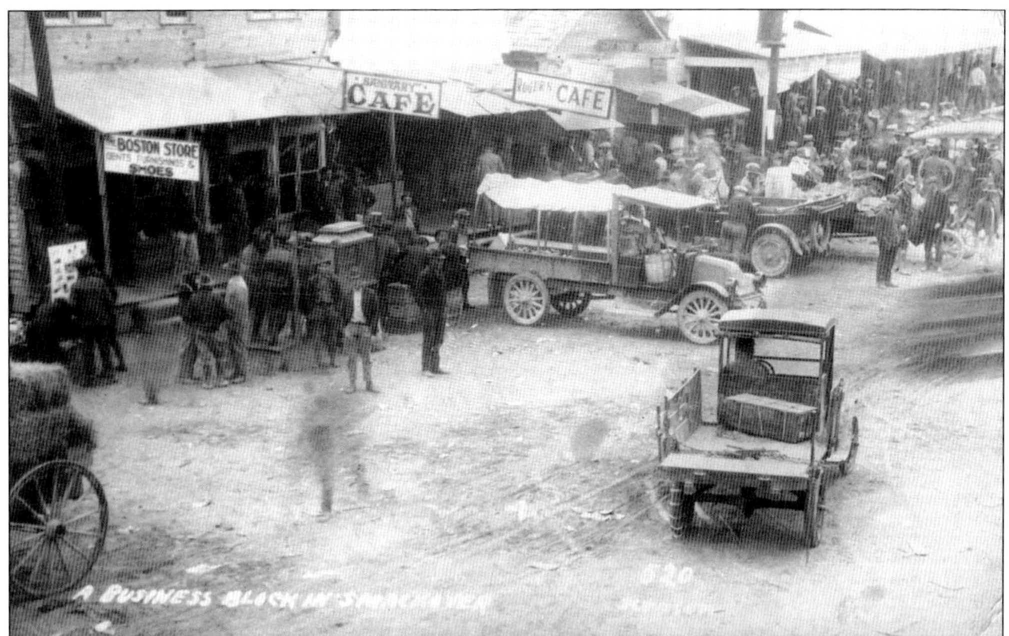

The photographer caught Broadway on a dry day, but still with a frenzy of people and a variety of vehicles. In this view, the Sanitary Café and the Rogers Café are seen side by side. To the left, the Boston Store promotes its shoes on a sandwich board sign propped on the sidewalk.

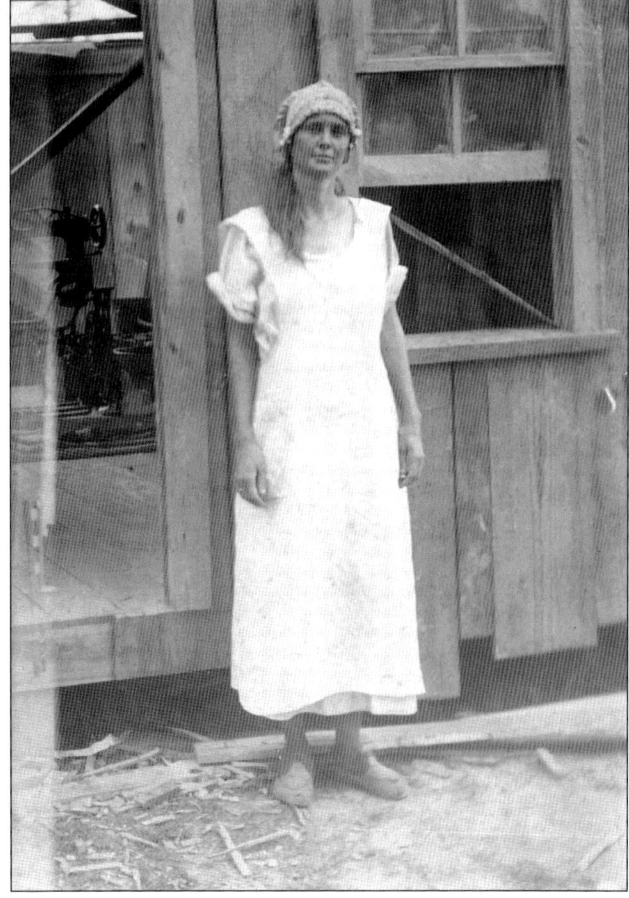

It took a lot of people working behind stoves in many kitchens to serve the thousands who had flooded the small town in search of riches. Seamstress skills were also in high demand, constructing clothing for the rough oil field work. This postcard shows Viola Schrimsher taking a break from her sewing machine as she poses outside the rough wooden building where she apparently spent her days.

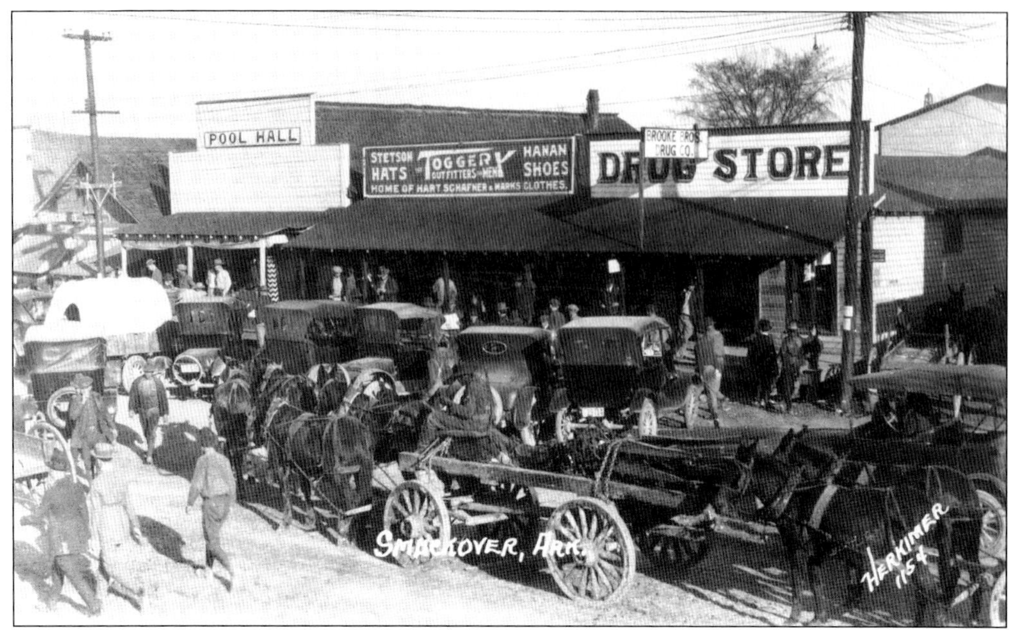

The crush of vehicles in Smackover ranged from Ford Model Ts to a covered wagon seen at far left to lines of mule-drawn wagons, which kept Broadway jammed most days. One of the businesses seen here in early 1923 was the Toggery Outfitters for Men, which offered Stetson hats, Hanan shoes, and Hart Schaffner & Marks clothes. The haberdashery was flanked by Brooke Brothers Drug Store and a pool hall.

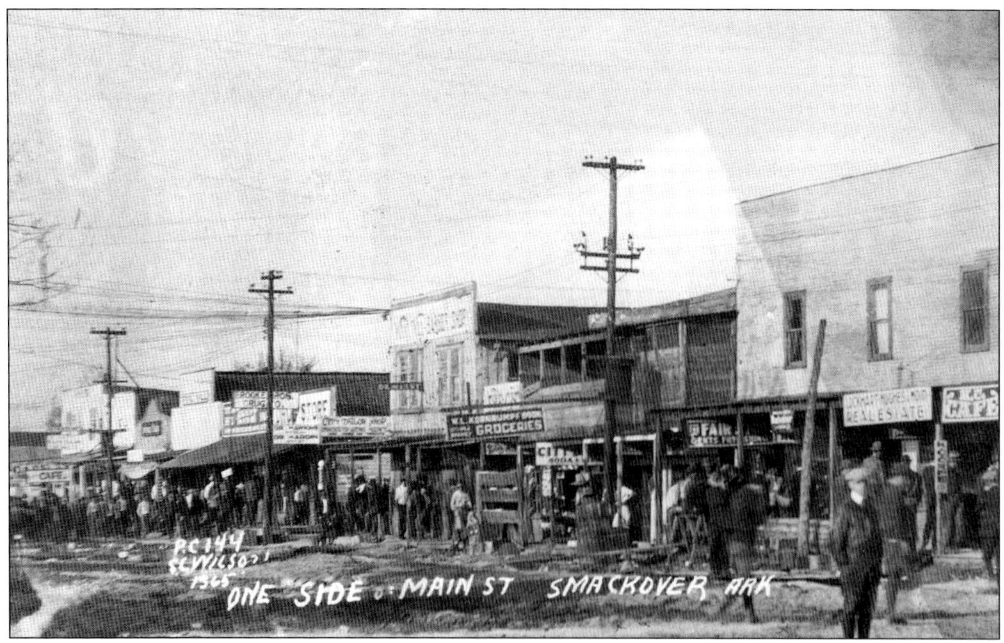

Photographer S.C. Wilson offered a view labeled, "One side of Main Street," showing Broadway in a muddy condition, with dozens of men on the sidewalk. This view captured the next block up from the Toggery, with signs noted for City Tailor Shop, W.L. Kornrumpf & Son Groceries, and the KC Café. Almost all of these frame buildings were lost in the fire of 1923.

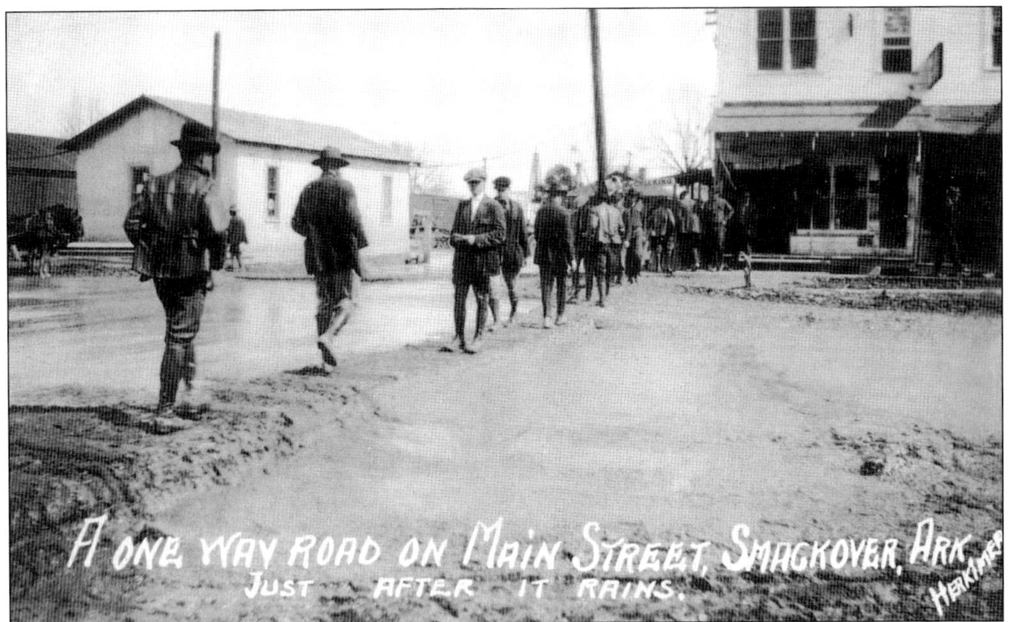

Pedestrian traffic was heavy on Broadway, and avoiding the mud while crossing the street was a challenge. One solution was to keep bulldozed up an elevated path of wet earth topped with sections of two-by-four lumber. Unfortunately, this type of crosswalk was often cut by heavy iron wagon wheels and the hooves of mule teams hauling equipment.

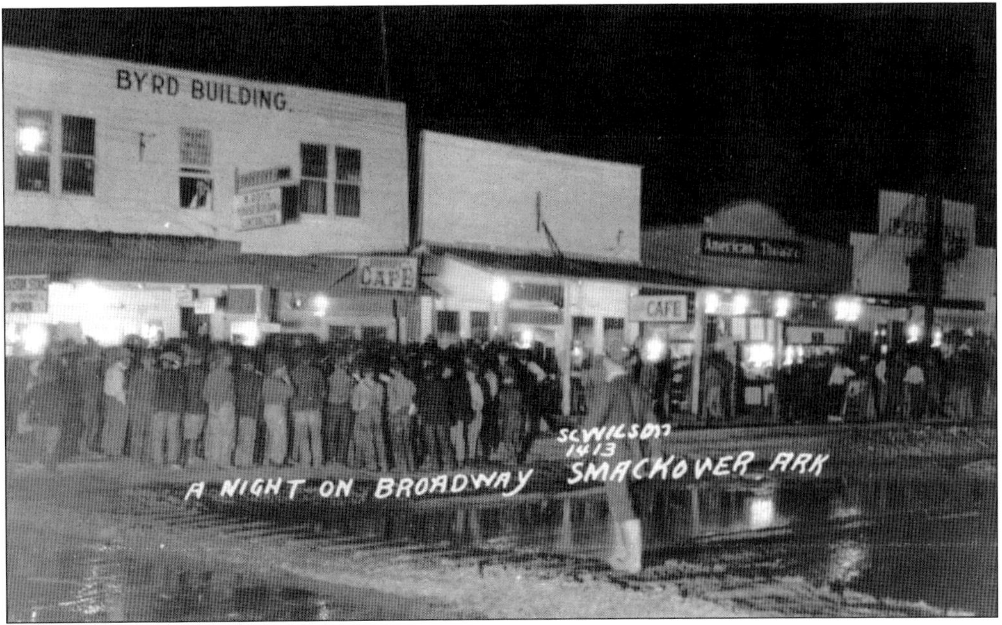

Smackover's Broadway saw fewer vehicles at night but rather was clogged with crowds of rough men blowing off steam after hard days on the outlying oil rigs. The laws of Prohibition meant little, as moonshine flowed freely while prostitutes plied their trade. The town's law enforcement officers could do little but try to stem the frequent violence as it erupted.

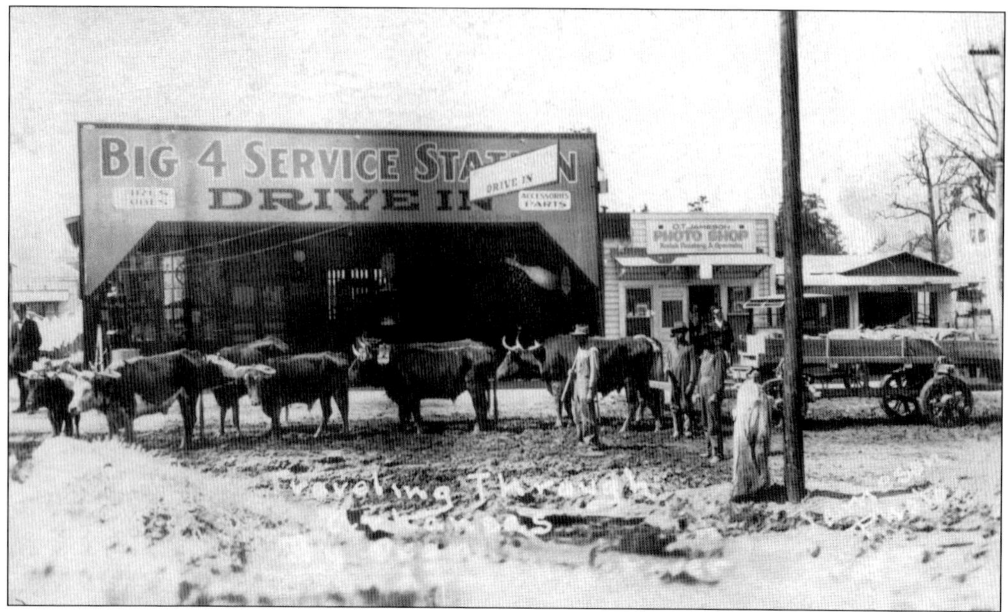

By July 1923, the Big 4 Service Station was operating at one end of Broadway; it had a large open front, where pretty much anything with an engine could be pulled in for repairs. Next door to the service station was O.T. Jameson's photography shop, which offered "Kodak Finishing" and likely produced a lot of postcards of the oil boom community.

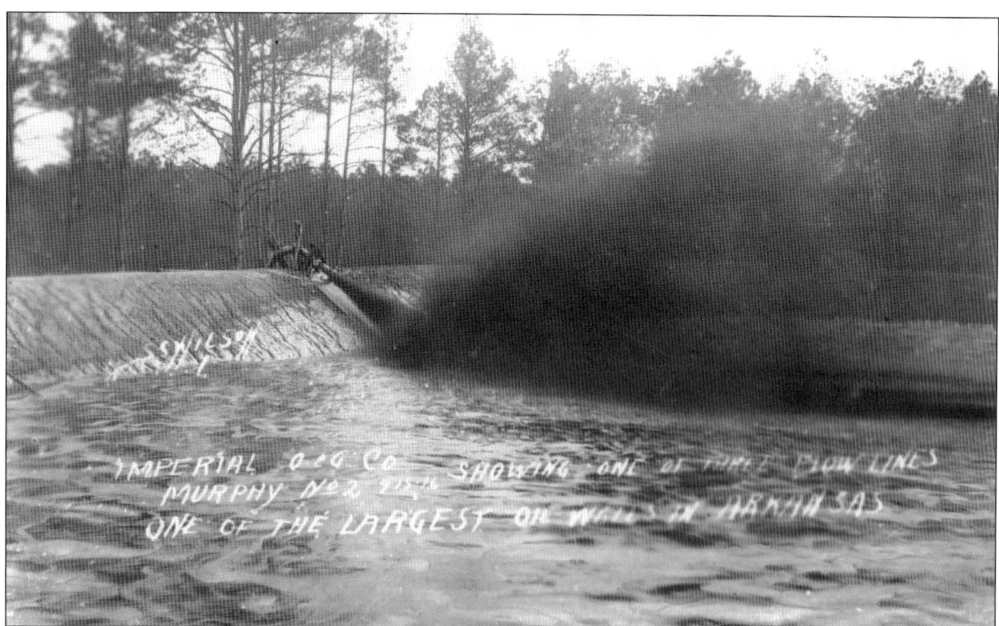

Some of the Smackover fields produced more than 50,000 barrels of oil a day, and storing it became a huge challenge. Huge pits dug into the ground were soon filled with oil pumped from the well heads.

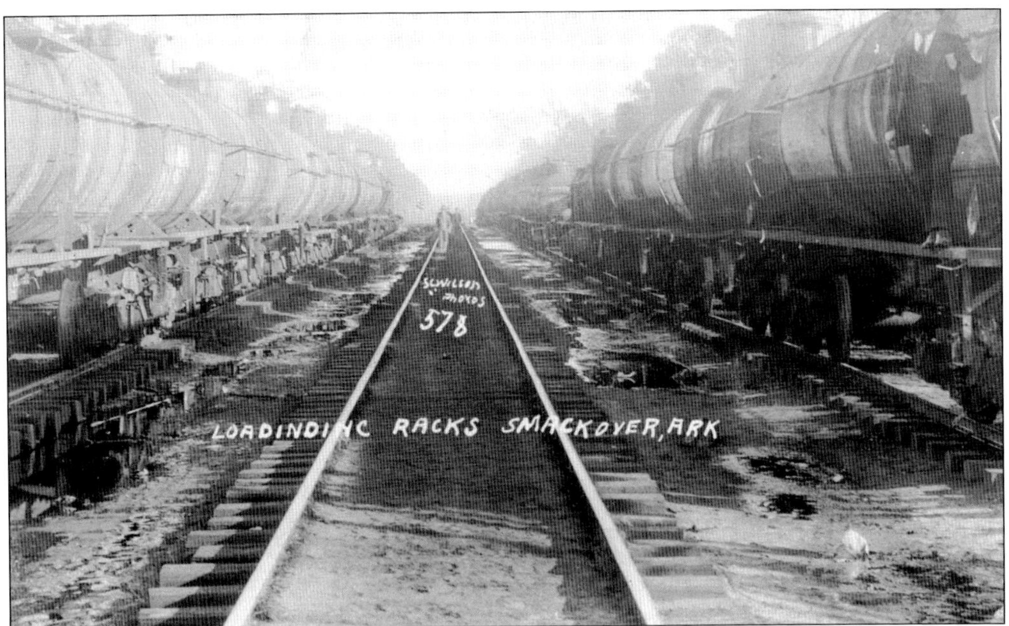

Once rail tank cars could be secured, oil was pumped into the cars and transported to refineries, some of which were opening in El Dorado. Eventually, pipelines were laid to transport the oil. By 1925, nearly 3,500 wells were pumping 69 million barrels of oil around Smackover. As in the El Dorado boom that started earlier, the oil flow around Smackover eventually ebbed.

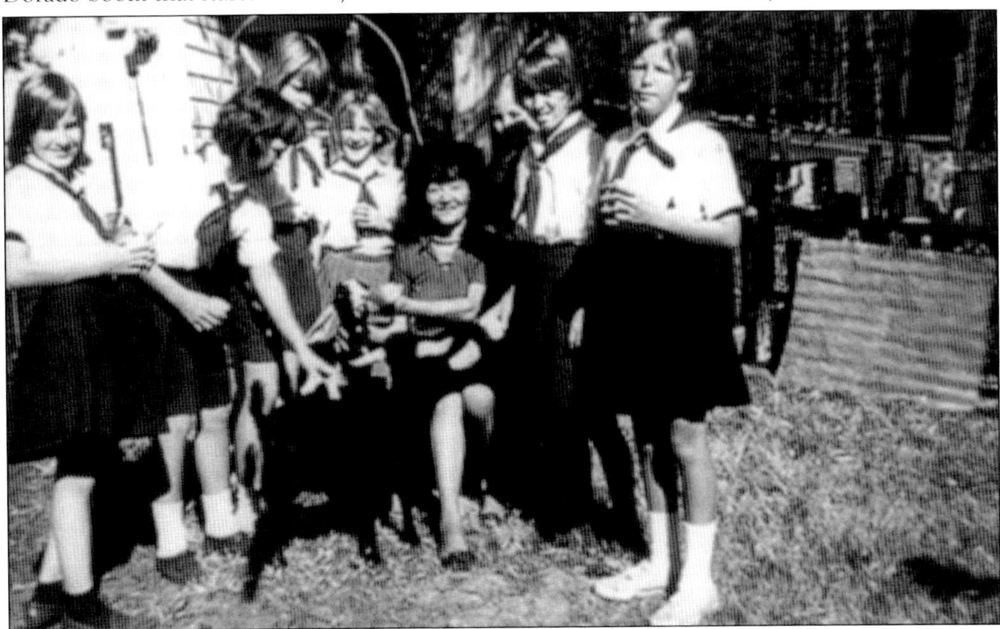

Among the memorable residents of Smackover was Rhena Salome Miller Meyer, known as the "Goat Woman." She toured for a time with the Barnum & Bailey Circus, doing an act in which she played as many as eight musical instruments at one time. Rhena married the circus business manager, and the couple settled in Smackover. They kept a circus wagon along with their goats and offered shows to entertain children and adults alike. Rhena and her goats could even be heard singing together on the local radio station. (Courtesy of the Encyclopedia of Arkansas.)

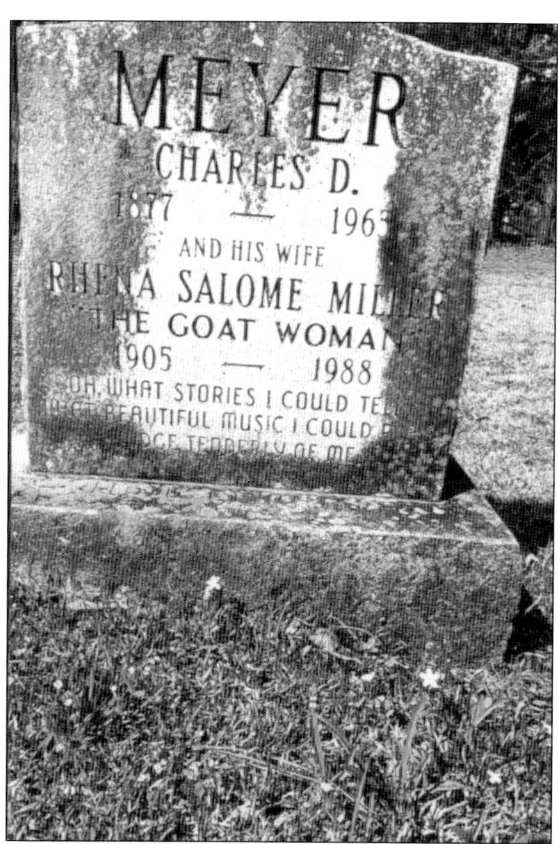

After her husband died in 1963, Rhena Meyer continued performing for Scout troops and birthday parties. By 1984, she gave up her circus wagon and moved into a nursing home; she died in 1988. Her monument in the Liberty Cemetery in Louann, Arkansas, notes her nickname of "The Goat Woman" and includes the inscription "Oh What Stories I Could Tell—What Beautiful Music I Could Play—Judge Tenderly Of Me." (Photograph by Ray Hanley.)

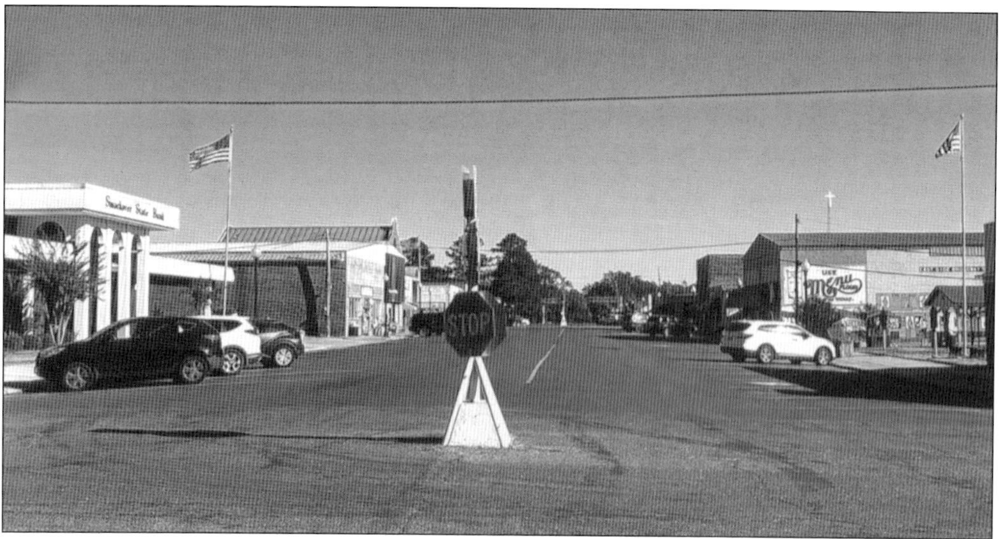

Smackover in 2024 finds Broadway a far cry from the muddy mired street of a century earlier. Most of the brick buildings still stand, which had replaced the wooden ones lost in the fire of 1923; several are adorned with colorful murals depicting the oil boom days. The town's population today is around 1,500, enjoying a slow life in a pleasant small town, far removed from the frenetic pace of the 25,000 population of 1925. Some oil is still produced in the area with "pump jack" wells. (Photograph by Ray Hanley.)

Four

Iconic Leaders and Companies of the Oil Boom

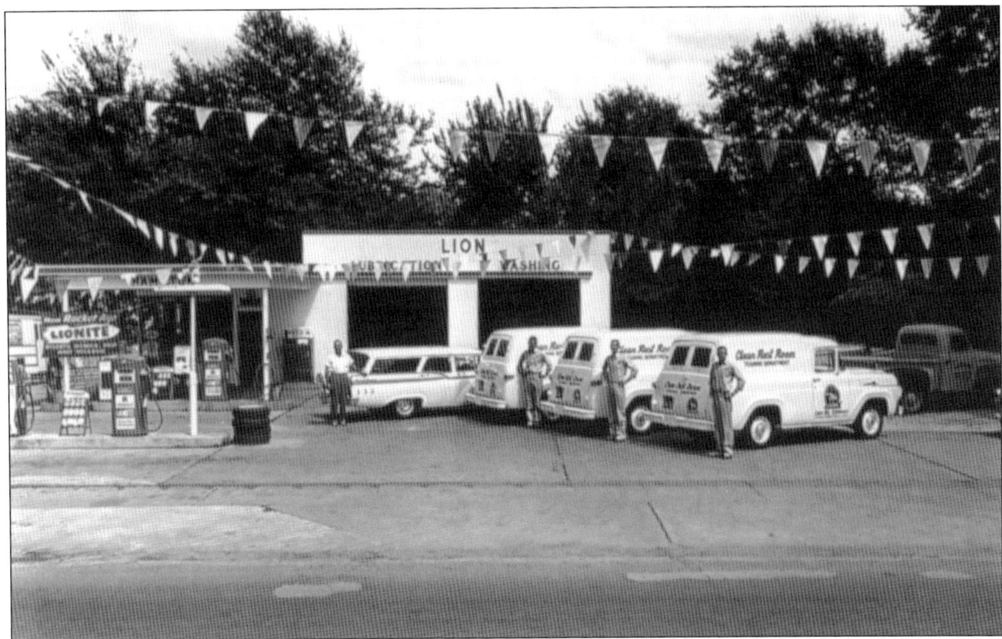

The photographs from the oil fields and muddy clogged roads of Union County tell only part of the oil story there. Behind those images are remarkable individuals who took chances investing in the area. In the process of establishing their fortunes, several of these investors founded iconic oil companies. One such company was Lion Oil, which not only produced oil and refined gasoline but also operated hundreds of service stations across the South.

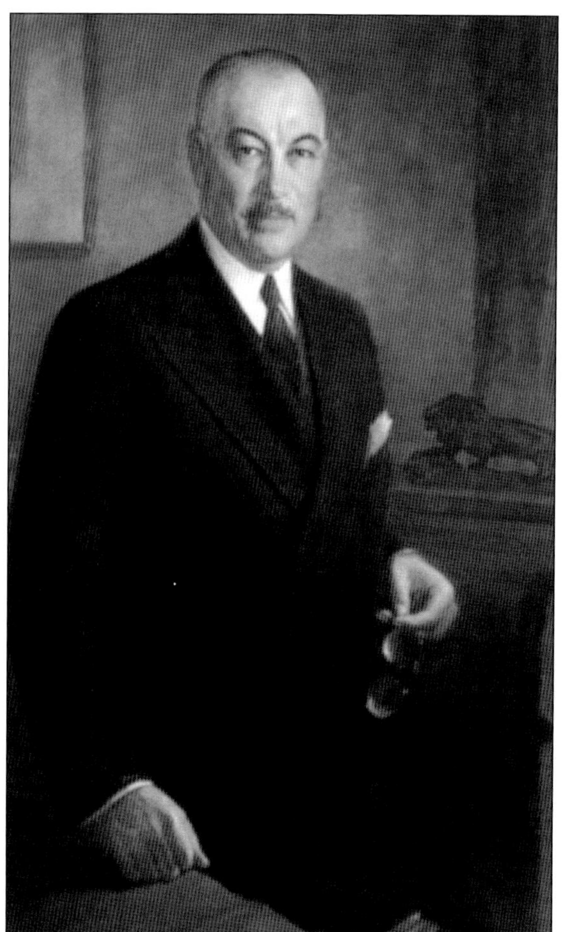

Col. Thomas Harry Barton came to El Dorado from Texas and began to invest in the oil business. He took over a small refinery in 1922 and named it Lion Oil. The man liked wordplay, as "lion oil" is a palindrome, spelled the same forward or backward. Initially, Lion Oil produced 2,000 barrels a day and employed 25 people, but much bigger things were to come. (Courtesy of SAHPS.)

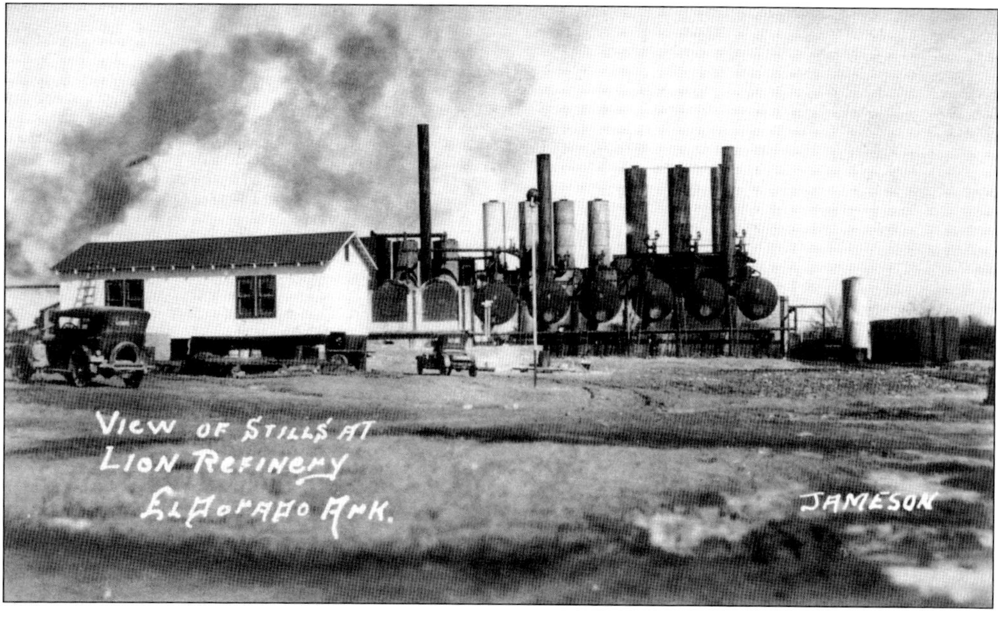

Lion Oil signed some 1,600 acres worth of leases in the Smackover field and was soon pumping 12,000 barrels of oil a day. It built a 12-mile pipeline from those fields to its refinery in El Dorado, seen here. During the first six months of 1924, Lion Oil's 85 wells pumped out 1.4 million barrels of oil.

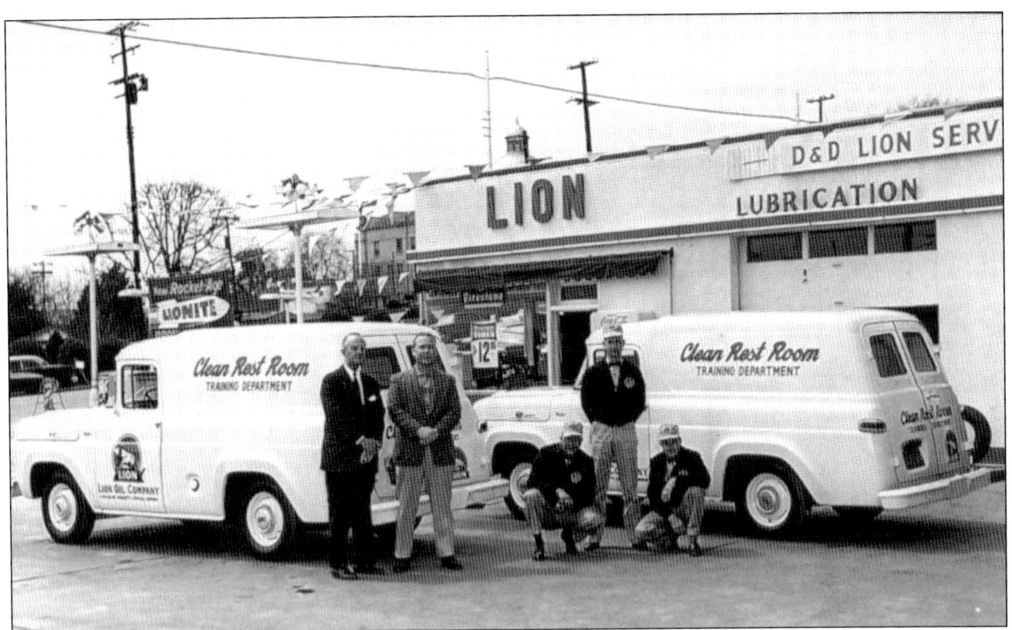

In 1929, Lion Oil started the wholesale marketing of oil and then began to sell gasoline. By 1932, there were 441 service stations under the Lion sign and by 1935 almost 800. Seen here is the D&D Lion Service Station, location unknown, as it was getting its visit from the company's "Clean Rest Room Training Department." At the time (around 1957), the average cost per gallon of gas was 31¢. According to the sign in the window, Firestone tires went for $12.95 each.

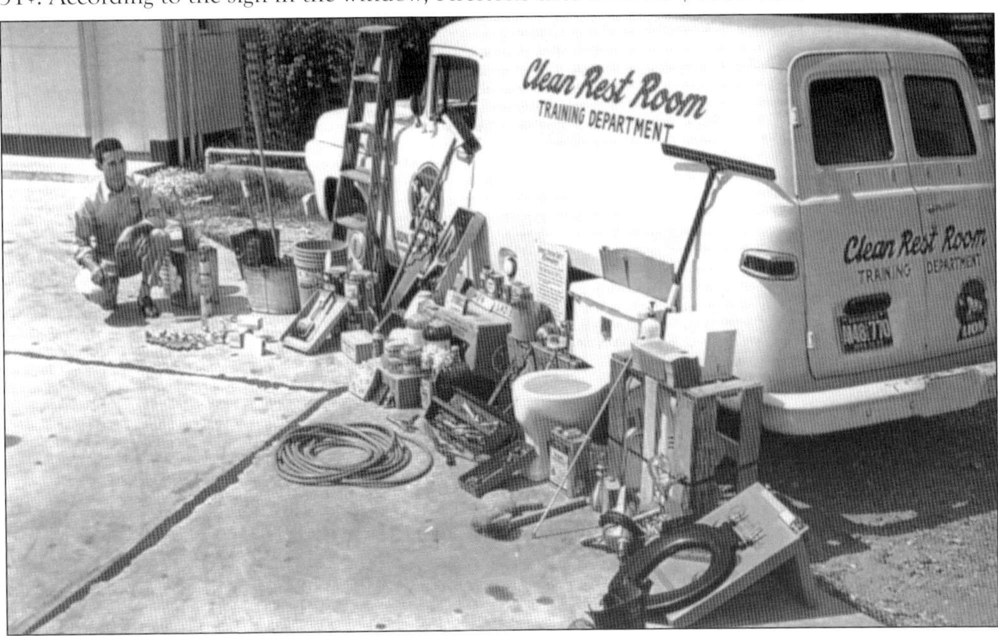

Lion Oil was clearly serious about the quality of its service station restrooms, as it put training teams on the road to inspect and train station managers on how to keep clean, well-equipped facilities. In 1939, Lion Oil became the first Arkansas company to be traded on the New York Stock Exchange. At its peak in the early 1950s, there were almost 2,000 Lion service stations, mostly in southern states.

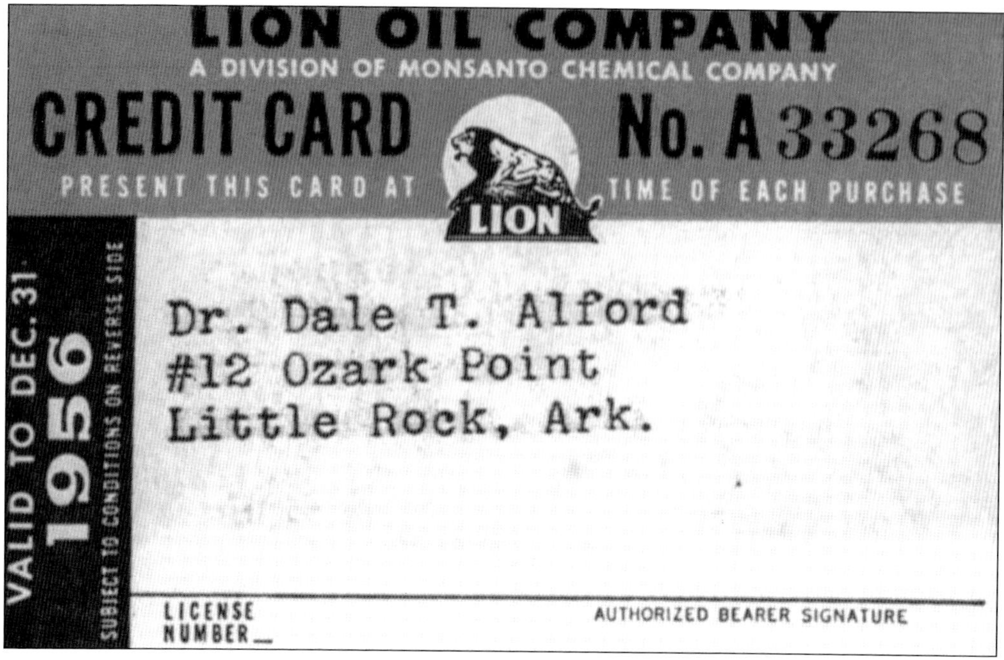

Lion Oil missed little in the business of selling gasoline, including issuing credit cards. Magnetic strip technology was decades away in 1956 when this credit card was printed on cardboard. The card shown belonged to Dr. Dale Alford, an ophthalmologist who also served as the US congressman from Little Rock. Perhaps with this Lion Oil card in his wallet, Dr. Alford posed for the advertisement postcard, below, during his campaign for reelection in 1958. In 1960, he mounted the first of two unsuccessful runs for the governor's office. Born in 1916, Alford died in the year 2000.

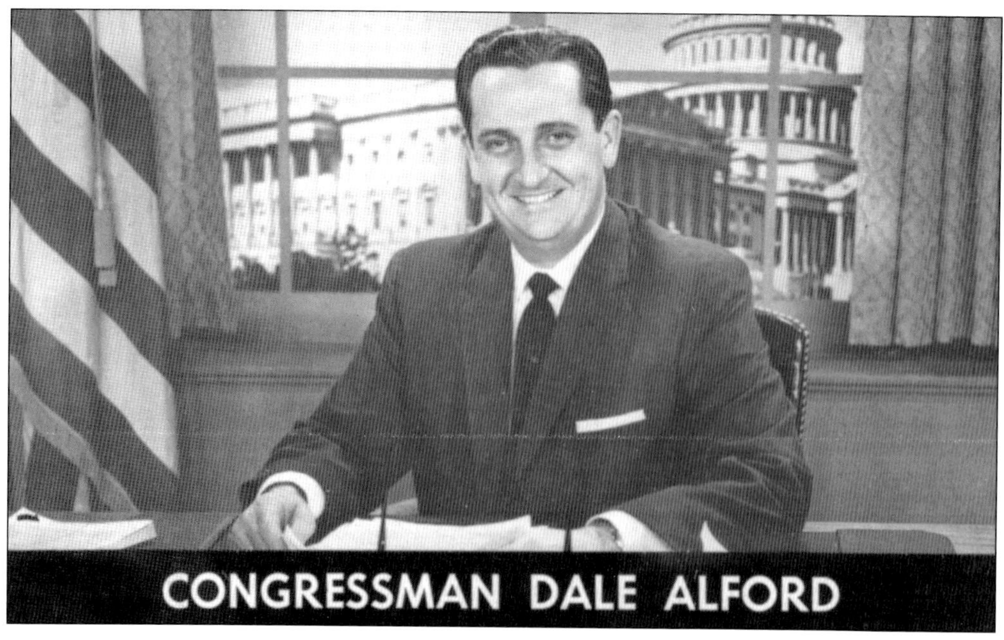

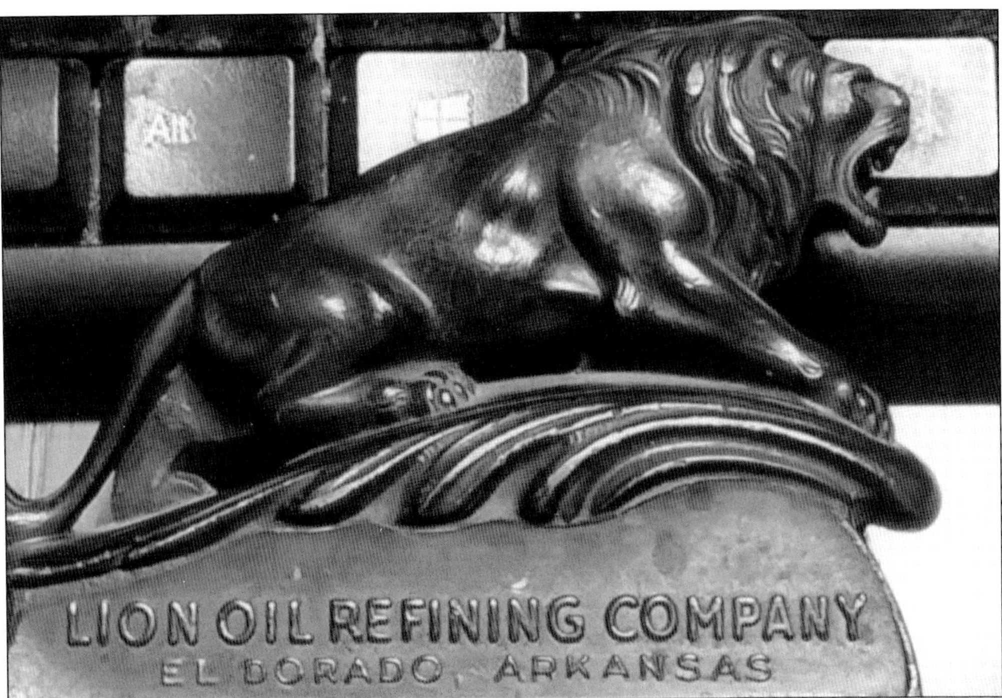

Lion Oil president T.H. Barton and his salesmen gave a number of brass Lion Oil paperweights to favored customers. The bronze sculptures today are sought after as collectibles, selling for as much as $100 in online auctions.

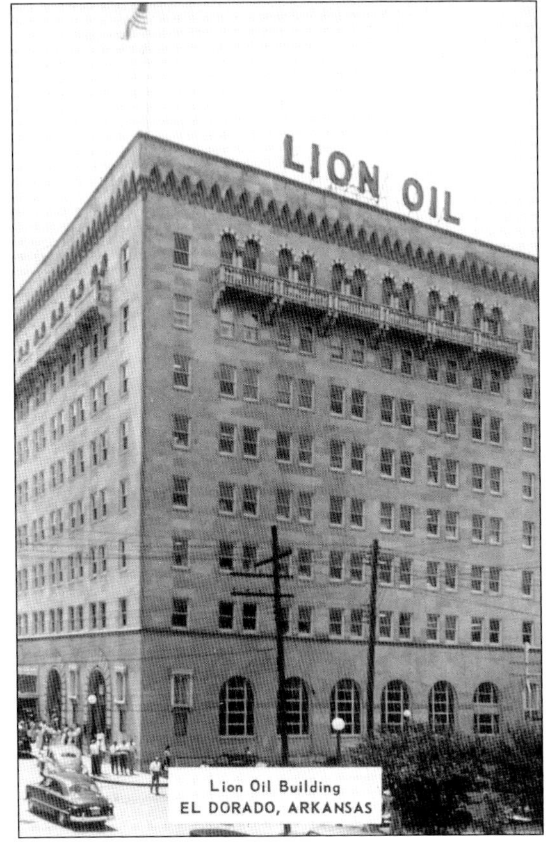

With the onset of World War II, Lion Oil created a subsidiary, the Ozark Ordnance Works, to make anhydrous ammonia for use in combat explosives. After the war, the company began to make ammonia and nitrogen fertilizers. The rapid growth of the company ensured full use of the El Dorado headquarters, an impressive eight-story "skyscraper" (by Arkansas standards) designed by George Mann and completed in 1927. Later known as the Exchange Bank building and now the First Financial Building, it remains the tallest structure in the region.

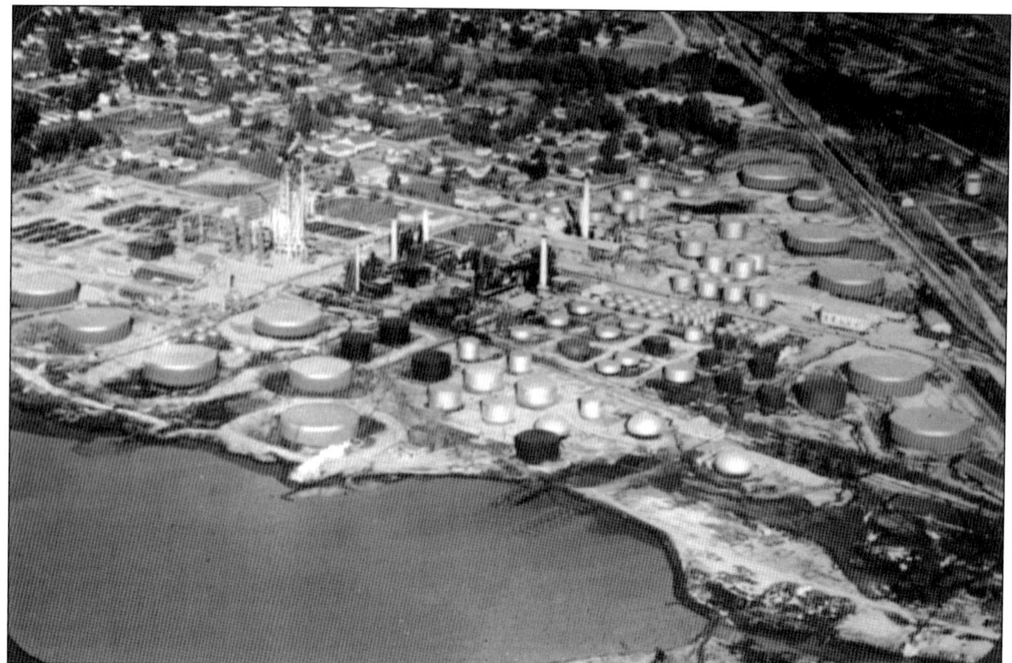

This aerial view of the Lion Oil refinery gives an idea of how large a presence the company maintained in El Dorado. In 1955, Lion Oil was acquired by Monsanto Chemical Company. The Lion logo slowly disappeared, as Monsanto sold off or closed down the service stations; a series of owners held the refinery, which continued to produce gasoline. Delek US Holdings, the American branch of Israeli-based Delek Ground, acquired 100 percent of Lion Oil in 2011.

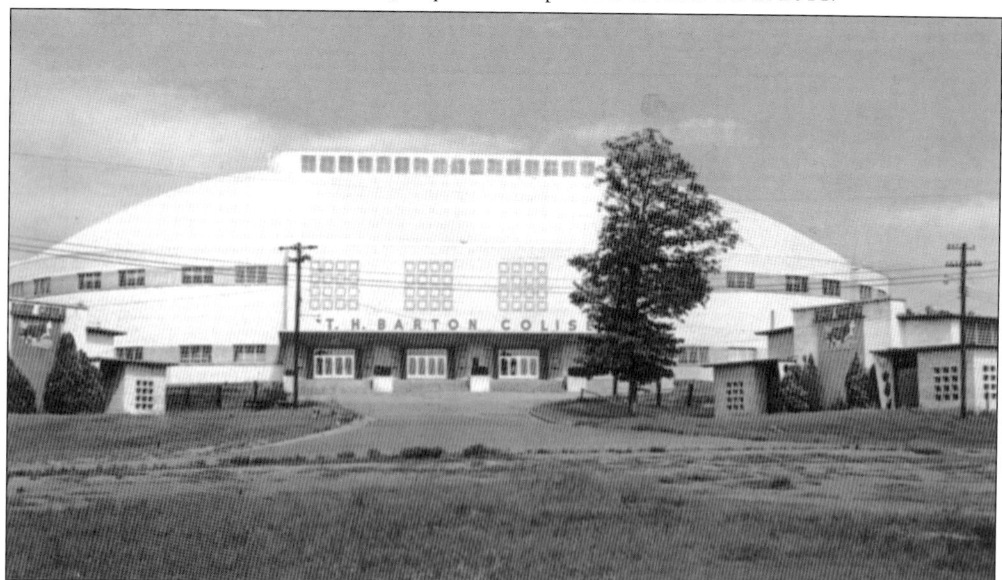

An enduring legacy for Lion Oil's T.H. Barton was erected in Little Rock in the early 1950s. Barton had long been involved with the Arkansas Livestock Association, which was in need of a larger setting for its annual rodeo and livestock show. The Arkansas State Fair was also in need of a new home. With major help from Barton, one of the largest arenas in the nation was built and given his name, T.H. Barton Coliseum. Barton died in 1960.

Charles Haywood Murphy arrived in El Dorado in 1904 when the town's population numbered about 4,000. He and his family's legacy had a lasting impact on Union County. Initially invested in banks and timberlands, Murphy eventually got into the oil business. In the early 1920s, he and his partners controlled about 100,000 acres in Union County.

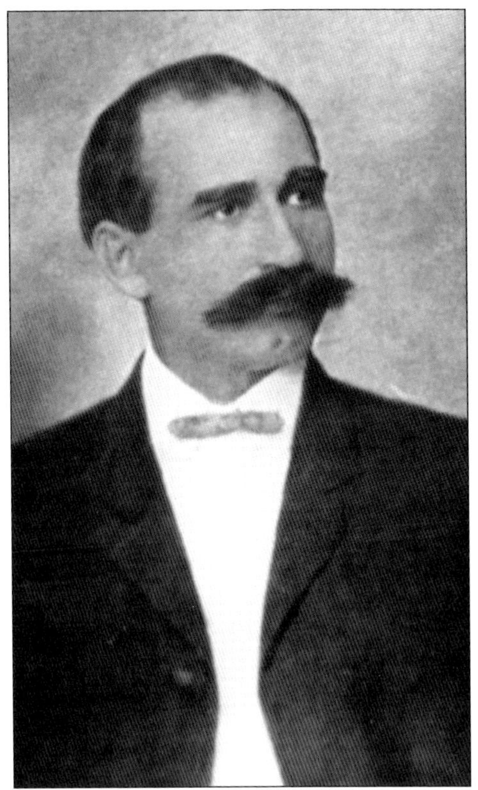

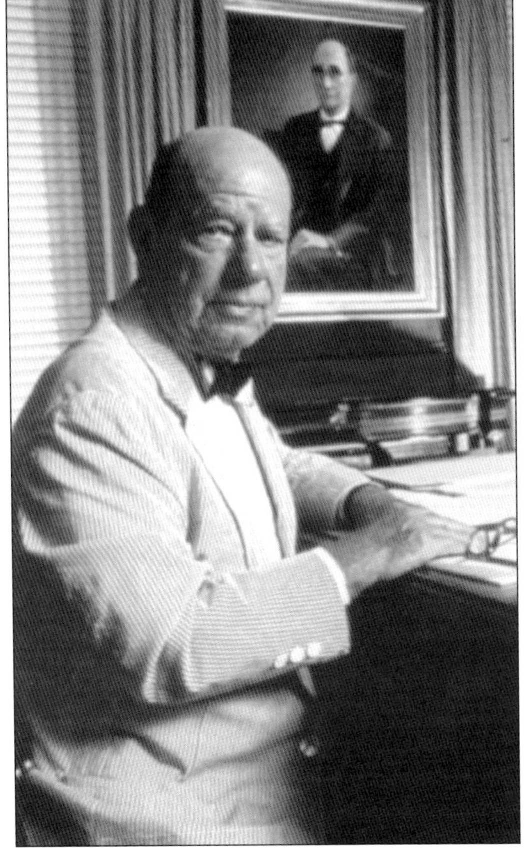

After his father suffered a stroke in 1941, Charles H. Murphy Jr. became the leader of the Murphy family business at the young age of 21. With his siblings, the 1938 El Dorado High School graduate formed C.H. Murphy & Company, which would go on to drill for oil around the globe. Upon Charles Murphy Jr.'s death in 2002, his son Madison said of his father, "The world is much duller without him." (Courtesy of the Encyclopedia of Arkansas.)

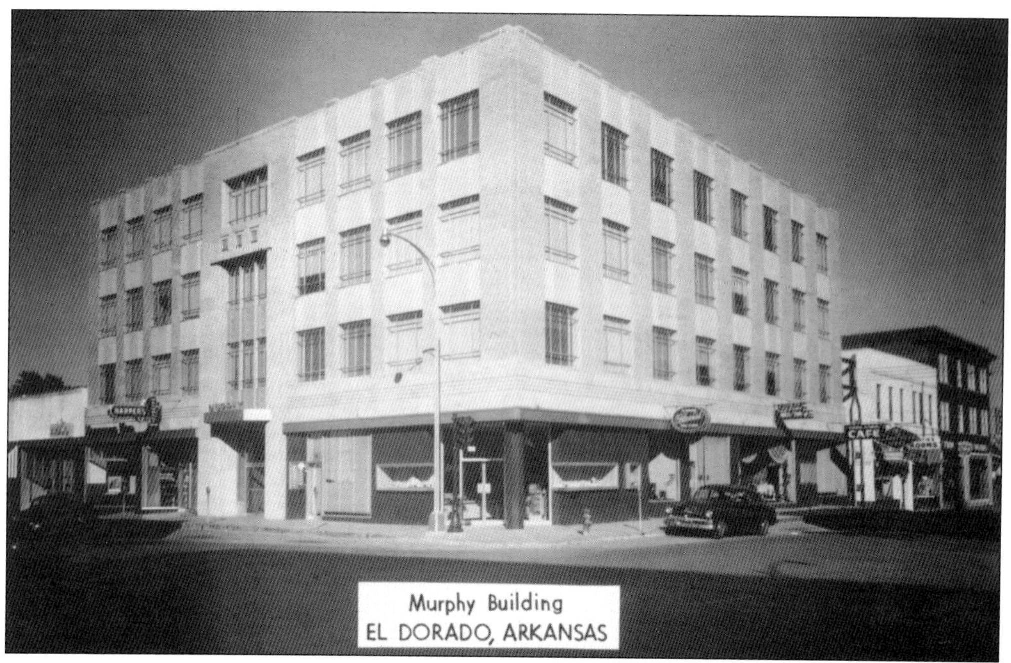

As C.H. Murphy & Company, now known as the Murphy Oil Corporation, prospered, it constructed a headquarters building downtown on Jefferson Street near the courthouse. By the 1950s, Murphy Oil was producing oil in Canada, Libya, and Ecuador, among other places. The planning and execution of what became a global enterprise was directed from this building in downtown El Dorado.

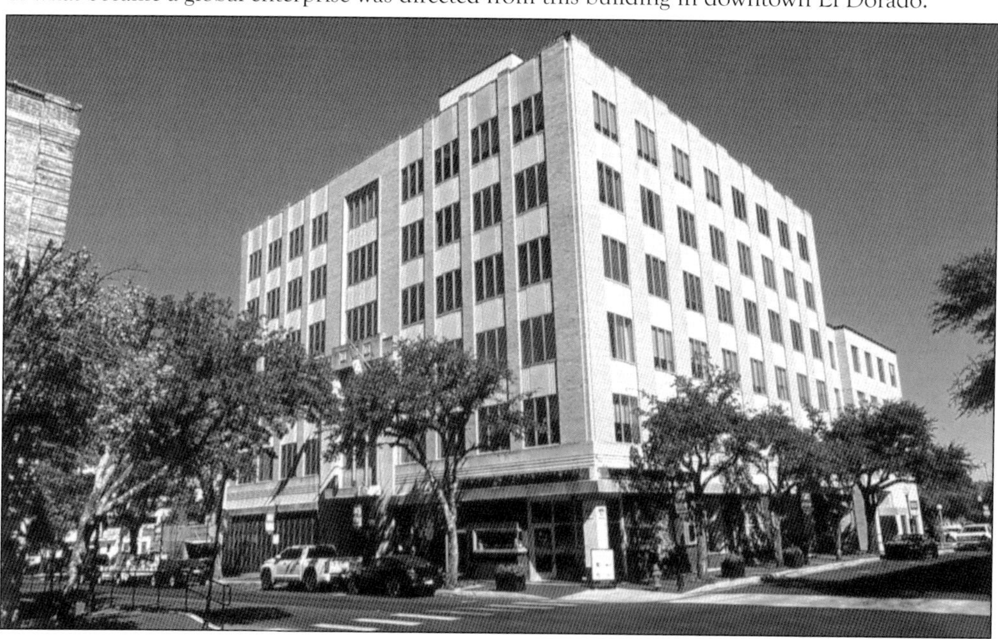

Murphy Oil's success led to the addition of two more floors to its building, as seen here. In 2020, after decades in the town of its birth, Murphy Oil announced it was relocating its headquarters to Houston, Texas, the nation's oil center. The Murphy Building today houses a variety of offices. Though its business headquarters have moved, the corporation continues to promote the "El Dorado Promise" scholarship fund it created for all local graduates. (Photograph by Ray Hanley.)

Five

El Dorado after the Oil Slowed

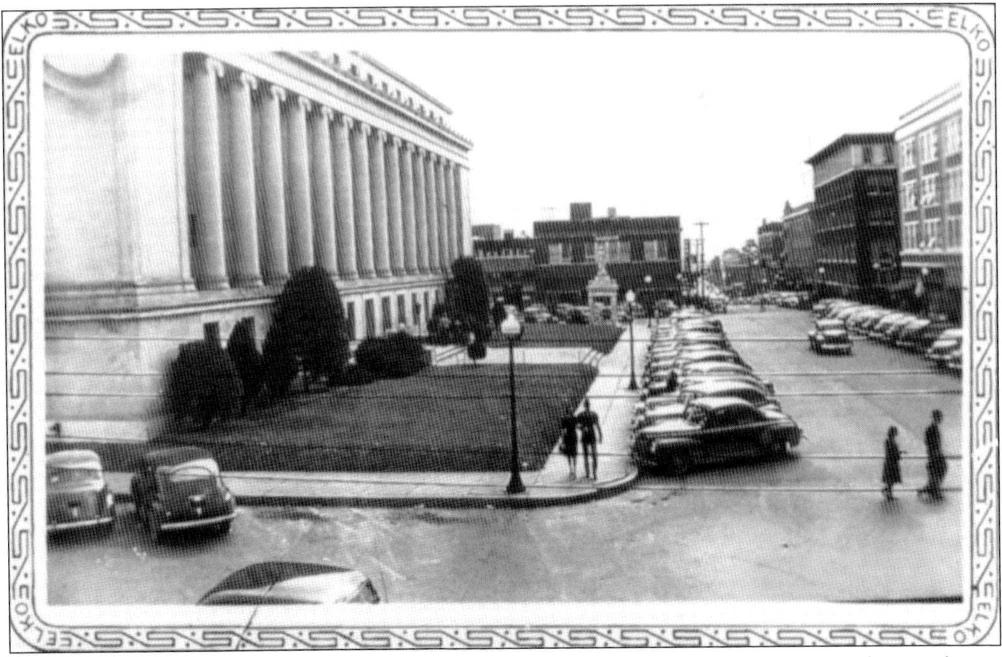

In 1925, a record 73 million barrels of oil were tapped in the El Dorado fields, but the rapid pace of extraction and improper storage led to a falloff in production. Attention shifted to the newer fields around Smackover. Still, oil would remain a part of El Dorado's economy into the future; the town was diversifying its industrial base, and by 1940, it was becoming a first-class city.

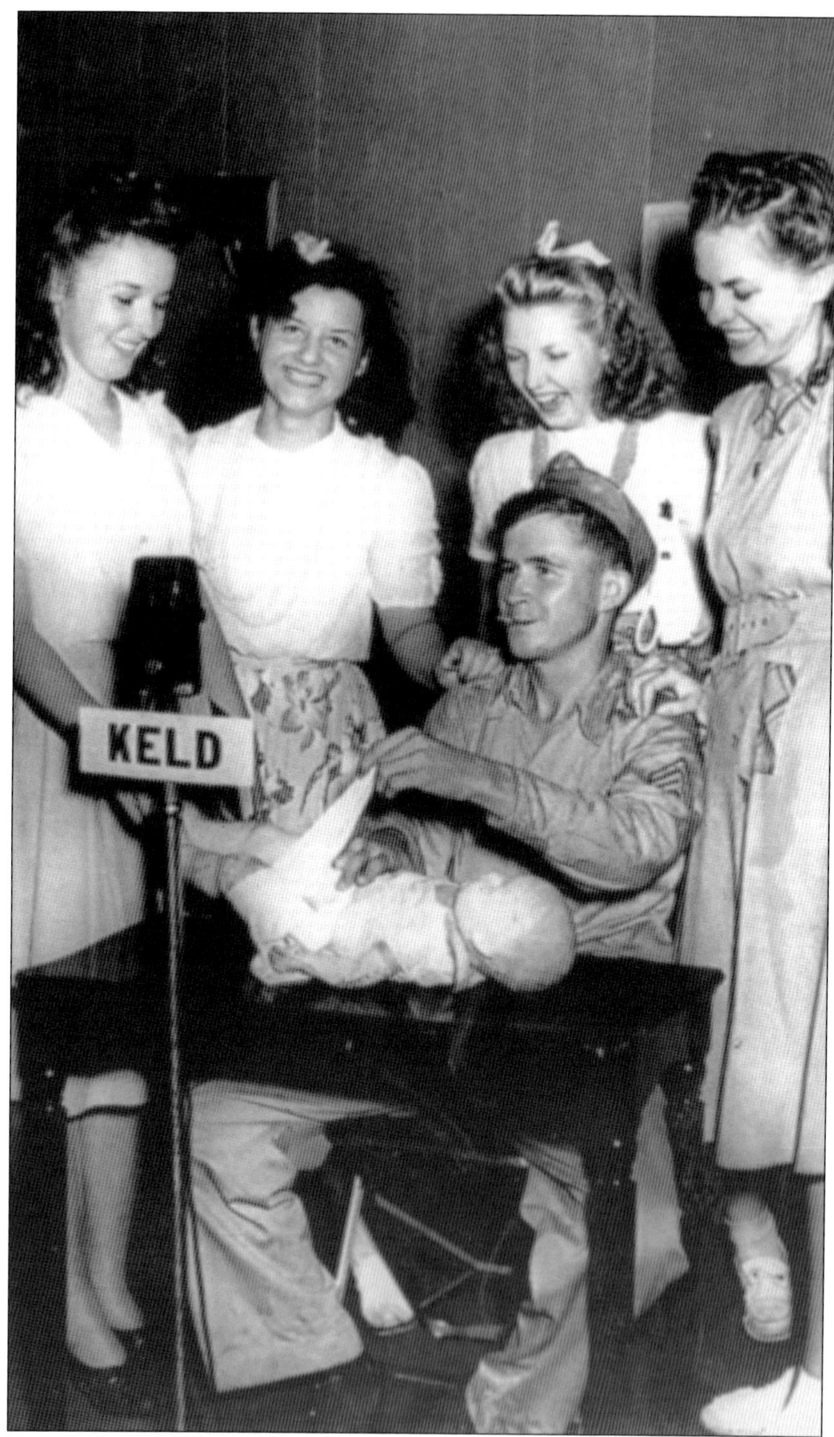

During World War II, a sprawling ordnance and ammunition plant was operated by the federal government near El Dorado, with hundreds of soldiers working or training there. In this publicity shot, Army Air Force nurses are photographed giving a young soldier from the facility lessons in changing diapers. (Courtesy of SAHPS.)

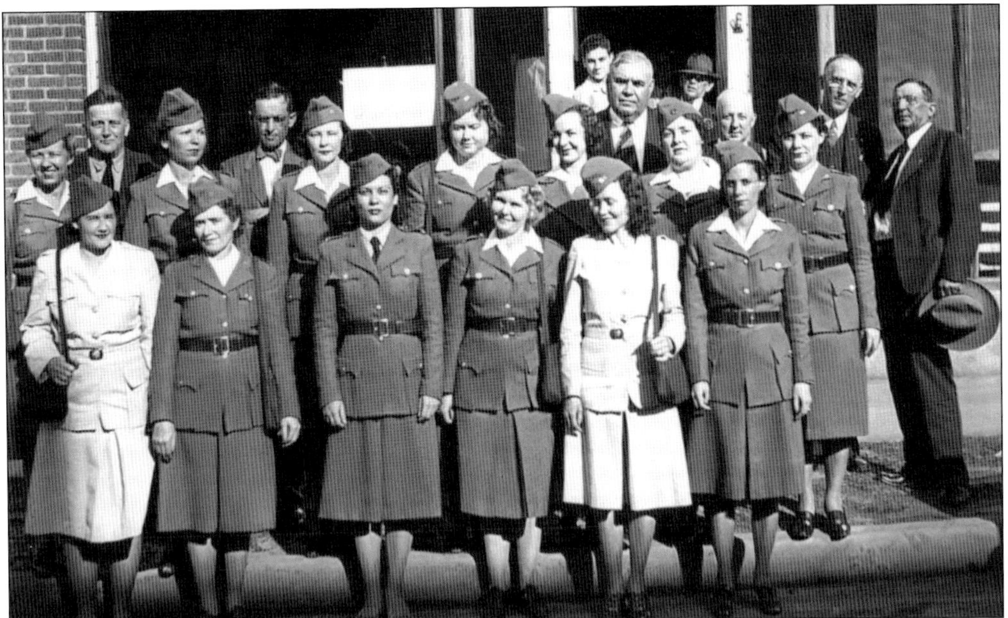

Warner Brown/Sisters of Mercy Hospital School of Nursing graduated many nurses who joined the Army Corps of Nurses. This photograph was taken at the US recruitment office in El Dorado; the gentlemen pictured were with the local draft board, although these ladies had enlisted. Third from the right in the front row was LaVanda "Rue" Bishop Aquilina, who after the war wrote a book, *Unsung Heroes: Combat Nurses & Army Wives*, recounting her World War II service in the Pacific. (Courtesy of SAHPS.)

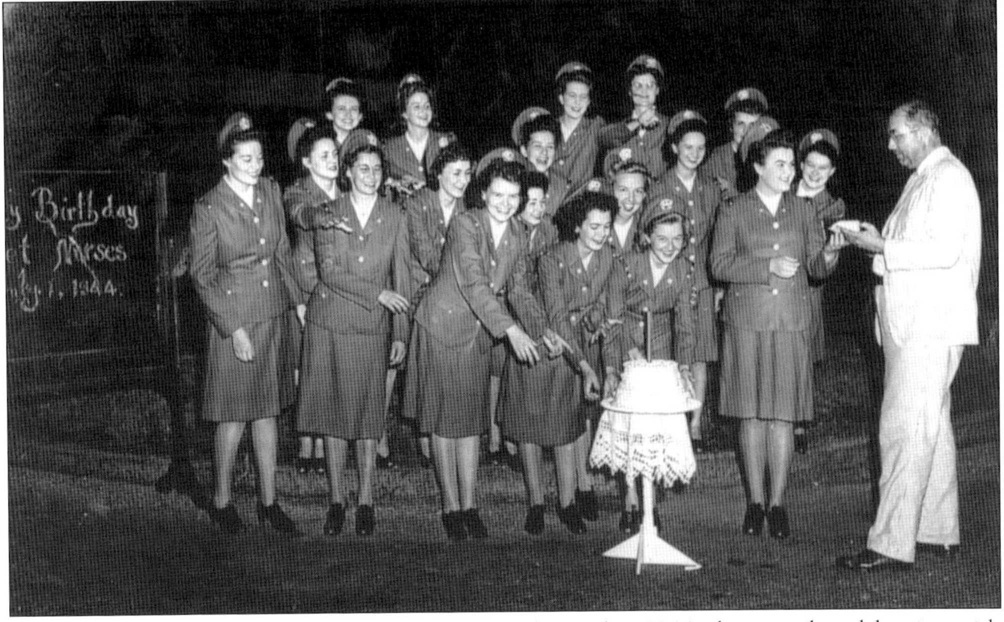

Col. T.H. Barton, head of Lion Oil, is seen at right in this 1944 photograph, celebrating with cadet nurses of the Warner Brown/Sisters of Mercy School of Nursing who had enlisted for the war effort. One of the nurses seems to be handing Colonel Barton a slice of the celebratory cake. (Courtesy of SAHPS.)

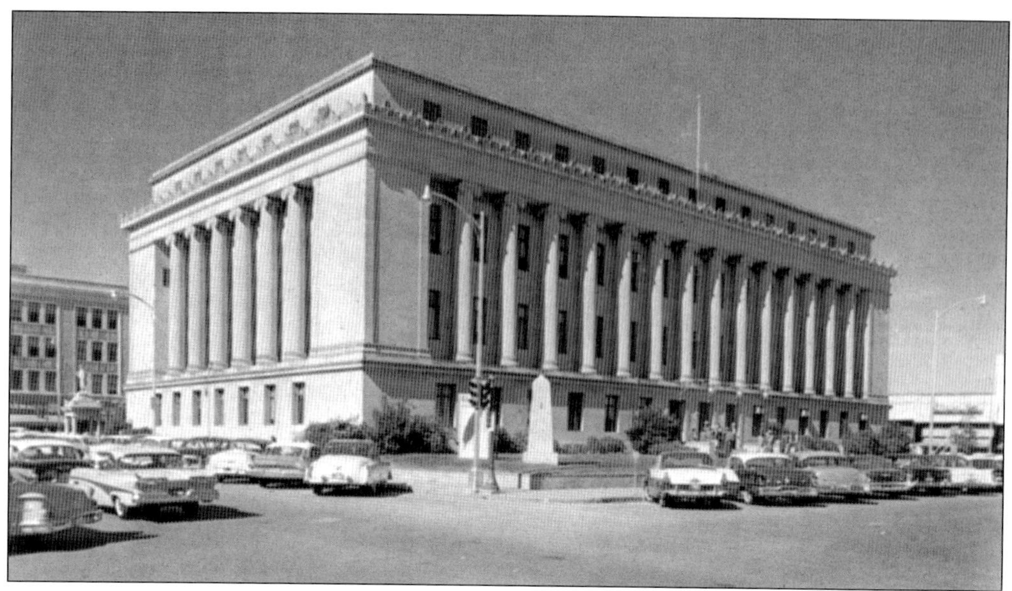

After oil was struck, there was a crush of county businesses needing to register records and file voluminous deed and title transactions. This factor, combined with an influx of county revenue, led to the construction of a new county courthouse in 1928, seen here around 1960. Constructed on the former site of a pioneer's log cabin and duck pond, the impressive new building was faced in dressed limestone, with 40 freestanding Ionic columns that would not be out of place in the nation's capital.

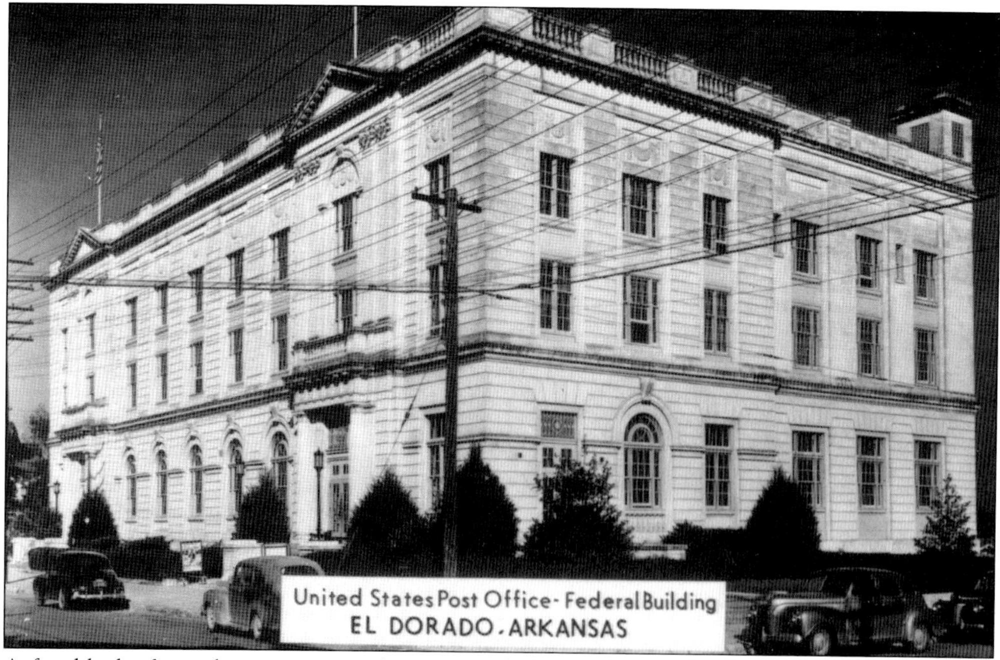

A few blocks from the county courthouse sits the federal courthouse, which, in the past, also housed the town's main post office. The impressive building, contained today within El Dorado's historic district, was completed in 1931 and continues to serve the US District Court for the Western District of Arkansas.

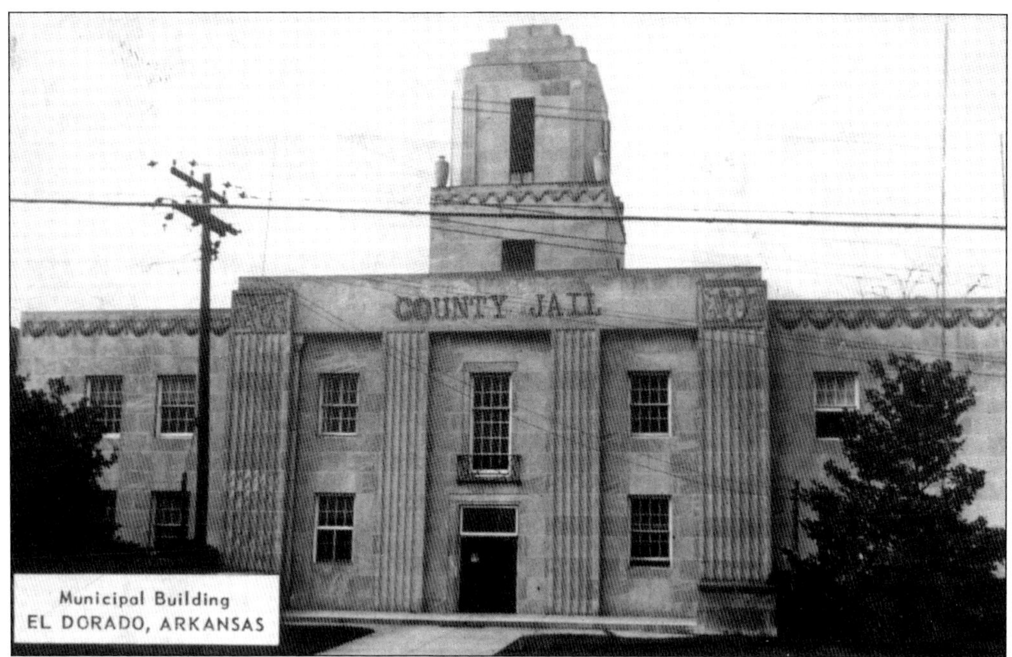

El Dorado's two-story Municipal Building was erected in 1927 and was designed by noted architect Eugene John Stern. The masonry construction carries a number of Classical Revival and Art Deco characteristics, with a three-story tower in the center. Today, it serves as the city hall. On this penny postcard sent to Cleveland, a prankster apparently used a typewriter to inscribe the words "County Jail" above the impressive facade.

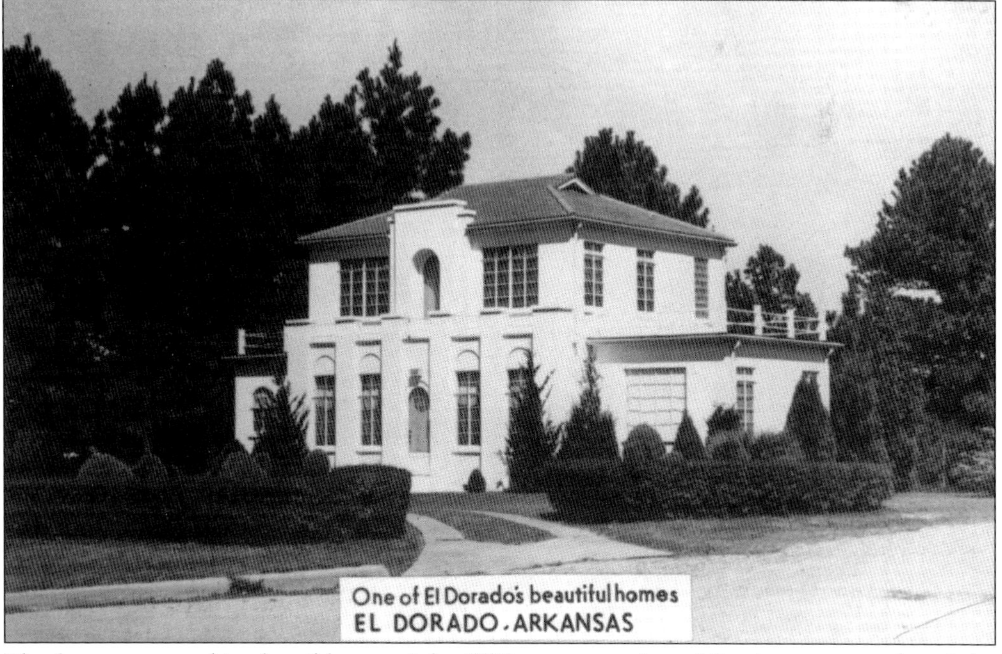

The fortunes earned in the oil boom of the 1920s saw a number of fine homes erected, and the city showcased them with pride. The postcard was tagged, "One of El Dorado's beautiful homes." Sadly, this home is gone today, as are too many others built a century ago.

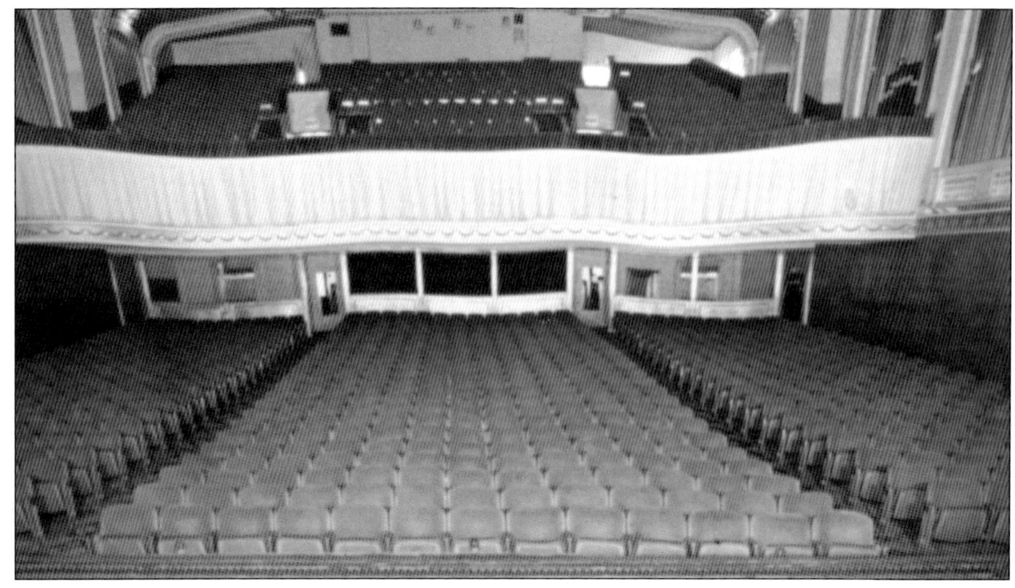

Guests of the Hotel Como or the Garrett Hotel could have walked a couple of blocks to take in a movie at the Rialto Theater on East Cedar. The theater was built in 1929 with some 1,400 seats; it was home to touring vaudeville acts, silent movies, and later, "talkies." Closed for much of the 1980s, it reopened as a three-screen theater that operated until 2006. The theater was purchased in 2012 by the Murphy Arts District and is undergoing restoration with the goal of reopening in the future as a multipurpose entertainment venue. (Above, courtesy of SAHPS; below, courtesy of Murphy Oil.)

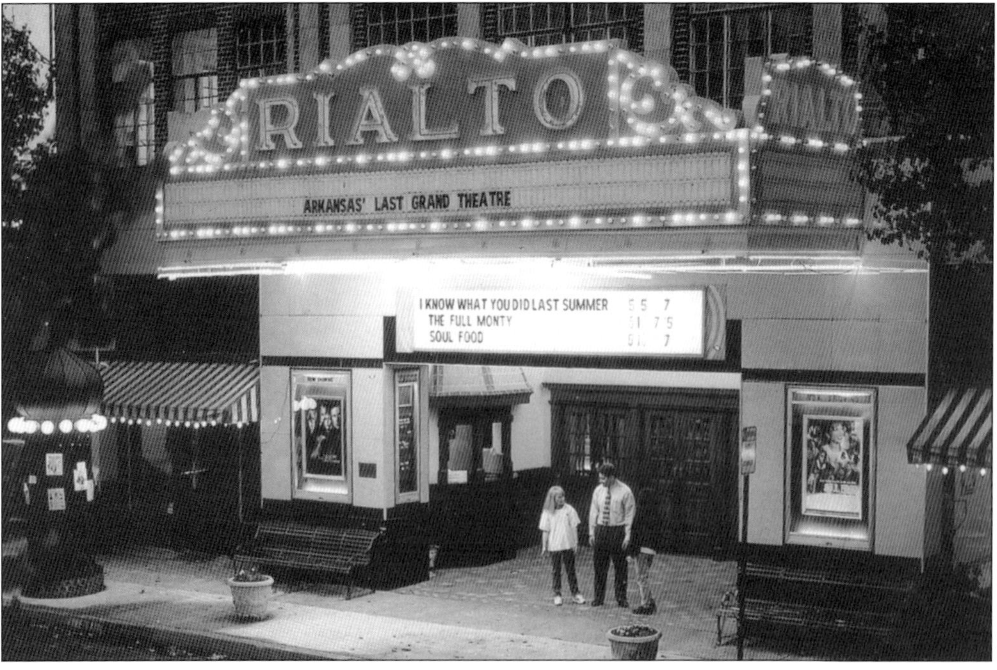

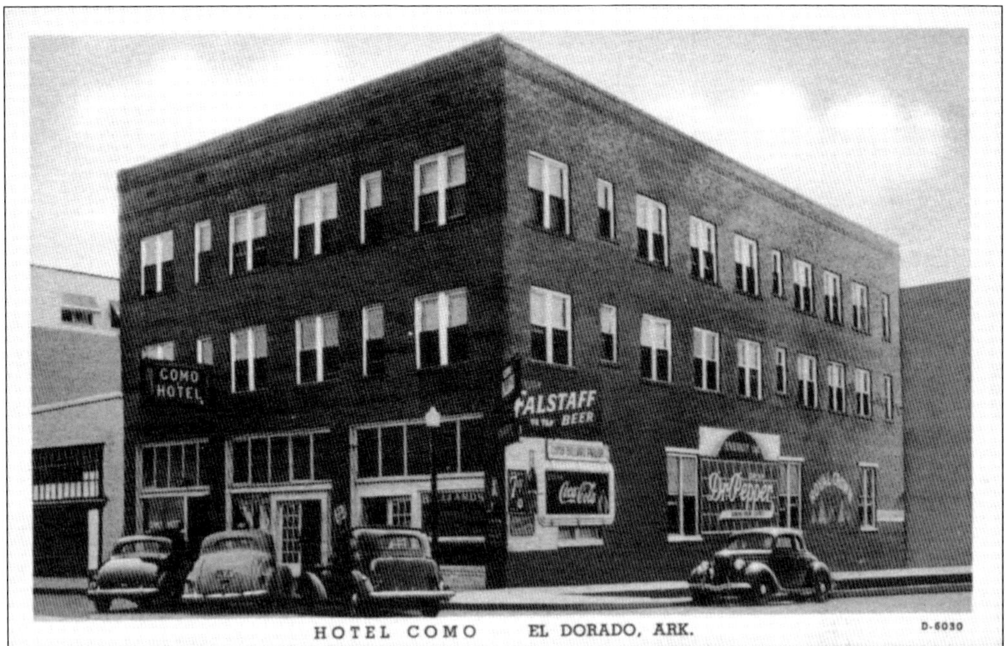

Traveling businessmen and others on a budget had newer lodging options by the 1930s, such as the Hotel Como with its large Falstaff beer sign over the Coca-Cola emblem on the corner. The hotel is gone today, and the site is now a parking lot.

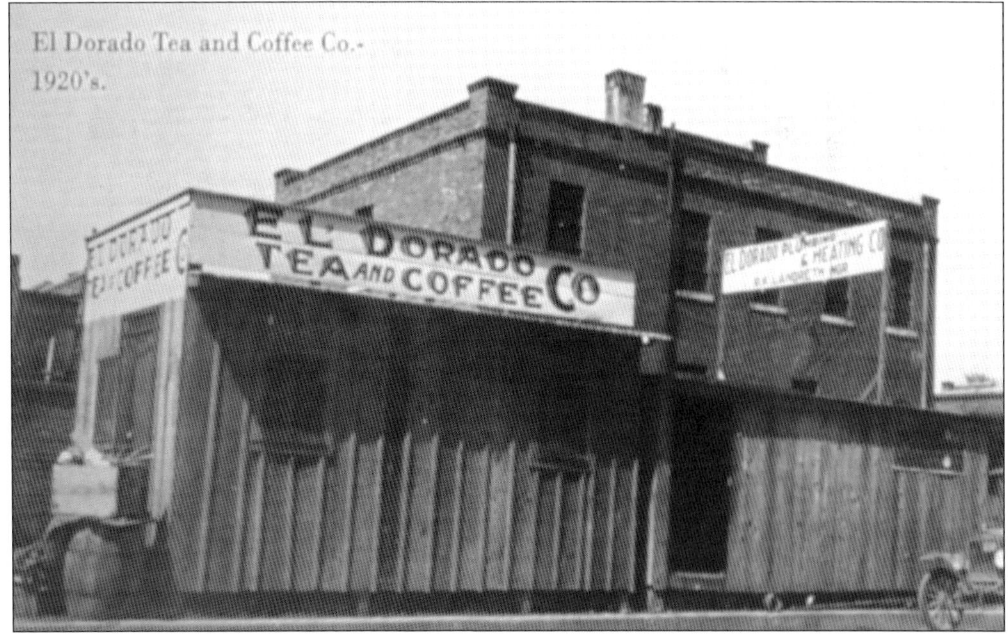

In the wake of the 1920s oil boom, dozens of new businesses cropped up, trying to profit from the thousands of people and millions of dollars that flooded into El Dorado. One such enterprise was the El Dorado Tea and Coffee Company, which shared a building with the El Dorado Plumbing & Heating Company.

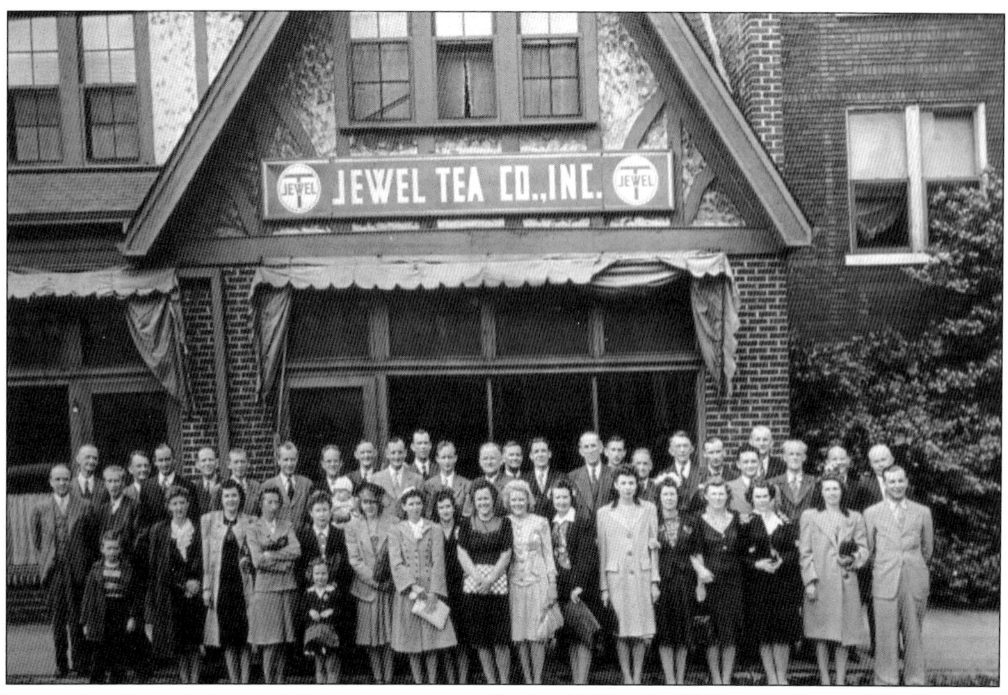

By the 1940s, the El Dorado Tea and Coffee Company had transformed into the Jewel Tea Company, housed in a large handsome building. The structure was razed in the 1950s, but today, several delightful coffee shops can still be found around the courthouse square.

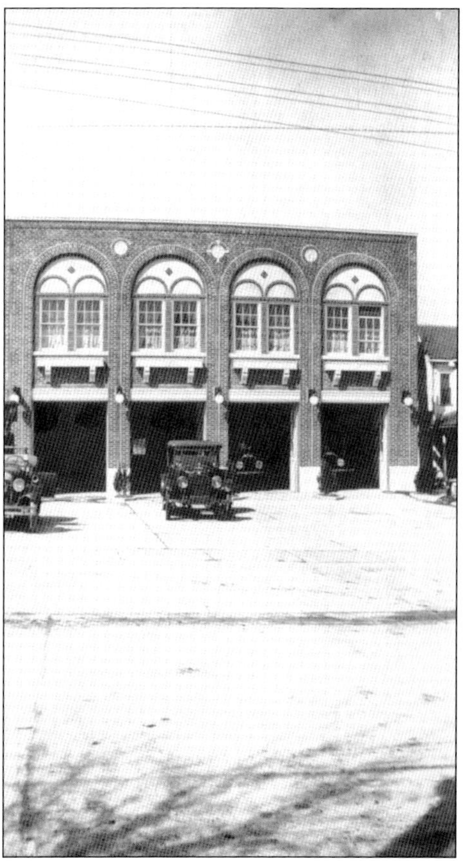

In the 1930s, the City of El Dorado opened a new fire station on North West Avenue; this photograph notes it was built by W.S. McDowell. The service of the El Dorado Fire Department goes back a full 125 years. The pictured fire station still serves today, unusual in that modern, larger fire trucks still manage to fit into the old building.

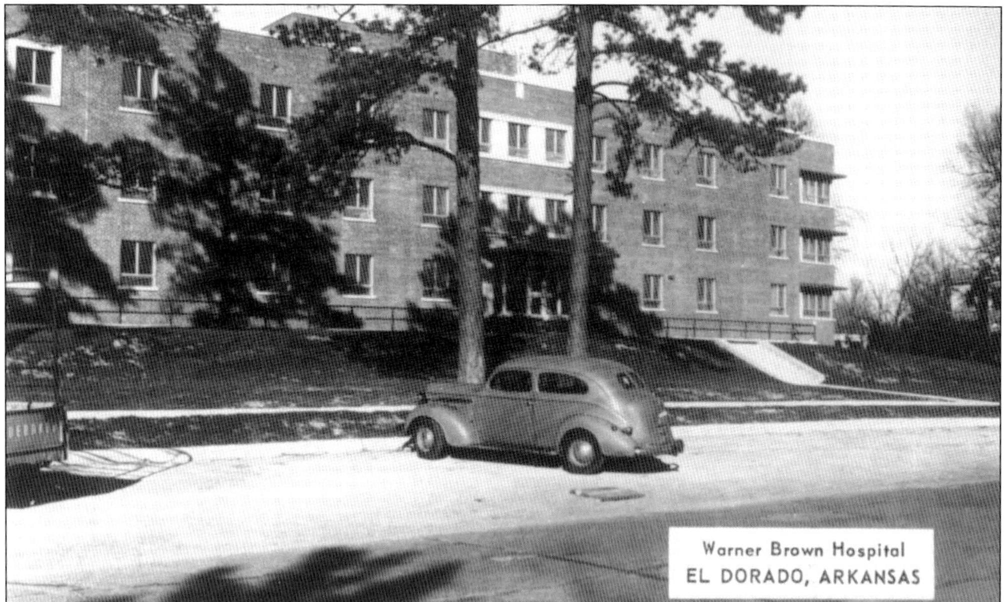

The Warner Brown Hospital had been opened in 1921, honoring one of El Dorado's early settlers. By the 1940s, the Sisters of Mercy, who ran the hospital, knew a newer expanded facility was needed. Thanks to donations from the community, government, and their religious order, this new annex opened in 1954 with 130 beds and a staff of 256. In 1971, the Sisters donated the hospital to the city and county. This structure was abandoned in 2015, and Union County is today served by the modern South Arkansas Regional Hospital.

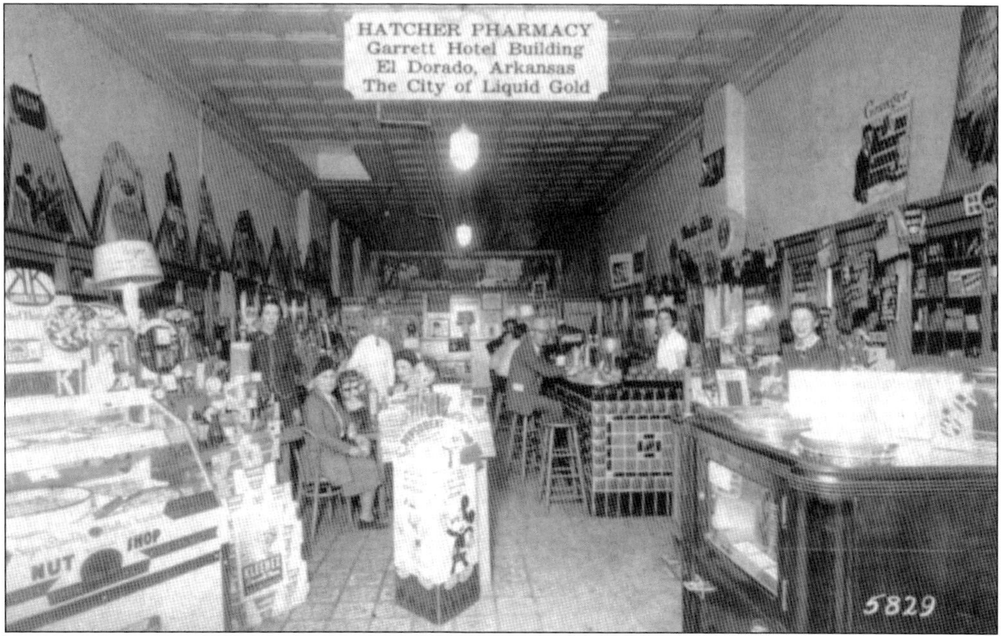

Around 1930, a patient with a prescription might have filled it at Hatcher's Pharmacy, located inside the Garrett Hotel. The pharmacy also included a lunch counter and soda fountain, common to the era. A display in the front center shows Mickey Mouse promoting Pepsodent toothpaste, which had first been marketed in 1915.

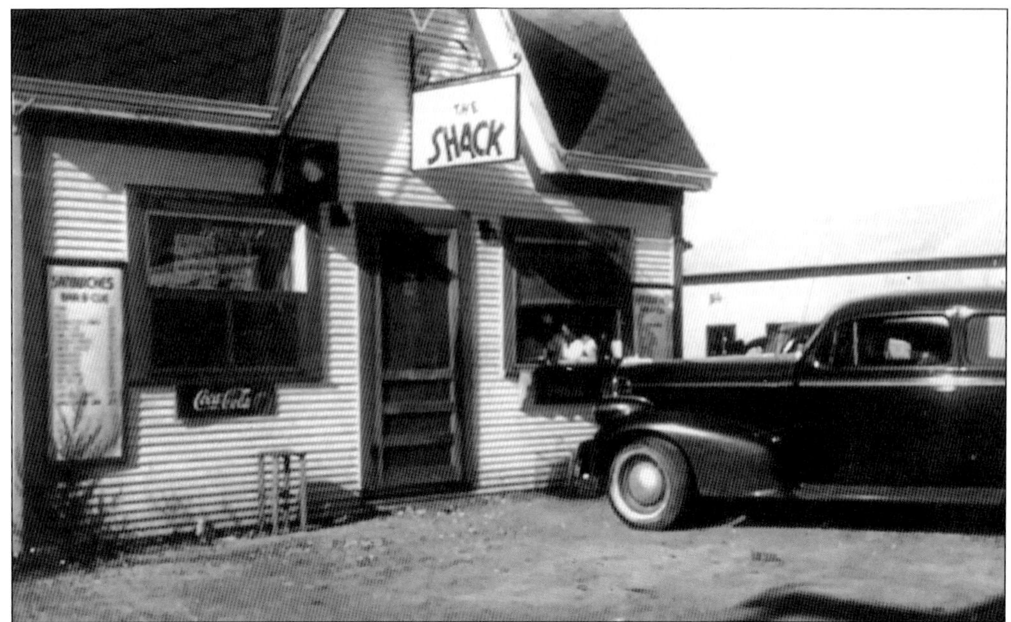

By World War II, Union County's industrial base had expanded so that it was less dependent on oil alone. One business serving workers at factories like the Ozark Ordnance Plant was the Shack, a barbeque and sandwich shop located out on Industrial Road. In this view, someone in a 1938 Oldsmobile enjoys their lunch.

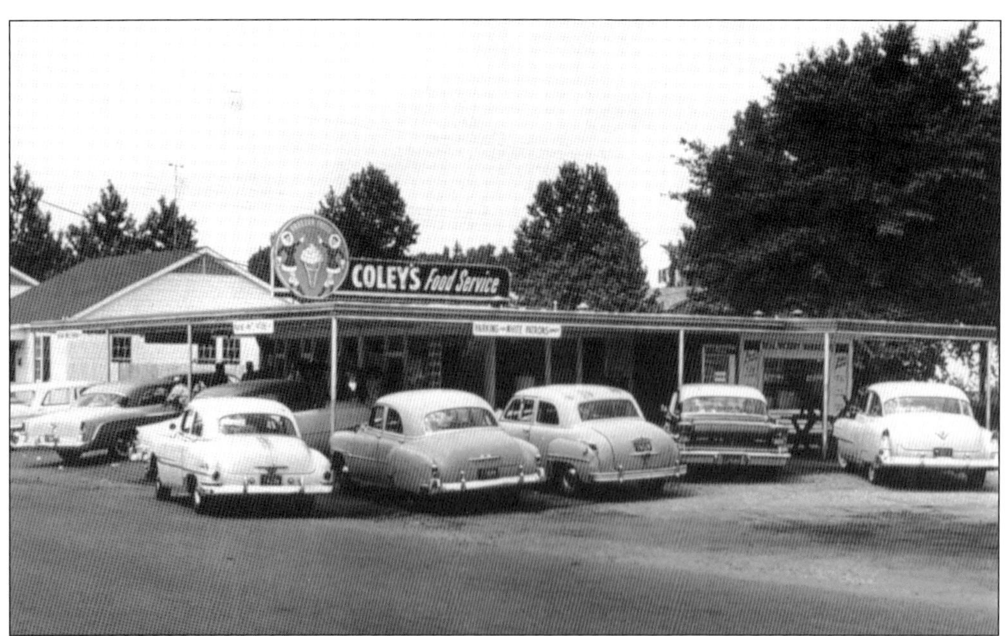

In the mid-1950s, Coley's Food Service at Parkway Drive and Northwest Avenue was a popular drive-in before the rise of today's franchised and branded fast foods. The white sign on the awning reads, "Parking for White Patrons Only," a sign of those segregated times in the South.

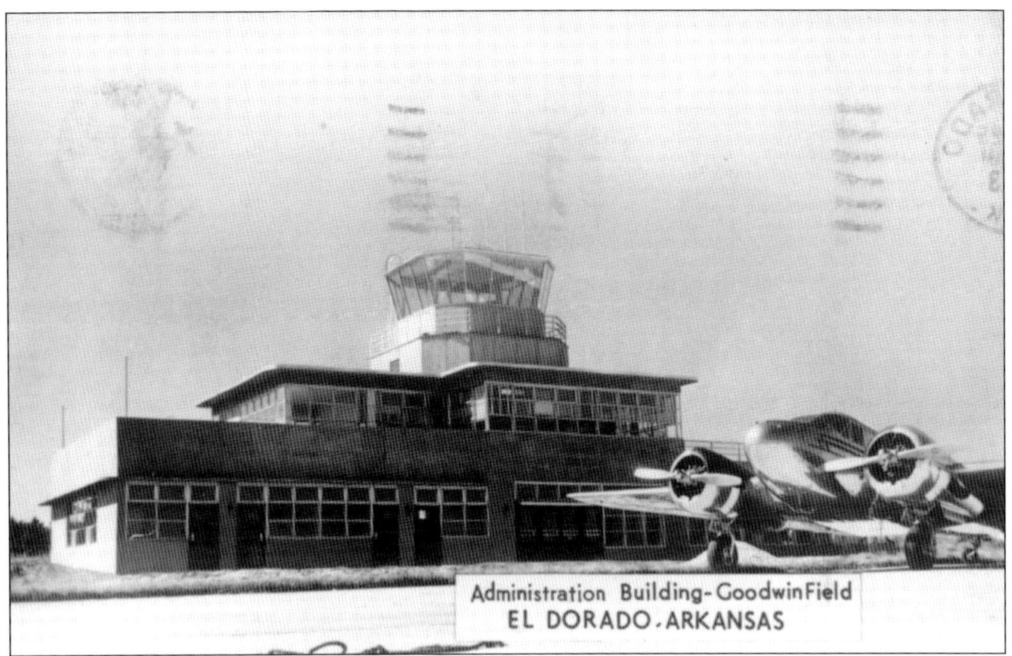

In the 1940s, the city of El Dorado was introduced to modern air service with the construction of the South Arkansas Regional Airport. The airport operates today for general aviation at Goodwin Field.

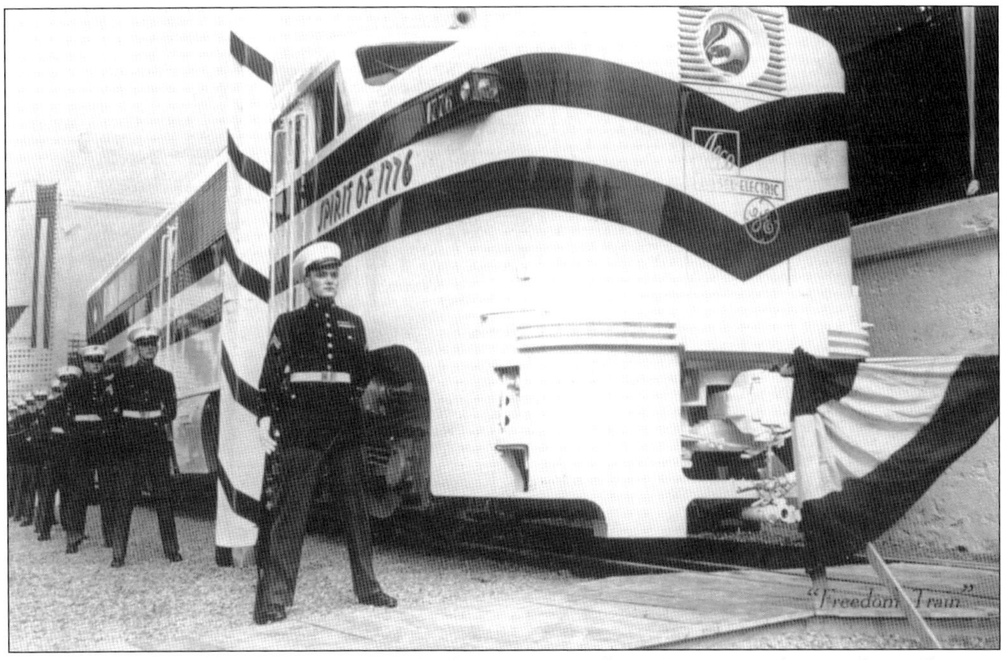

In 1947, El Dorado hosted a visit from the "Spirit of 1776" *Freedom Train*. The traveling effort was intended to be a show of patriotic pride in the years just after World War II. Controversy occurred in some places in the South, where local authorities required Black and White citizens to visit the train at different times. No such issues were reported in El Dorado.

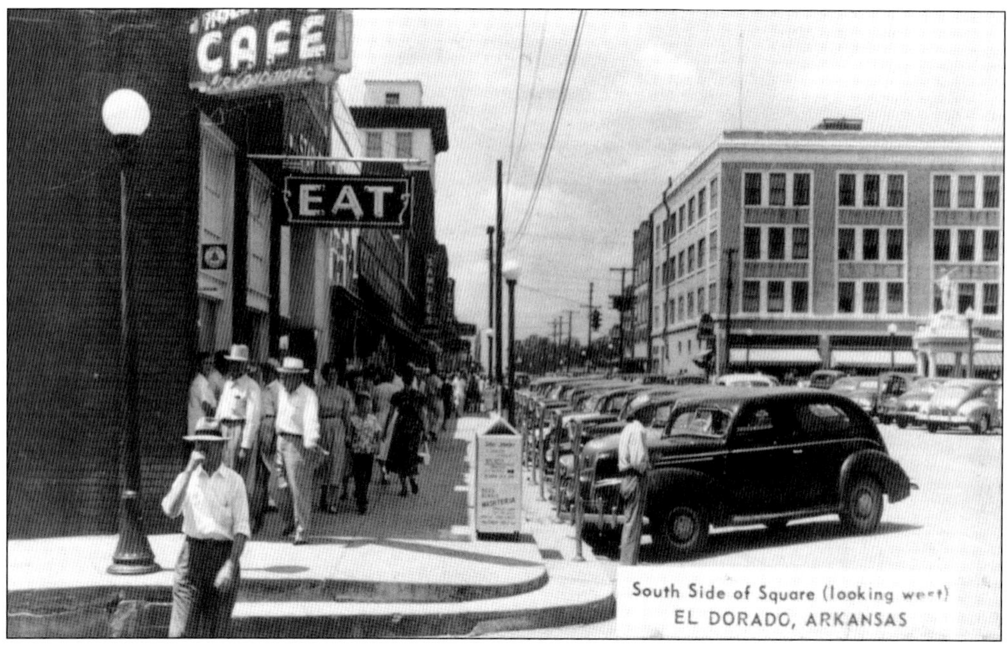

Around 1940, a man is seen picking his teeth as he crosses Jefferson Avenue, perhaps after lunch at the Hollywood Café with its "EAT" sign. This image appeared about 20 years ago in the Arkansas Postcard Past column printed in the *Arkansas Democrat-Gazette*. An inmate at Cummins Prison wrote the author to say that he was the small boy seen holding his mother's hand. He asked for a copy of the photograph for his cell and was sent an eight-by-ten-inch copy.

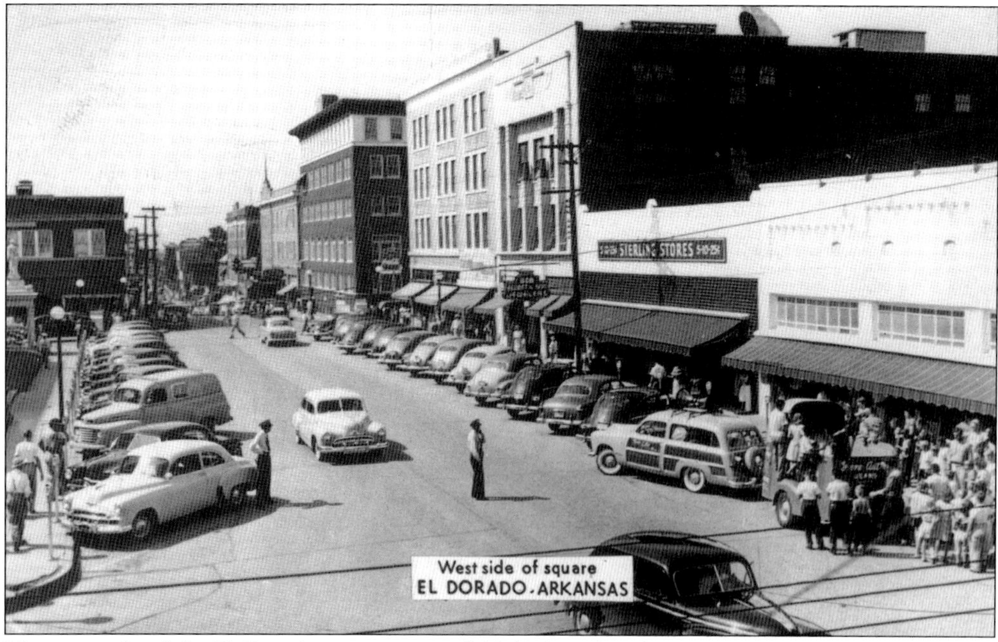

The west side of the El Dorado square around 1950 found parking at a premium on Washington Street, with Sterling's Store occupying the center of the block. At right, a 1949 Ford woody, a paneled station wagon, was pulling a trailer with a promotion for Gene Autry jeans in front of the B.W. Reeves Department Store. The courthouse is just out of view to the left.

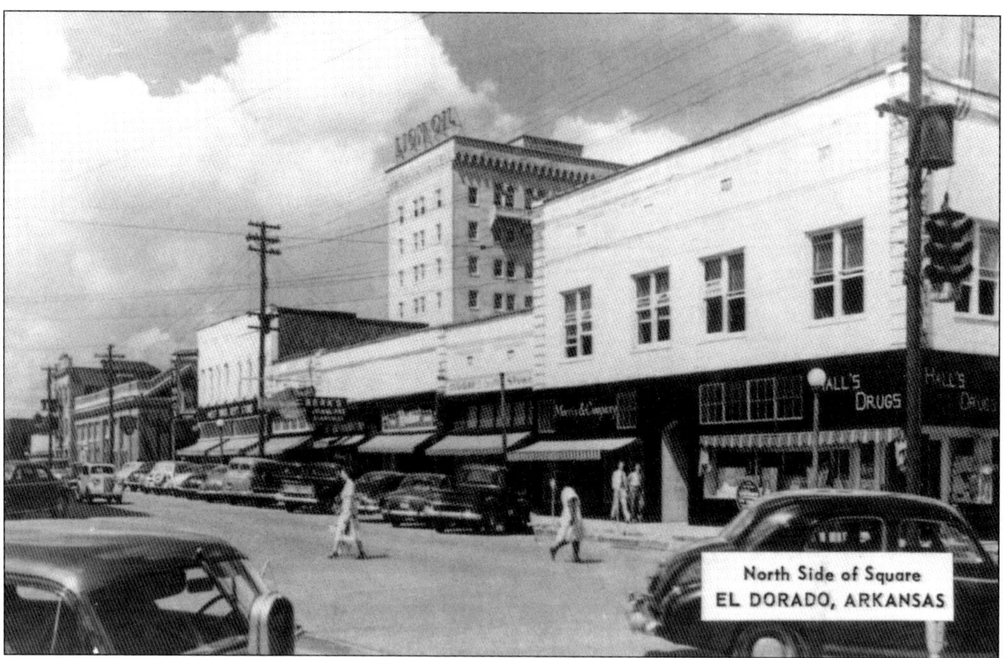

The north side of the square, seen here in the late 1940s, shows Elm Street anchored at the right corner by Hall's Drug, with Berk's Jewelers in the center of the block and the Elks Lodge on the far corner with Washington Avenue. Looming over the view was the Lion Oil building in the distance.

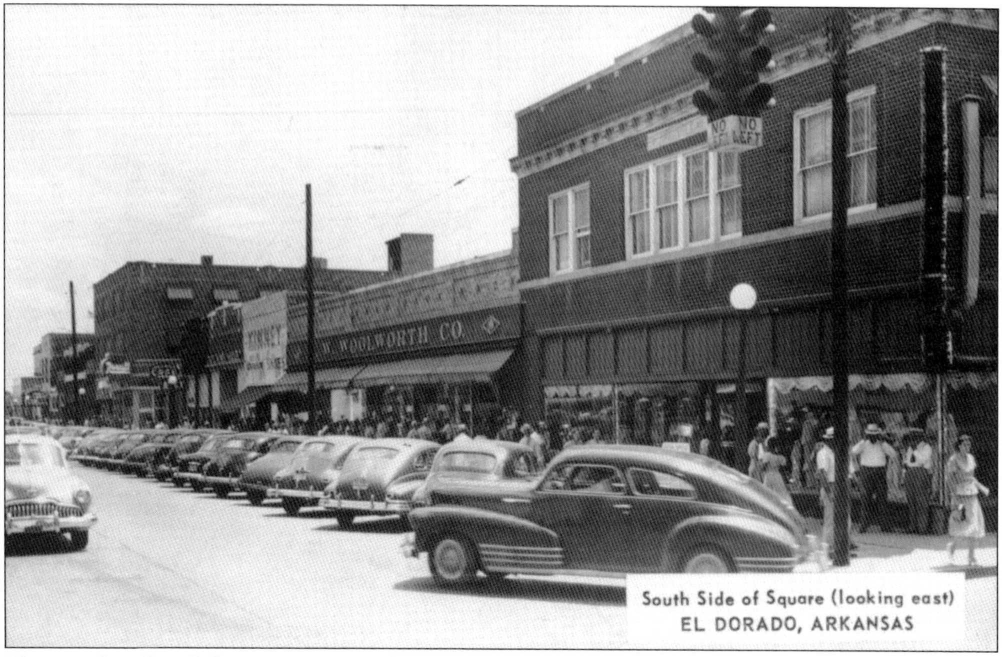

The south side of the square around 1950 was packed, with seemingly not a parking space to be had along Main Street. Anchoring the middle of the block was Woolworth's, once an iconic presence on main streets all across the South. Shoppers flocked to do business downtown in this era before the rise of shopping centers and big-box stores.

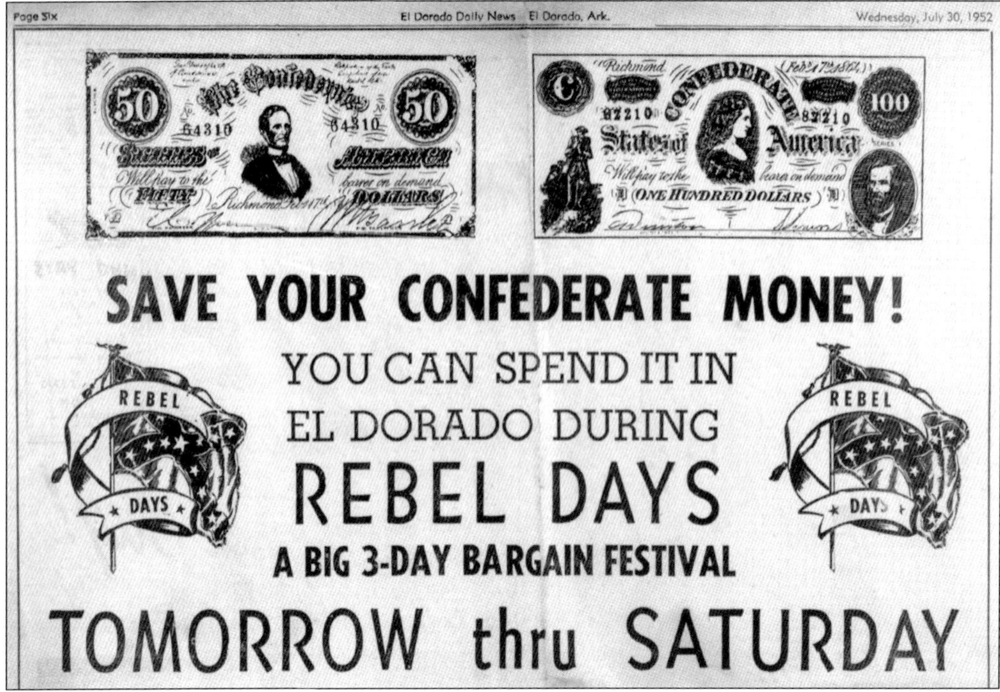

In 1952, the merchants of El Dorado banded together to promote "Rebel Days," a three-day festival of bargains to stimulate shopping. "Confederate money" was printed in the newspapers, and shoppers were invited to cut out the bills to redeem for value at the participating merchants. The Civil War had been over only about 85 years at that time.

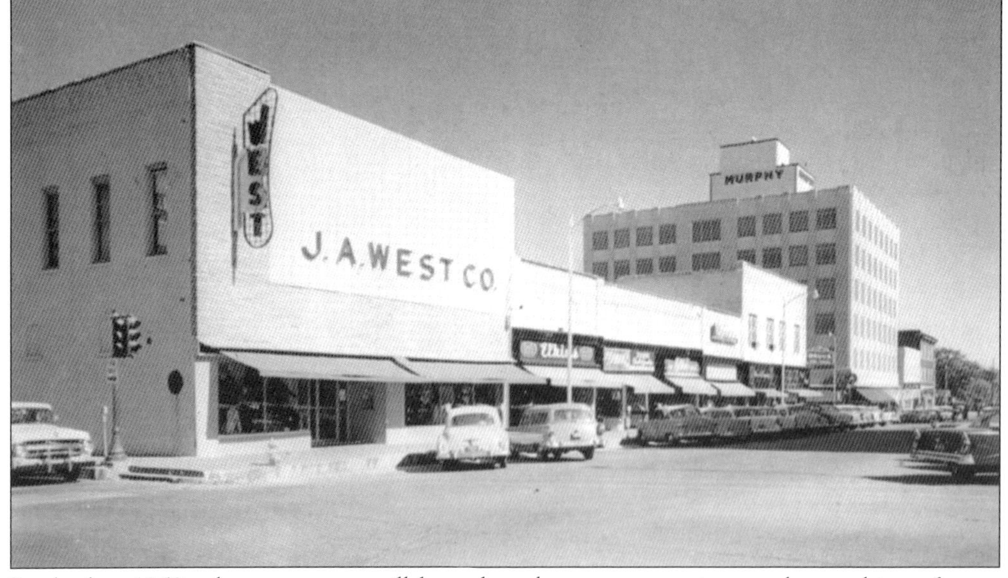

By the late 1950s, downtown was still busy, but change was coming on the outskirts of town with the completion of the first shopping centers. Elm Street along the square was anchored by J.A. West Co., sometimes just called West Brothers. The family-owned chain was once a fixture on small-town main streets, but in the age of Walmart, it is only a memory. The Murphy Oil headquarters building rises in the distance in this view.

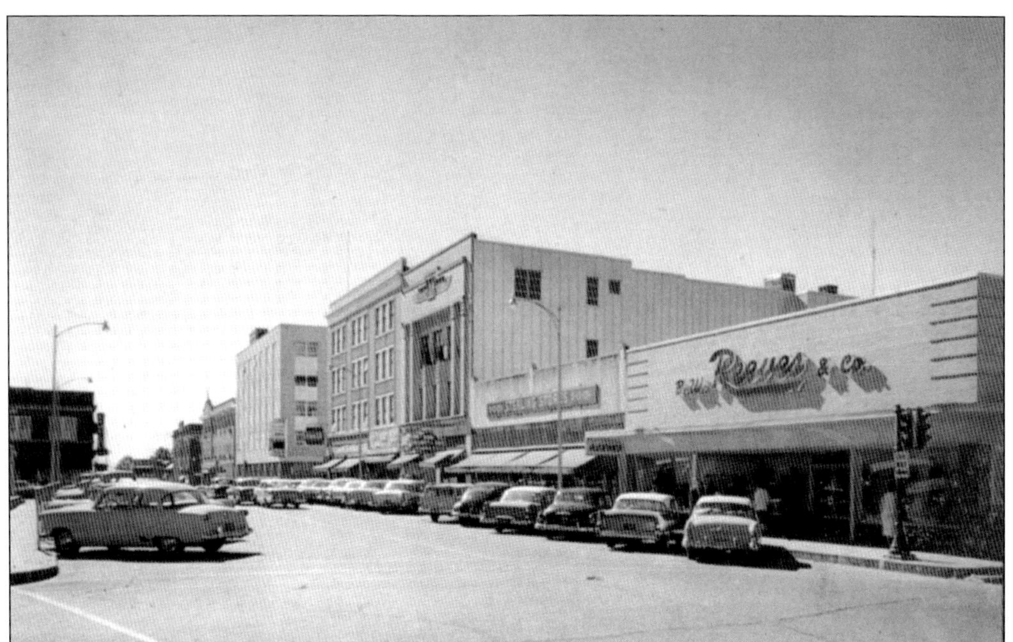

Washington Street on the west side of the square is seen here around 1960, about 10 years later than the view seen on page 88 of this book. The block was still hosting a vibrant retail business, anchored by the iconic B.W. Reeves store, a presence in El Dorado for decades. It shared the block with Sterling's Store and Elliott's Jewelers as well as the striking Masonic Temple.

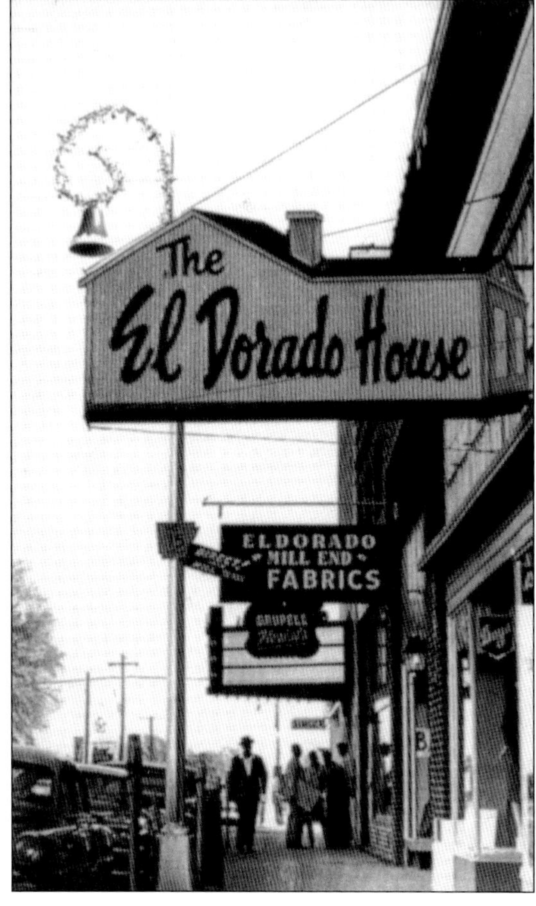

The most popular women's store in south Arkansas may have been the El Dorado House on East Cedar Street, downtown. Generations of ladies got their prom dresses, wedding dresses, and party outfits there. On occasion, the store used models to show off their dresses. A business called El Dorado House still occupies the space today but now sells vintage clothing, antiques, and collectibles. (Courtesy of SAHPS.)

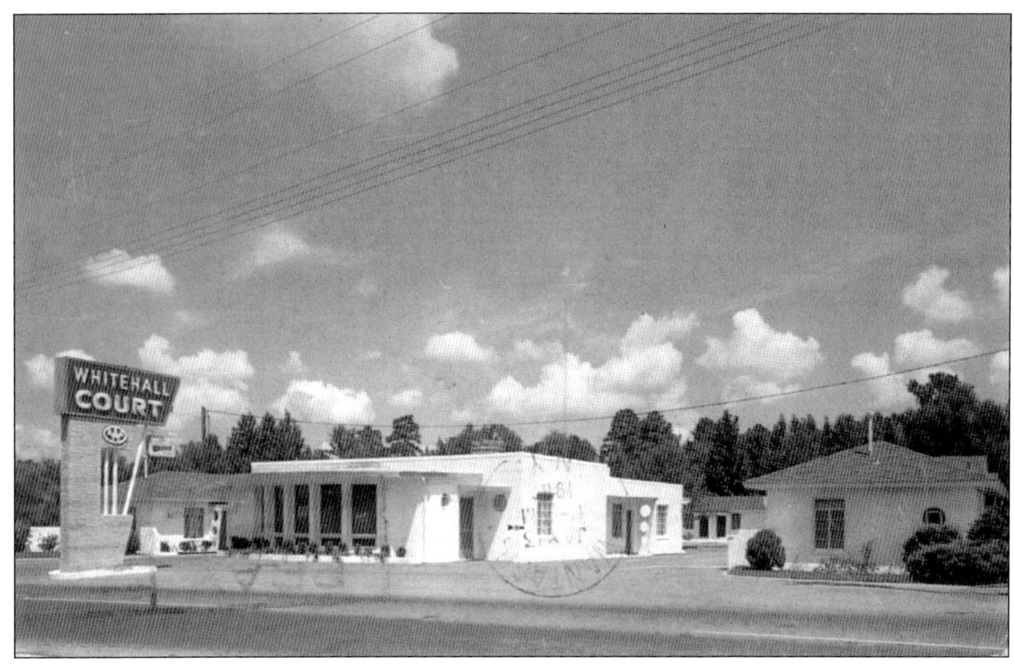

Today, the highway bypasses around El Dorado are dotted with the same national brands of hotels and motels as seen elsewhere in the nation. In the 1950s, however, the mom-and-pop motels and courts were the norm. One of these was the Whitehall Court, a dozen blocks from downtown on Highway 82. It operated under the aegis of both AAA and Best Western Motels. The advertisement postcard seen here promises "40 lovely rooms" with coffee, television, and phone in each and shows off a well-tended swimming pool. Rates for a single room were listed at $4 to $6. The motel was razed years ago.

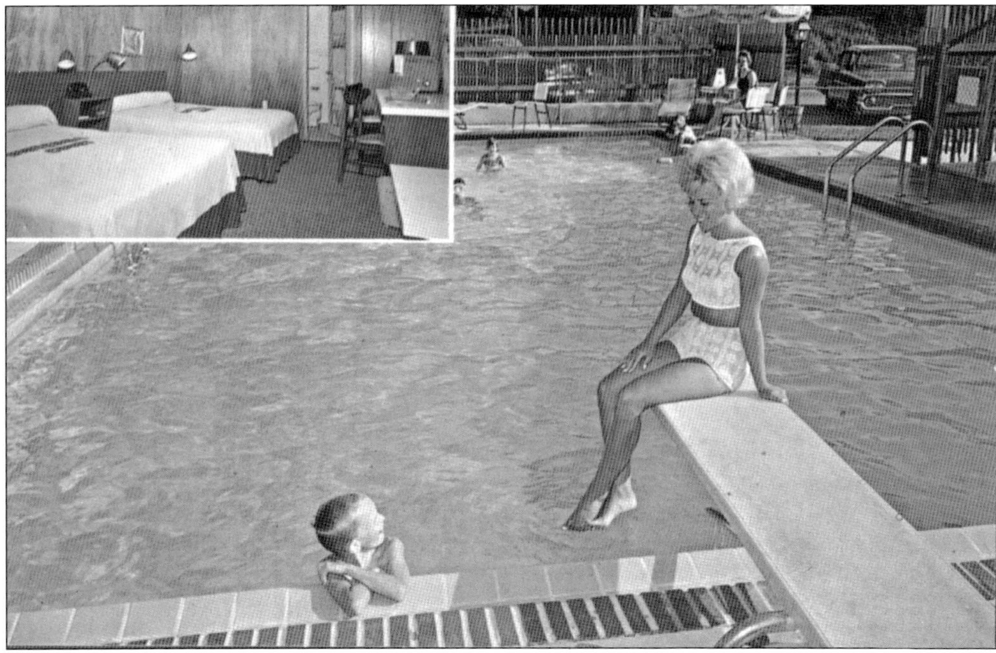

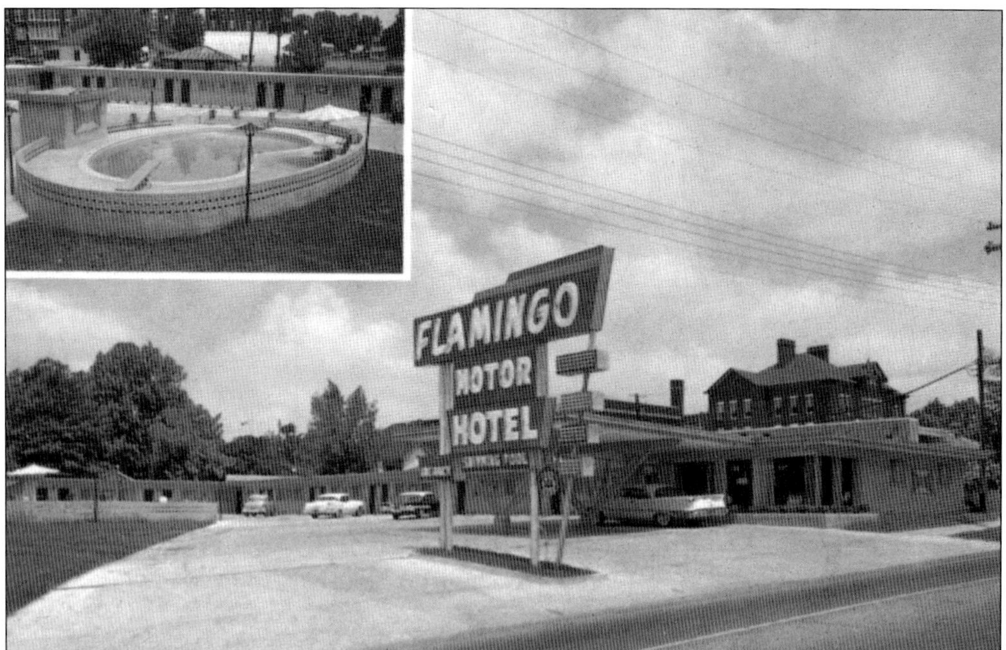

The year 1960 saw the opening of the Flamingo Motor Hotel, "El Dorado's newest and finest" and close to downtown. The town's high school is seen in the distance. Now called the Flamingo Motel, it still does business today, often housing oil field and construction workers as much of its clientele. The big sign still stands but is not lit at night, for its neon has gone dark.

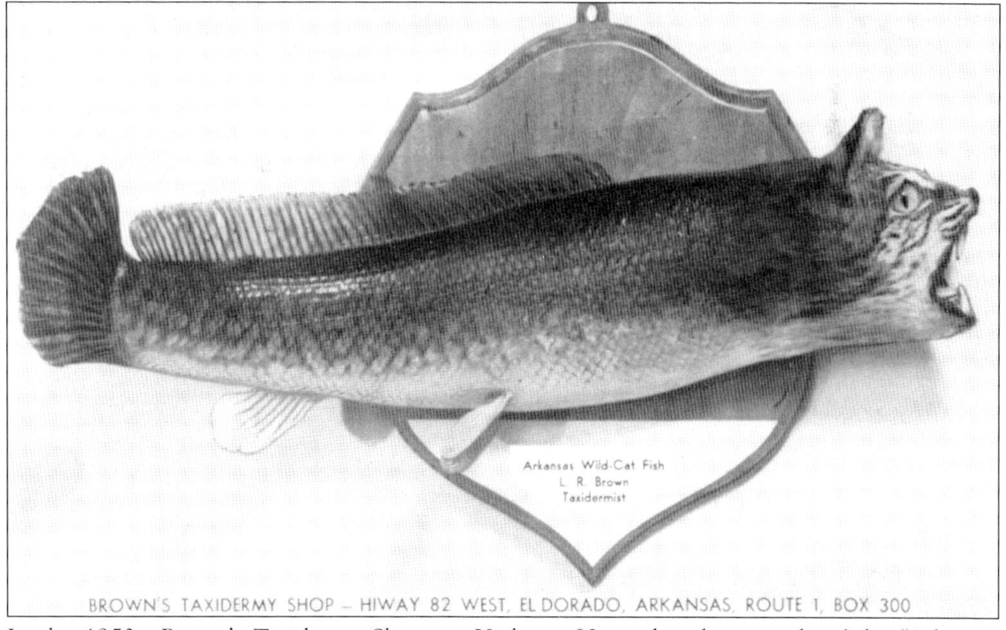

In the 1950s, Brown's Taxidermy Shop on Highway 82 produced postcards of the "Arkansas Wildcat Fish" in an effort to showcase Brown's workmanship. The back of the advertisement card notes that the creature was a combination of a Grinnell fish and a wildcat's head "blended in our workshop by our highly trained taxidermists."

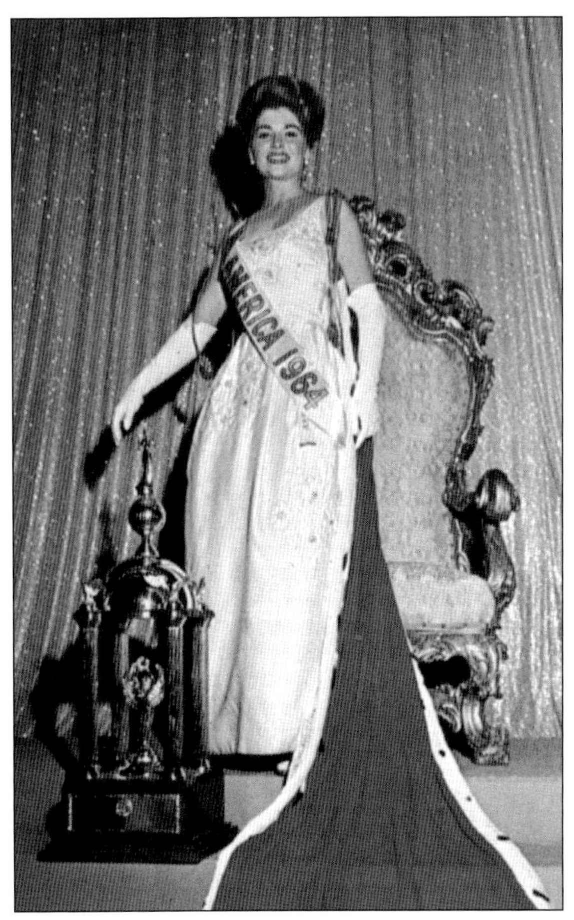

One of the biggest news stories in El Dorado since the days of the oil boom may have been in 1964, when hometown girl Donna Axum was crowned Miss America. She claimed that entering beauty contests was the way she dealt with "an inferiority complex." At age 16 in 1958, she was crowned Miss Union County; as a student at the University of Arkansas in 1963, Axum won the title of Miss Arkansas. She was the first contestant from Arkansas to ever be crowned Miss America. After a career in broadcasting and philanthropy, Axum passed away in 2018.

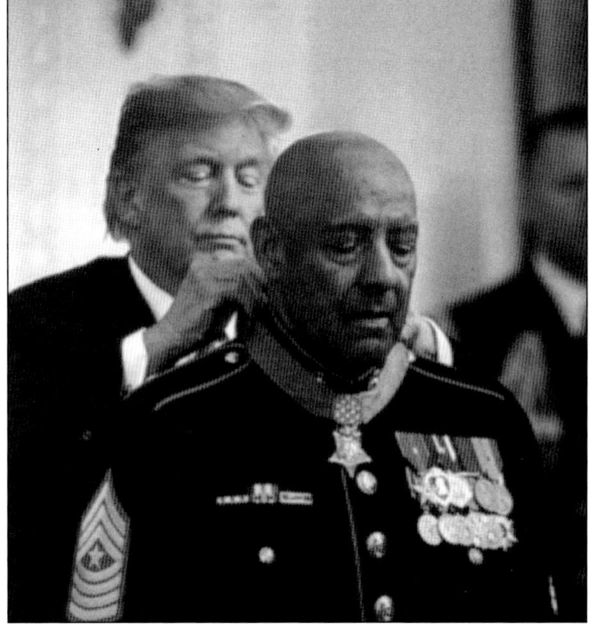

A story with deep Union County roots began with the birth of Johnny Lee Canley in the tiny Union County hamlet of Caledonia in 1937. Canley grew up to serve as a Marine gunnery sergeant during the Vietnam conflict. In 1968, as his unit moved along the highway toward Hue City to relieve surrounded American troops, Canley fought off multiple enemy attacks. On several occasions, despite his own wounds, the young Marine rushed across fire-swept terrain to carry the wounded to safety. In 2018, fifty years after these and other repeated acts of valor, President Trump bestowed on John Canley the Medal of Honor. Canley died in 2022 in Bend, Oregon. (Courtesy of SAHPS.)

Six

HAMLETS AND SMALL TOWNS OF UNION COUNTY

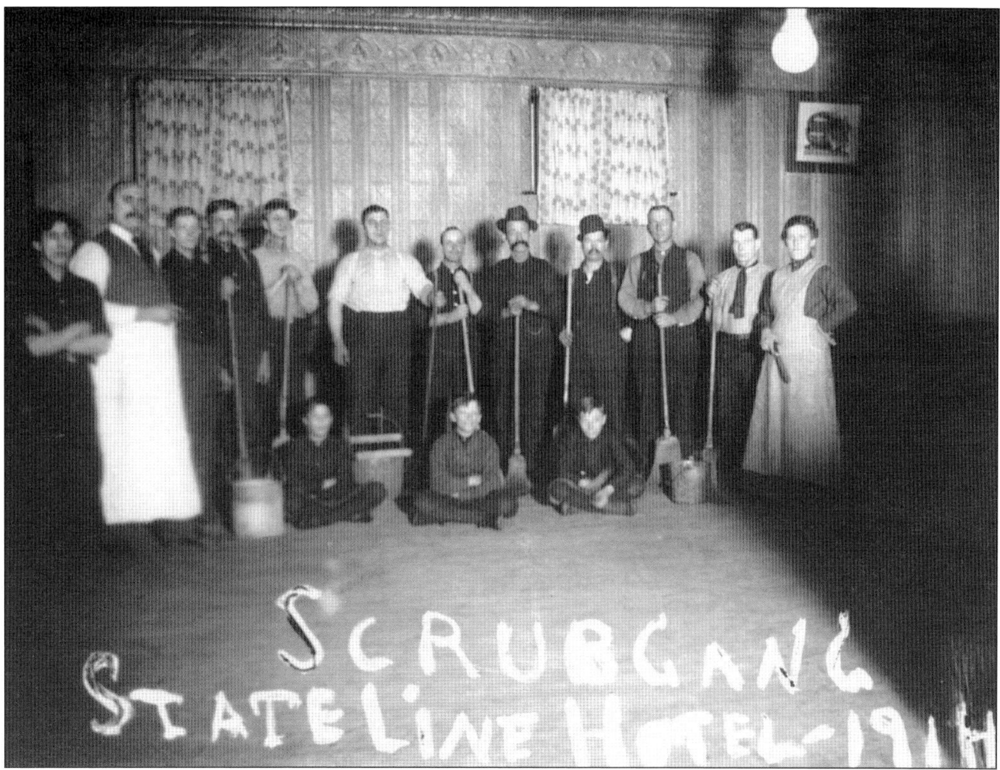

El Dorado and then Smackover got the most mention in the press and history books when anything about Union County was printed. There were, however (and still are), some interesting small communities in Arkansas's largest county. While oil was not often within their boundaries, other interesting industries and even some famous people did emerge from these dusty crossroads. One of these was the community of Cornie, which came into being in the 1850s in the deep woods southwest of El Dorado. It boasted the Stateline Hotel, seen here in 1911, with the "scrub gang" posing for the photograph.

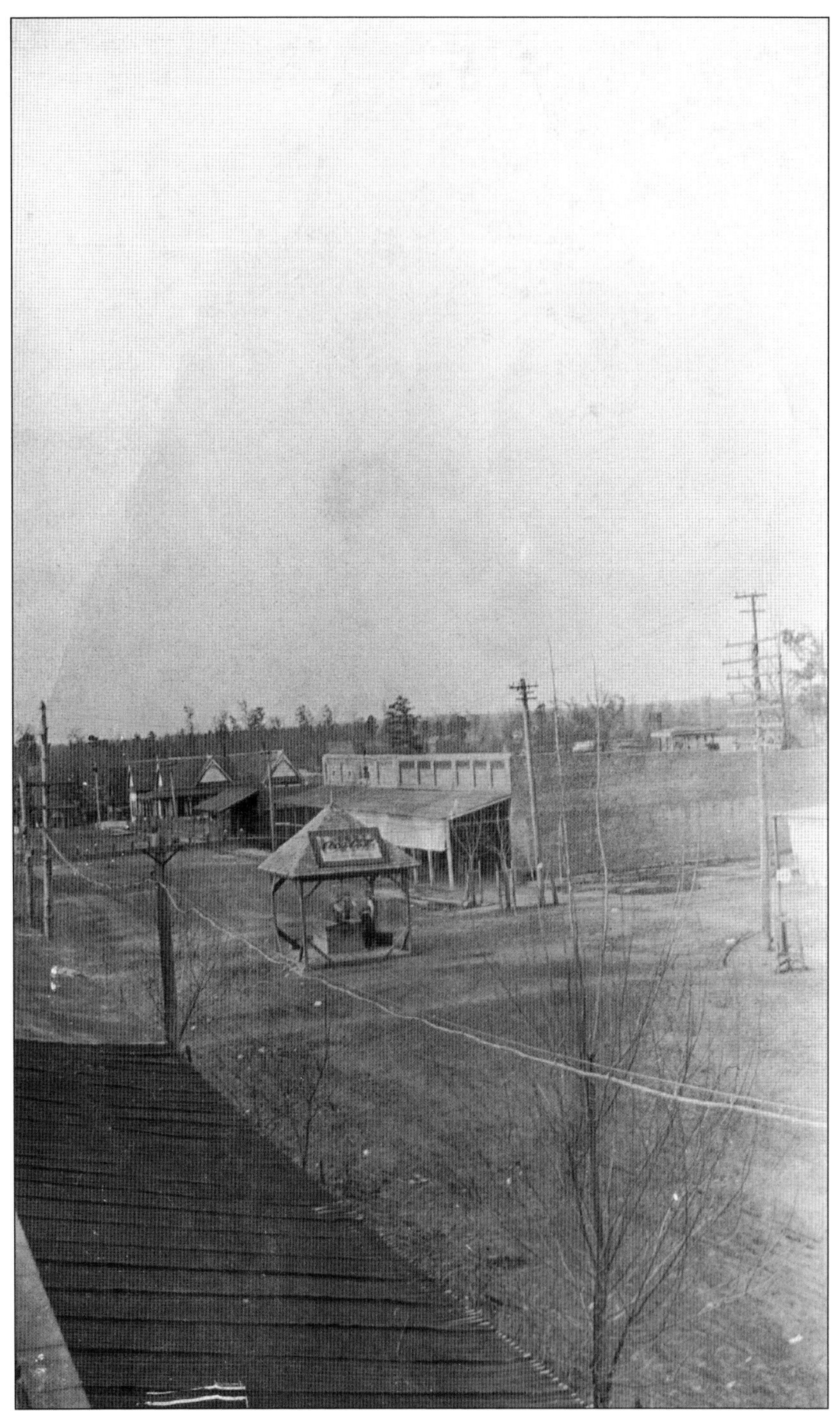

Junction City lies some 17 miles south of El Dorado and straddles the state line with Louisiana; the state line actually divides the city. As seen in this c. 1900 photograph, Junction City's town well had been built on the state line in the center of Main Street. At that point, one could stand with one foot in Arkansas and the other in Louisiana. An early version of the Coca-Cola logo is seen painted on the roof of the well, which has been gone for most of a century.

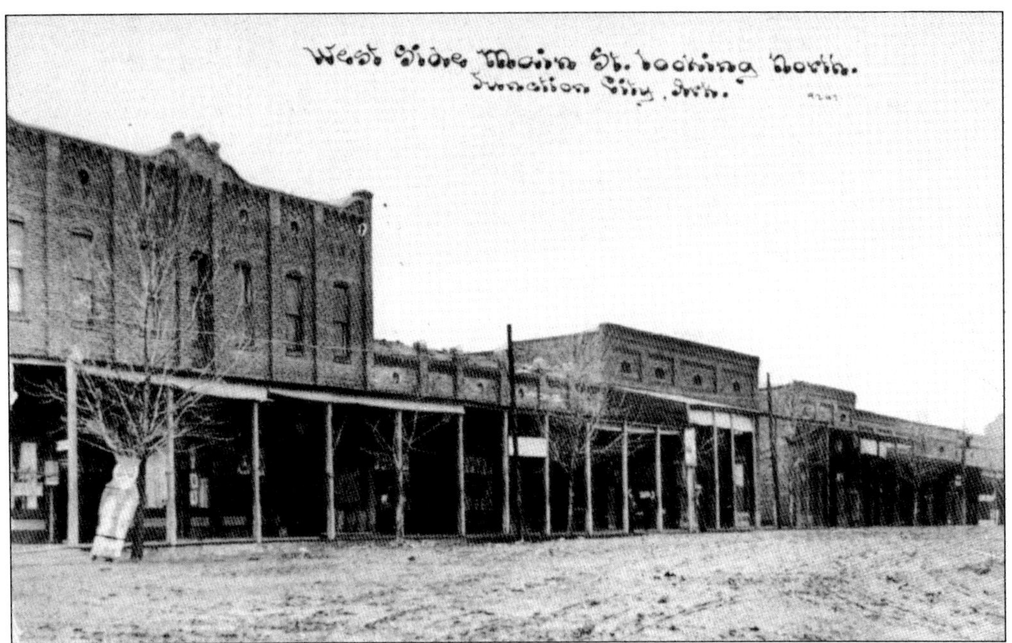

The town of Junction City was created by the Arkansas Southern Railway Company and was platted in 1894. Lots were auctioned at a public barbeque. Originally, it was a town of wooden structures, but several fires necessitated rebuilding in brick, as seen along Main Street around 1908.

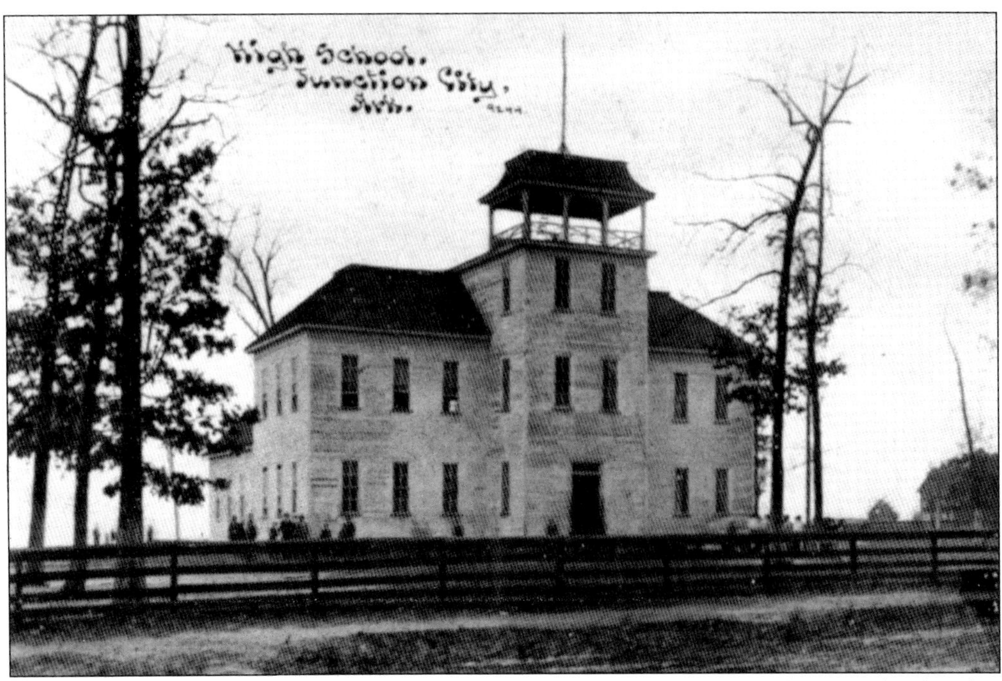

Junction City's High School was seen around 1908 when the average Arkansas schoolteacher earned about $275 for a 107-day school year. For many years, Junction City, Arkansas, and Junction City, Louisiana, have shared a common school district as well as a common fire department. (Courtesy of Butler Center for Arkansas Studies.)

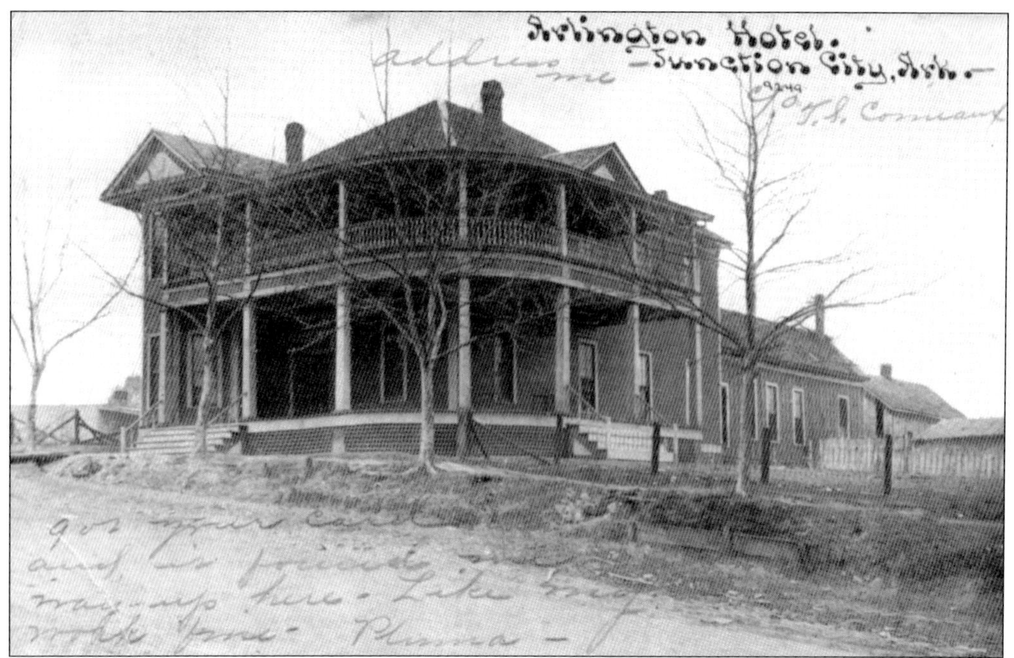

Visitors to Junction City seeking a place of lodging would have found their way to the Arlington Hotel, where a room in the rambling wooden building might have cost $2, and meals went for perhaps another $1 a day. "I like my work fine" is the note on the postcard, sent in 1908.

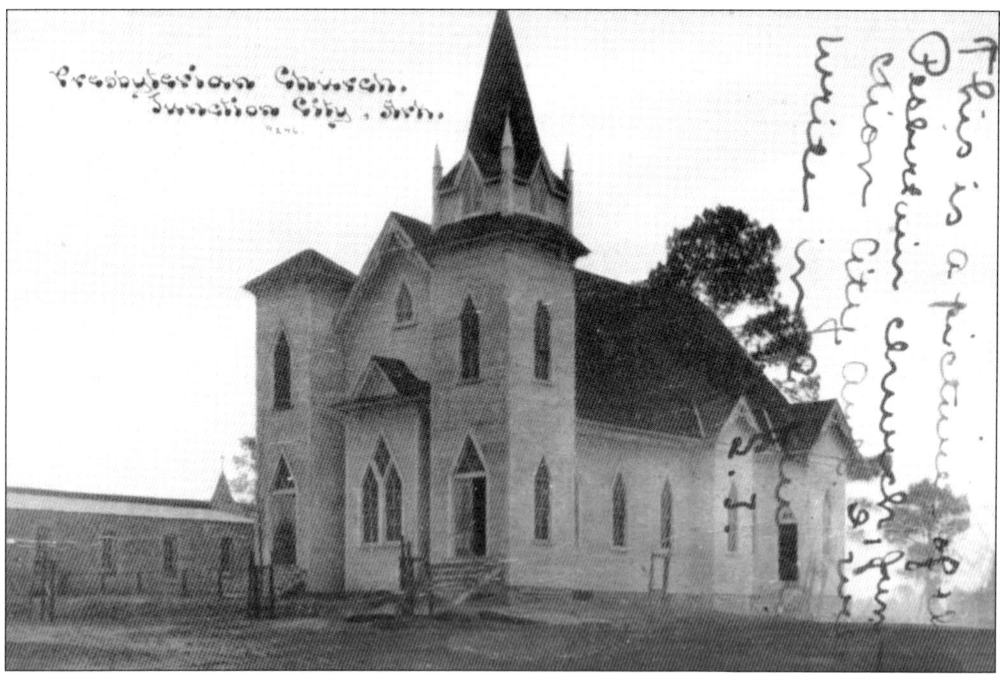

The population of Junction City was around 1,000 in 1910, a high-water mark never seen again. The town had about 500 residents in the 2020 census. The small town was blessed with several churches; the Presbyterian house of worship seen here has been gone for decades. The postcard was mailed some 2,000 miles distant to Washington state.

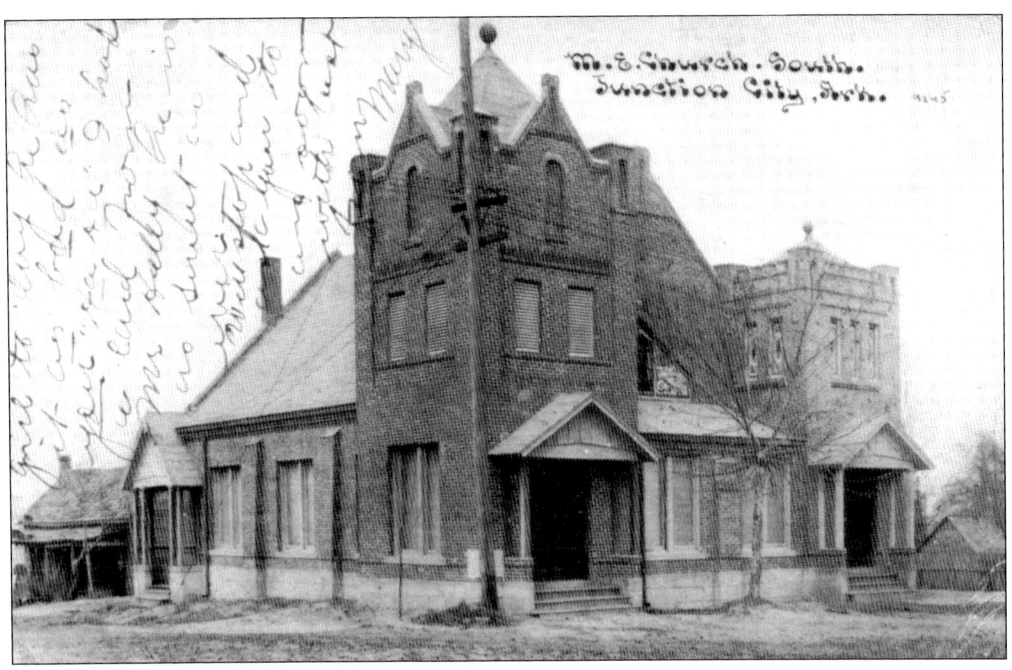

The Methodists built their own sturdy brick church in 1909, locating it in a residential neighborhood a block off Main Street. On the postcard, it is noted to be the "M.E. Church South" (Methodist Episcopal). Unlike the other churches in Junction City, the Methodist building seen here has somehow survived over a century. It has lost some of its original ornamentation with a reconfiguration of the rooflines but otherwise is remarkably unchanged. Now known as the Junction City First United Methodist Church, the venerable structure in its 116th year still hosts an active congregation. (Below, photograph by Ray Hanley.)

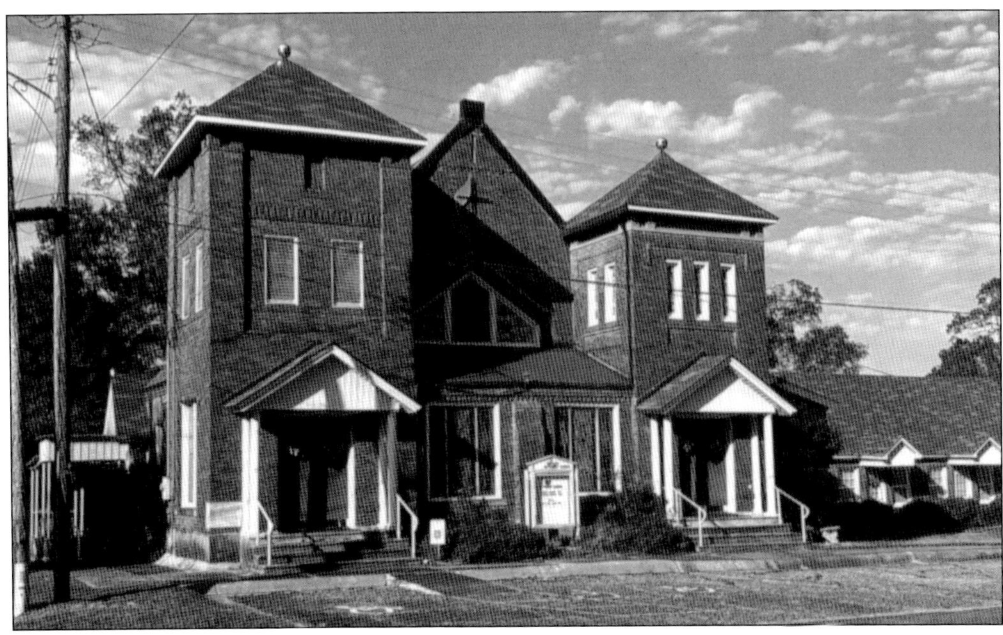

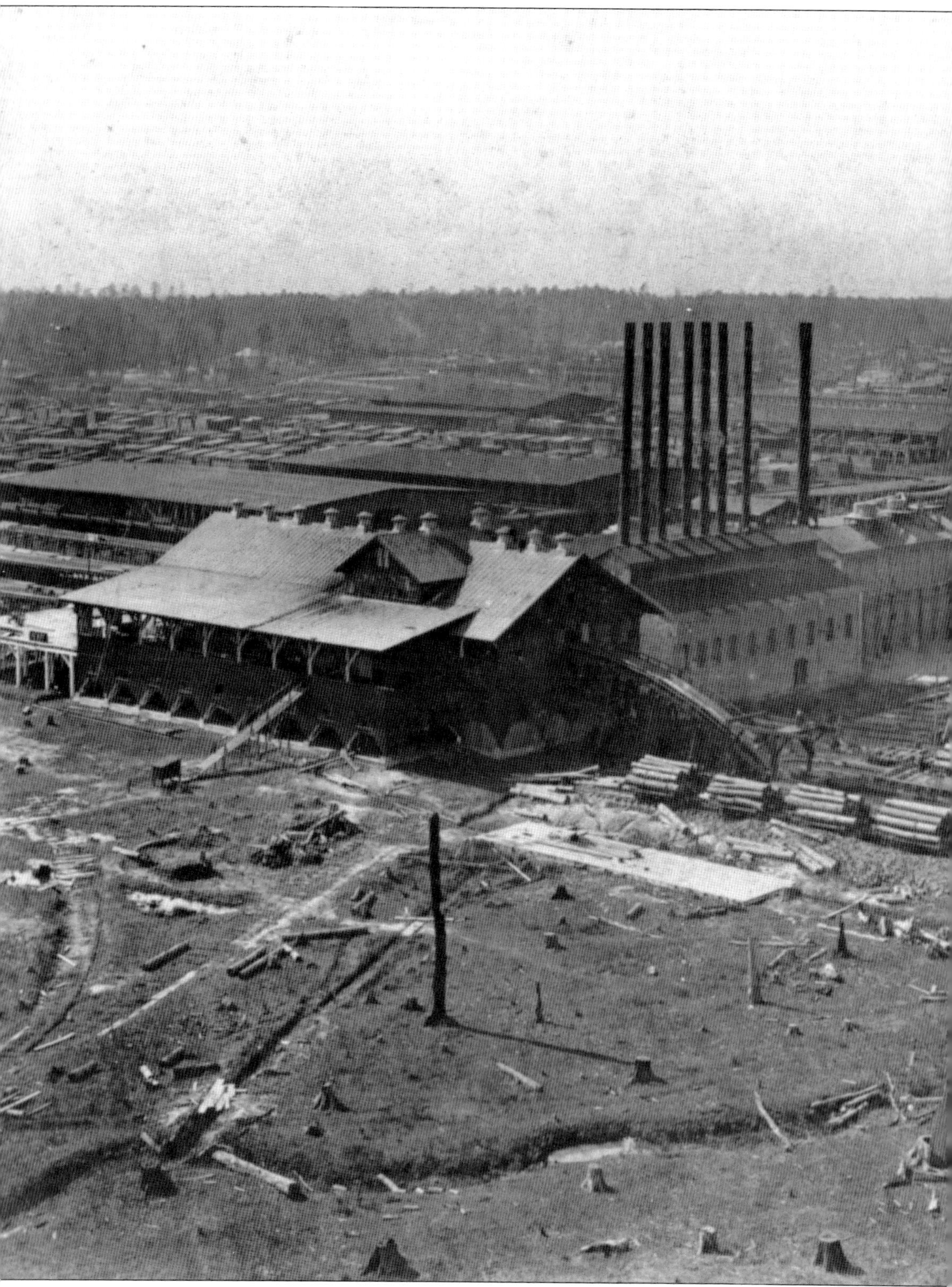

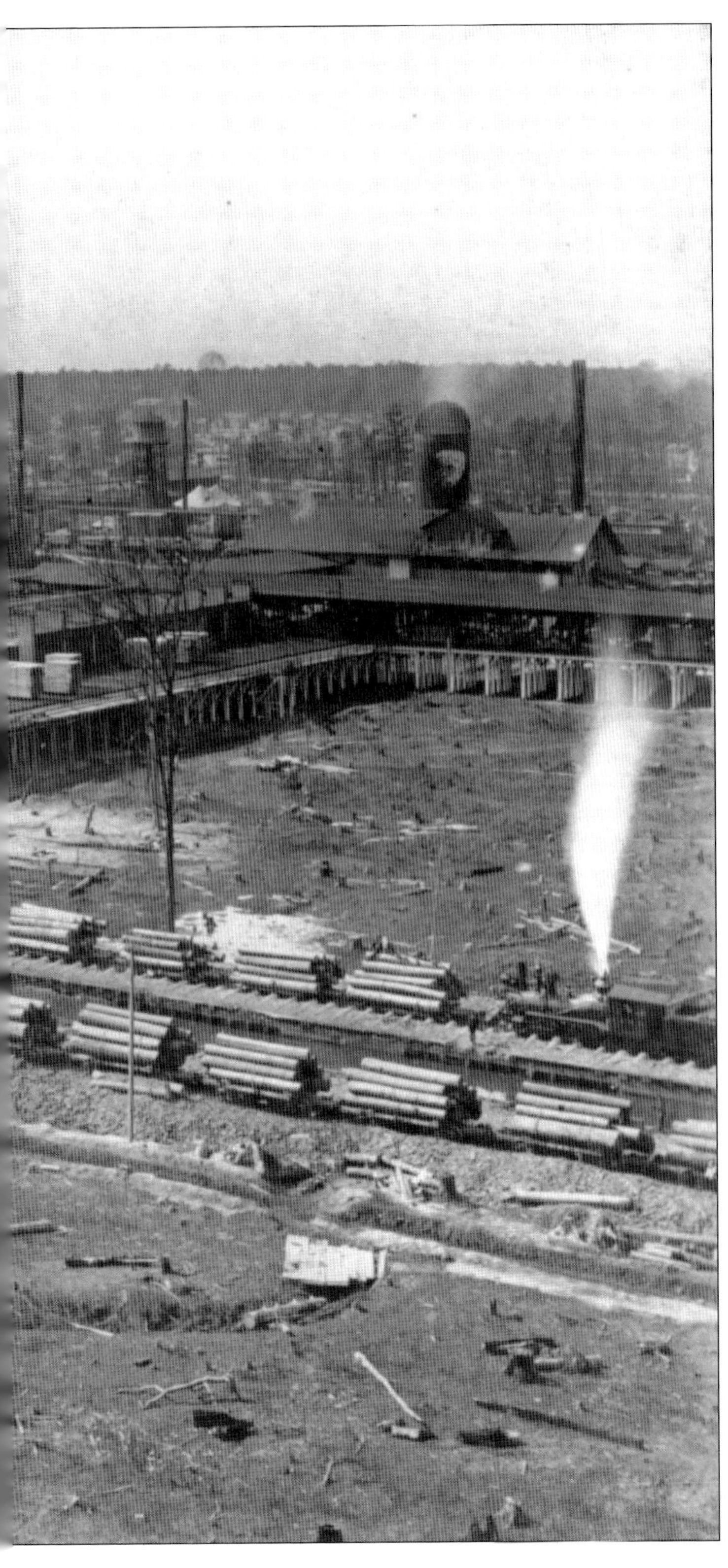

In the piney woods about 32 miles southeast of El Dorado, and only two miles from the Louisiana state line, rose the small sawmill town of Huttig. The Frost-Johnson Timber Company built a literal company town. It was named Huttig after industrialist William Huttig, a friend of the timber company's president C.D. Johnson. The Union Sawmill would grow to become one of the largest in the country. The view here was likely taken from a water tower; the train to the right had just delivered logs harvested nearby. The sawmill has been bought and sold several times, most recently to the West Fraser Timber Company of Canada. The company shuttered the mill indefinitely in early 2024 because of depressed lumber prices. About 140 jobs were lost, and the entire small community was impacted. (Courtesy of the Encyclopedia of Arkansas.)

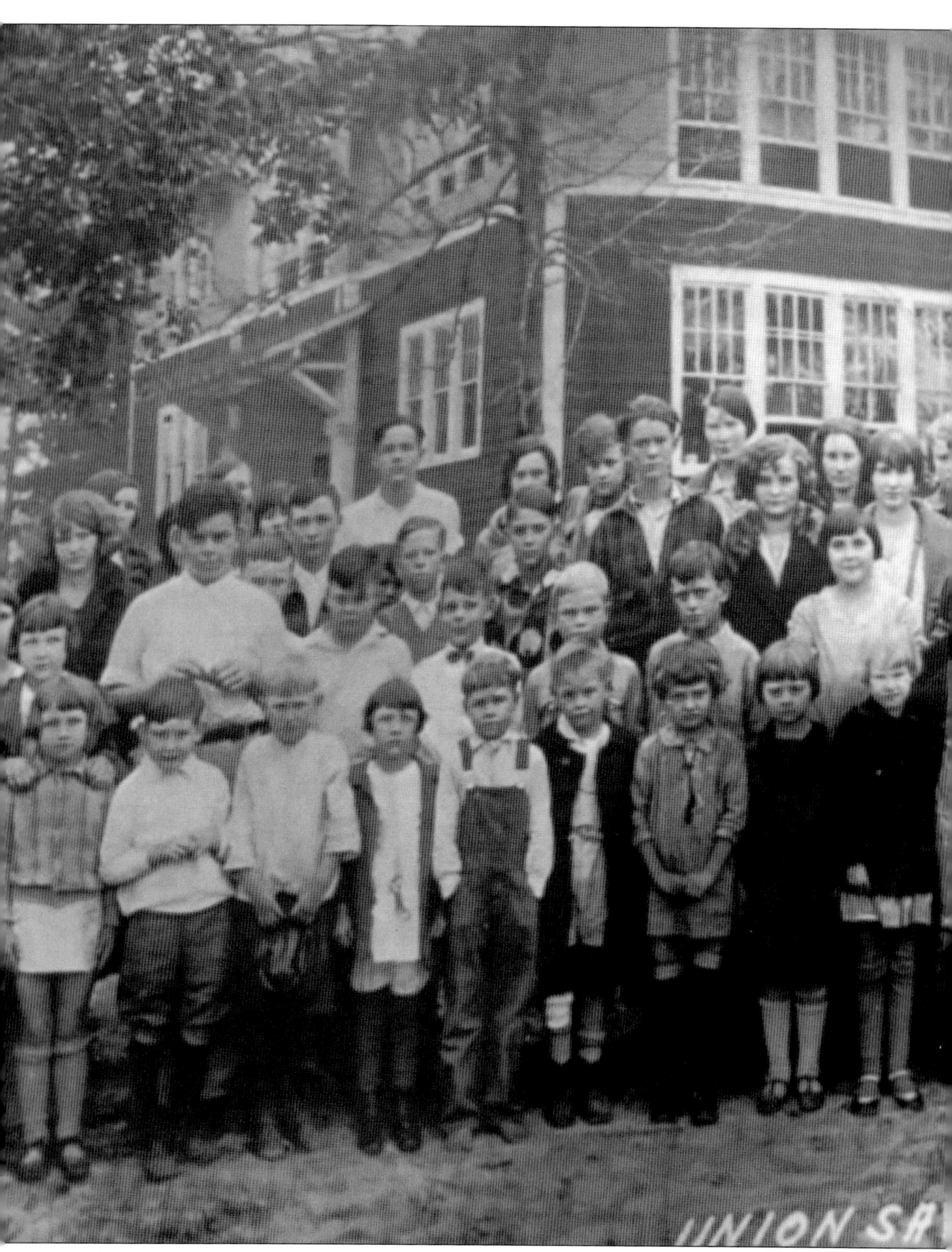

The company town of Huttig established a school for the local children, most of whom had fathers working in the huge sawmill. Seen here around 1920, the pictured students were part of the

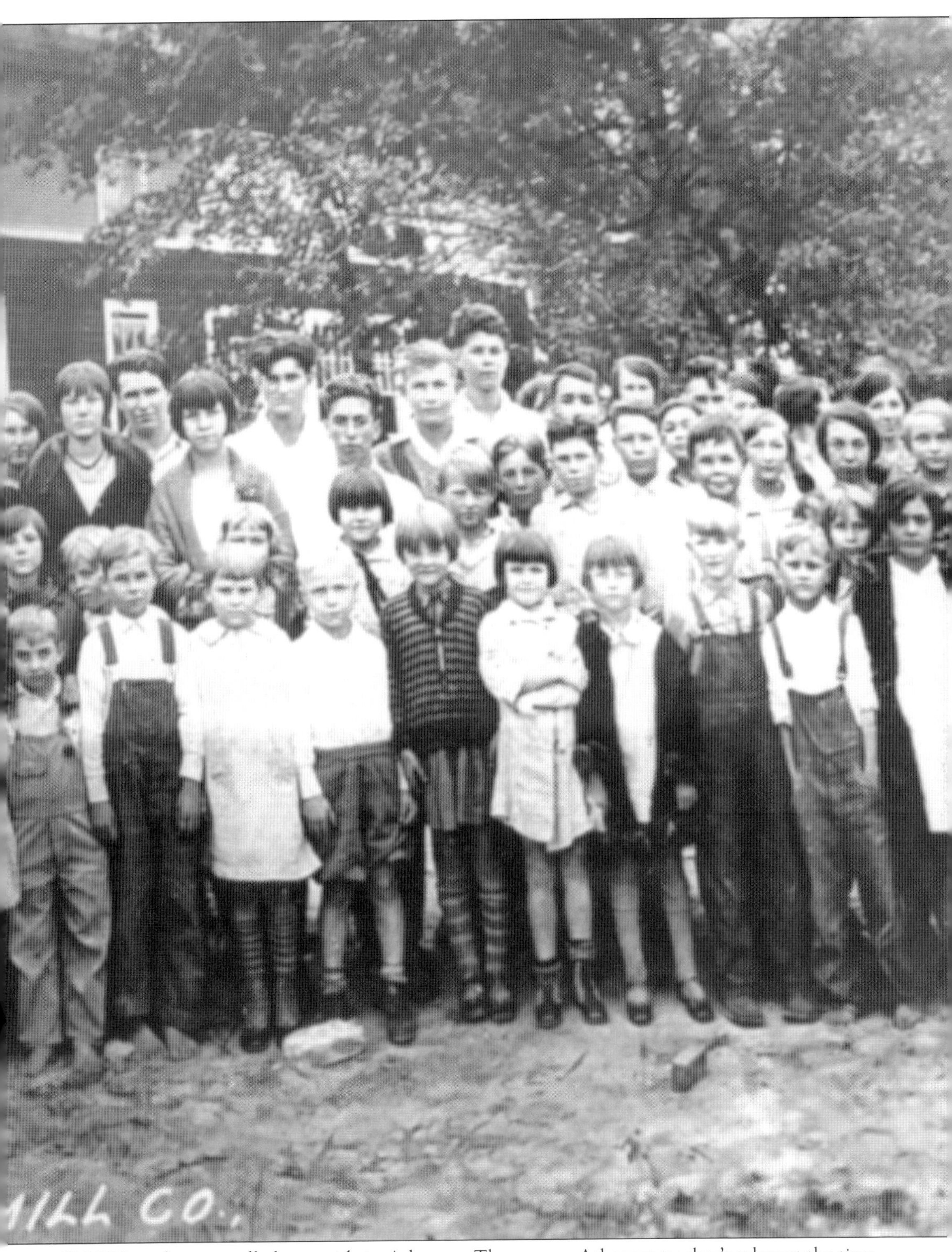

326,000 students enrolled statewide in Arkansas. The average Arkansas teacher's salary at the time was $476 for the school year. (Courtesy of Huttig Library.)

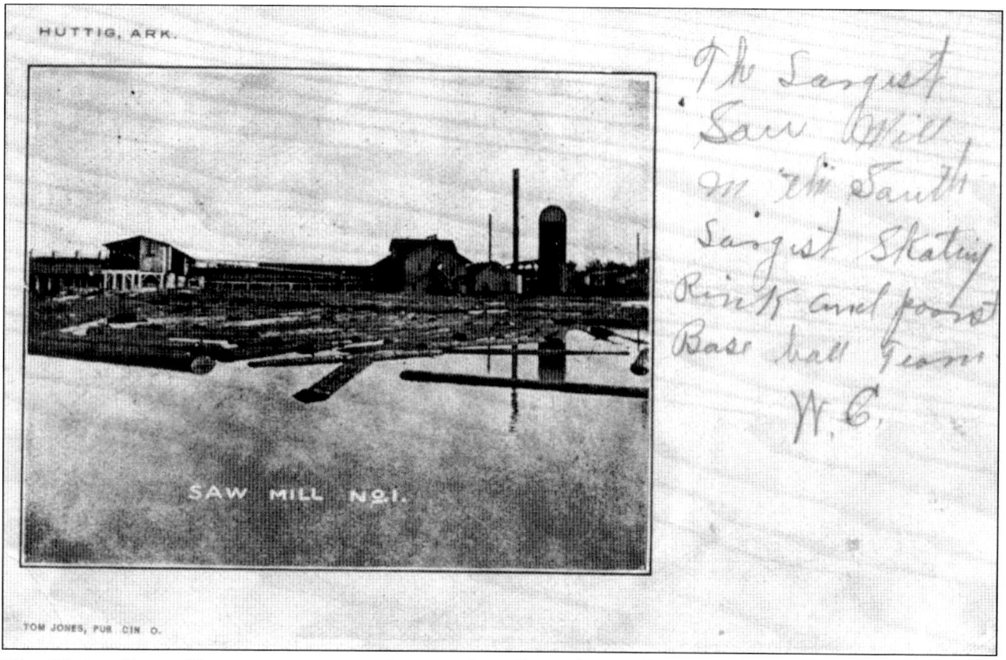

The Union Sawmill put out a postcard printed on "wood grain" paper; the image shows the pond where logs were held until ready for processing in the mill. The card's sender, in 1906, wrote on the front, "The largest saw mill in the south, largest skating rink and poorest baseball team."

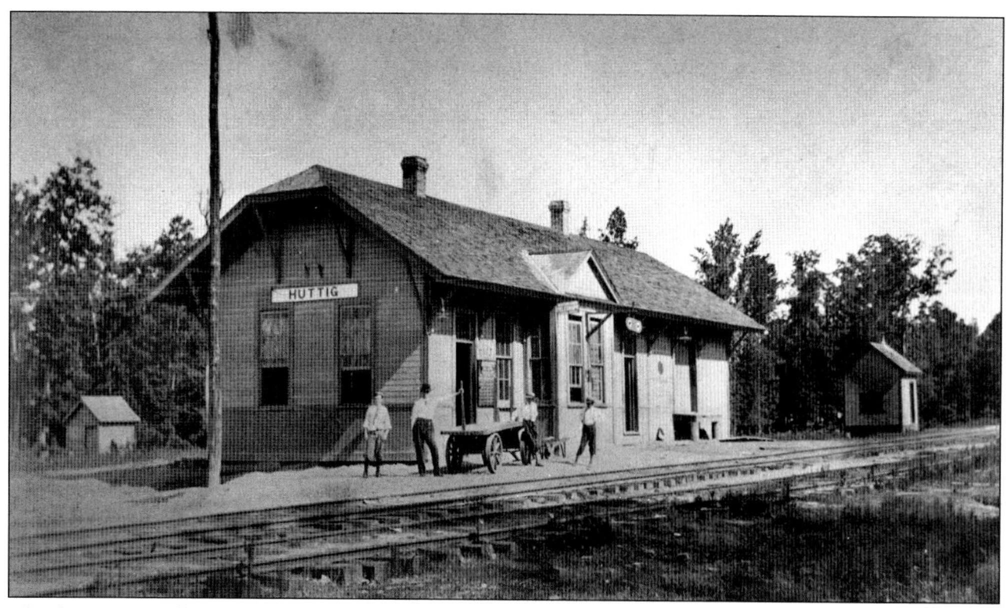

The huge sawmill brought people and supplies to Huttig daily, and the local Rock Island depot was a central point in the small community. Both the depot and the railroad have been gone for decades. (Courtesy of the Encyclopedia of Arkansas.)

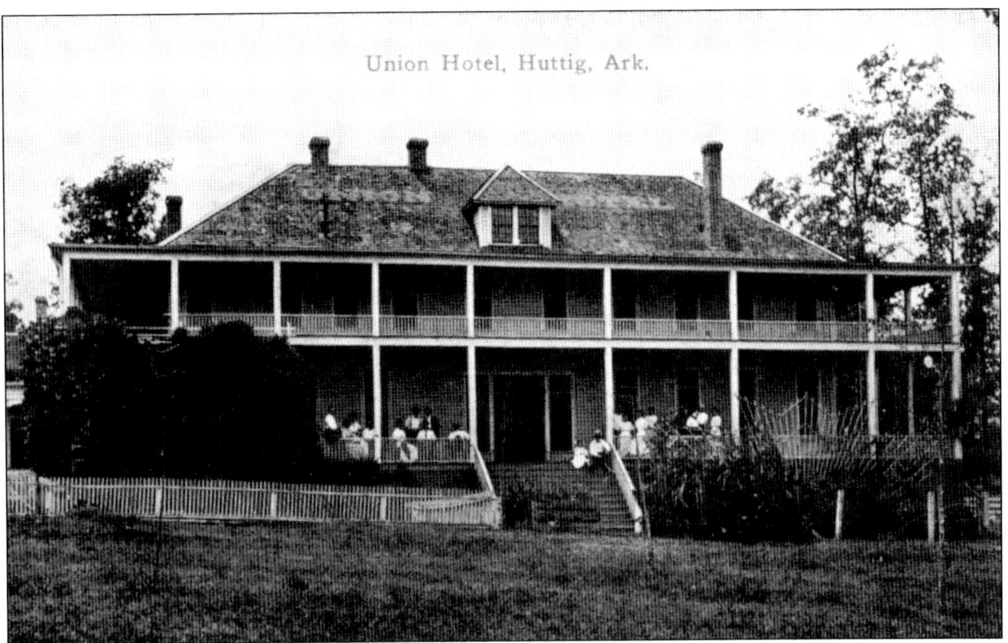

In the company town of Huttig, the rambling Union Hotel provided lodging for mill executives and visitors doing business in the bustling little town. The two-story hotel was named after the Union Sawmill; sadly, the wooden structure was later lost to fire.

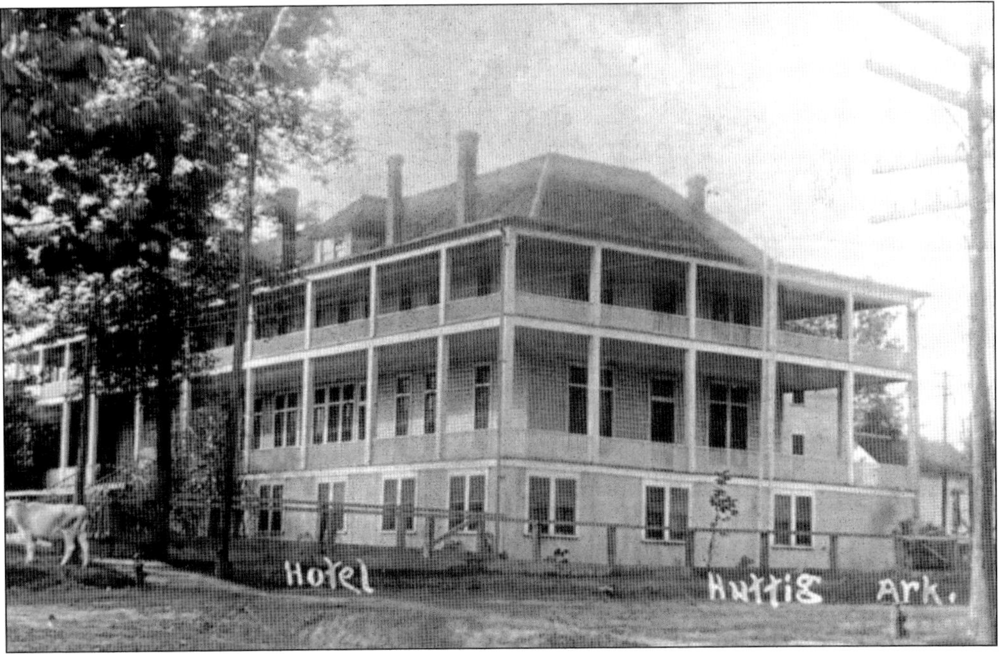

When the Union Hotel burned, an even larger hotel was immediately constructed to replace it. Such a project clearly indicates that Huttig was a busy town, with lumber brokers, salesmen, and families visiting regularly. The new Colonial Hotel, seen here, had three floors and was the largest hotel in Union County outside of El Dorado. To the left, a cow is seen ambling on the lawn. The hotel was torn down in 1957, and its lumber was used to build a new house.

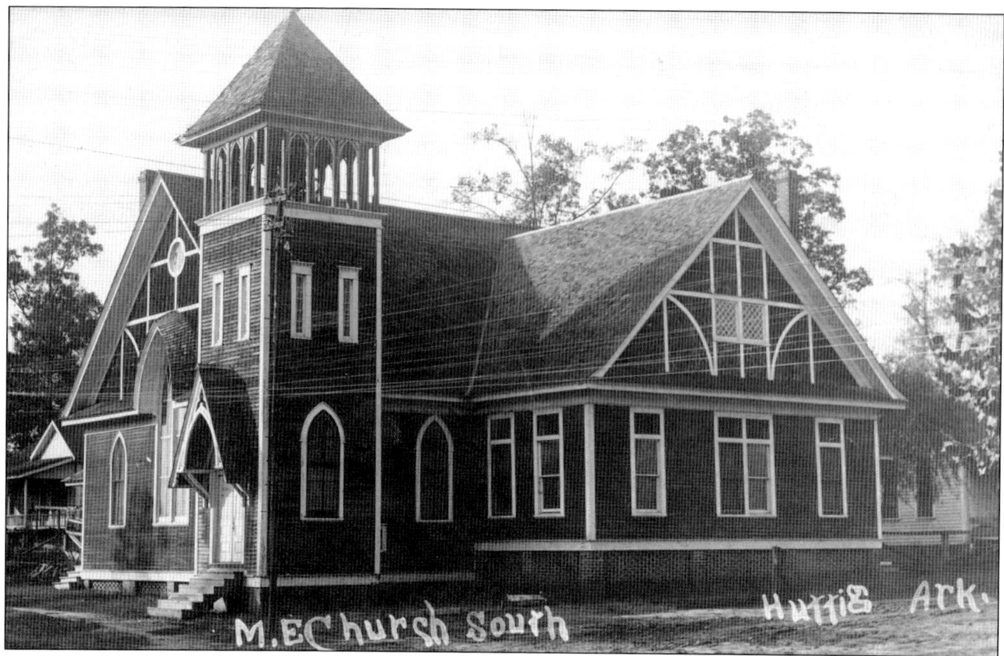

The company town of Huttig included several churches for its burgeoning population; this one was home to the Union Methodist Episcopal Church South. This denomination existed from 1846 to 1939, after a split within Methodism over the issue of slavery. The striking building was constructed from lumber harvested in the surrounding forests; its windows trimmed in white give it a unique appearance.

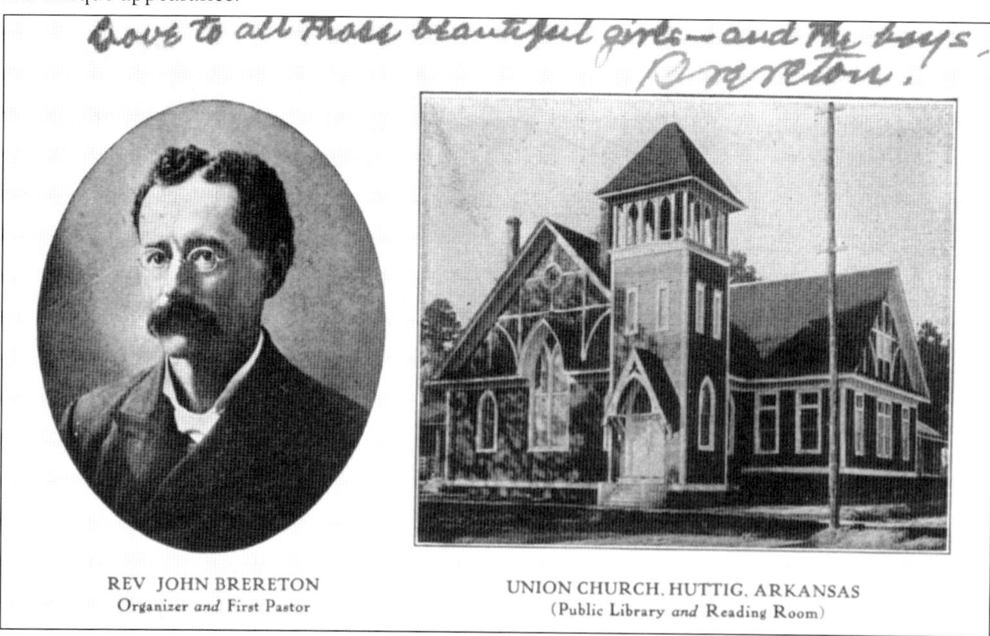

Rev. John Brereton was the organizer and first pastor of the Union Methodist Episcopal Church. He wrote at the top of the postcard, sent to Missouri: "Love to all those beautiful girls—and the boys." The postcard denotes an interesting dual use, in that the church also served as the town's public library and reading room.

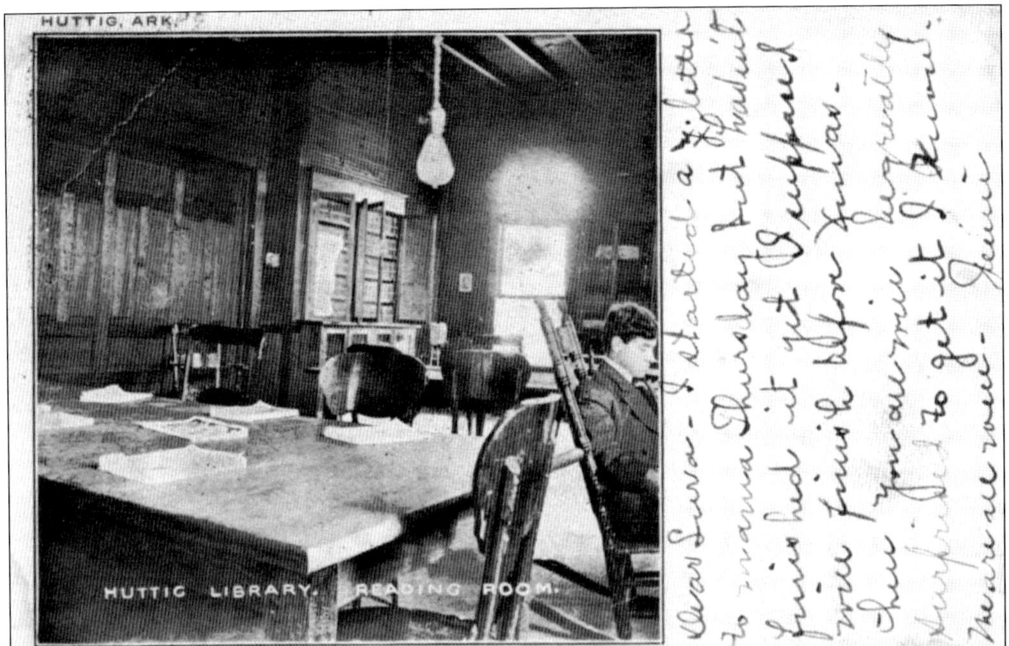

This 1909 postcard captured the inside of the Huttig Library and Reading Room, housed on the upper story of the Union Methodist Episcopal Church. The families of the mill workers could have used the library as well as the mill workers themselves in their off hours.

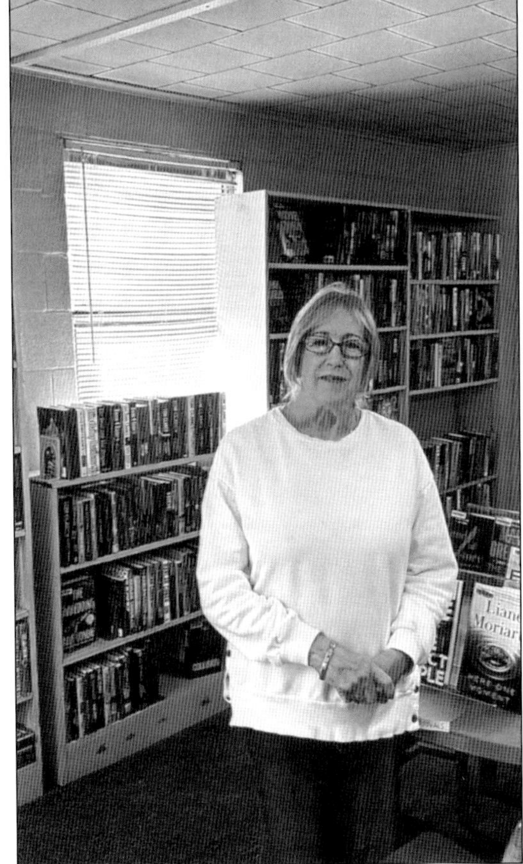

The Union Methodist Episcopal Church and its library and reading room have been gone for decades, but the little town now has a branch of the Union County Library System. Brenda Miller, Huttig's librarian and total staff, is seen here in 2024 at the library she oversees on Frost Street. (Photograph by Ray Hanley.)

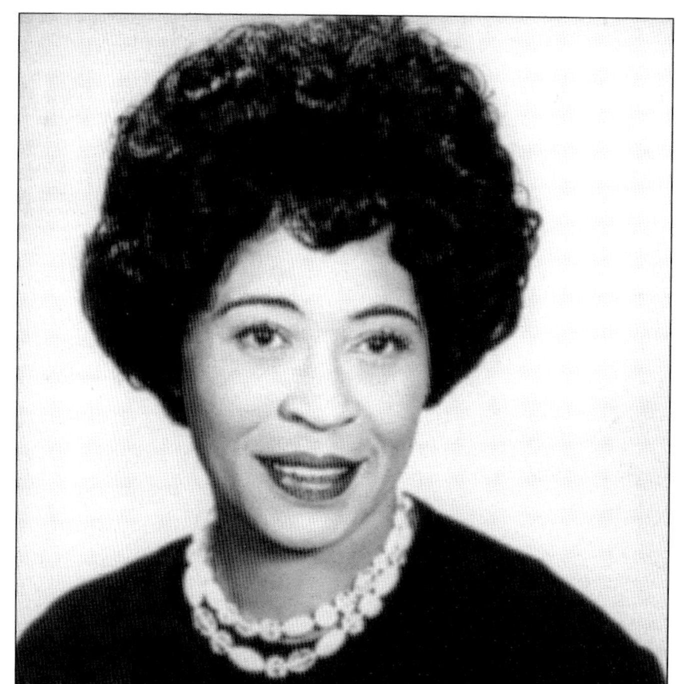

Tiny Huttig produced several people who went on to achieve fame. Daisy Gaston Bates was born in Huttig in 1914. She was orphaned at age seven and taken in as a foster child by a mill worker. Her fame began after her move to Little Rock, when she became a major spokesperson for civil rights. In 1957, Arkansas governor Orval Faubus closed Little Rock's Central High School rather than integrate it, and Bates spoke up. She lived near the campus and became the mentor of the "Little Rock Nine," the group of Black students who first attempted to integrate the school. (Courtesy of University of Arkansas Special Collections.)

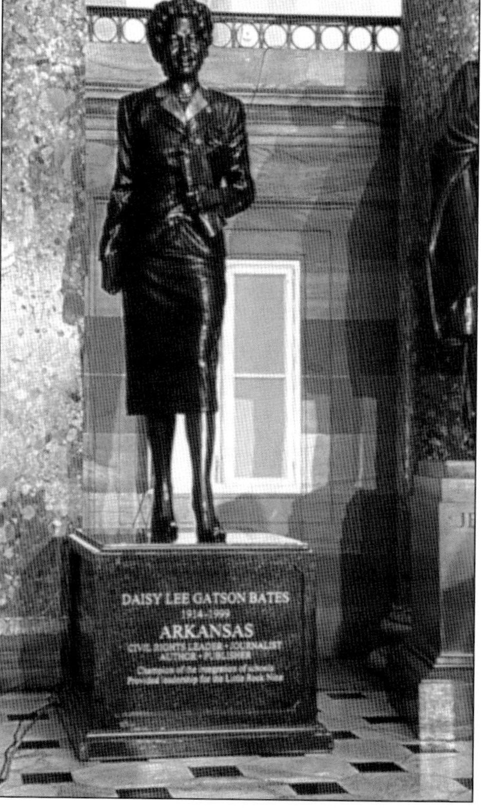

When Arkansas set about to replace its two representative statues in the rotunda of the US Capitol, it opted to replace the two White men from the 1800s with statues of Daisy Bates and Johnny Cash. Installed in 2024, the work recognizes Daisy Bates's life of civil rights advocacy as well as her career as a journalist and publisher. She and her husband published the *Arkansas State Press,* a newspaper promoting civil rights. Bates died in 1999. (Courtesy of Facebook group Huttig, Arkansas in Photos and History.)

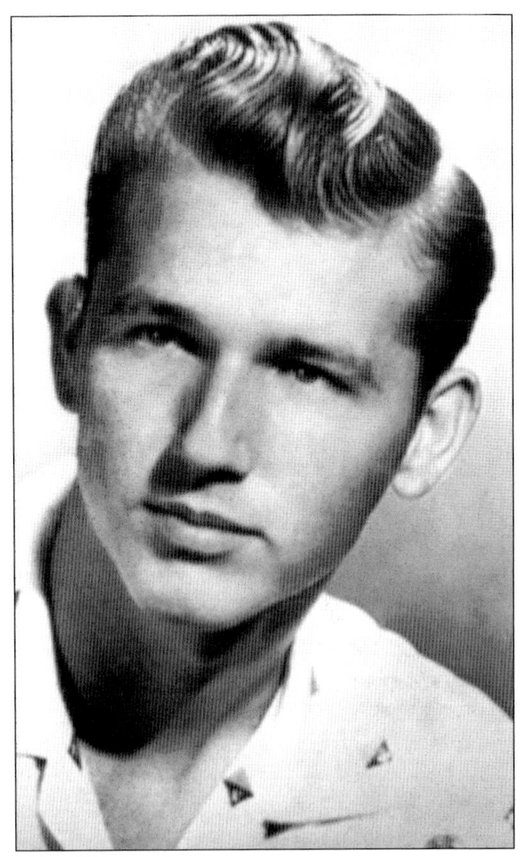

Born in Louisiana in 1933, musician Floyd Cramer grew up in Huttig; he learned to play the piano by ear beginning at age five. He played professionally starting at the Louisiana Hayride in Shreveport, then went on to become Nashville's top session keyboardist for many years. Cramer backed up such iconic stars as Elvis Presley, Jimmy Dean, Charley Pride, and Chet Atkins. Most famously, he developed the "slip note" technique showcased in his instrumental ballad "Last Date," which became his signature tune. Cramer died of cancer in 1997 at age 64. (Courtesy of Facebook group Huttig, Arkansas in Photos and History.)

Shoppers in Huttig during the 1930s and 1940s were often drawn to the Nash Store, operated by Orrin and Zena Nash. In this detailed interior view, a doll can be seen for sale in the glass case to the right. Seated on the counter was the Nashs' daughter Mildred, who died in 1938 at age 16, about 10 years after this photograph. Orrin died in 1957, while Zena lived to age 97 and died in 1996, almost 60 years after the death of her only daughter.

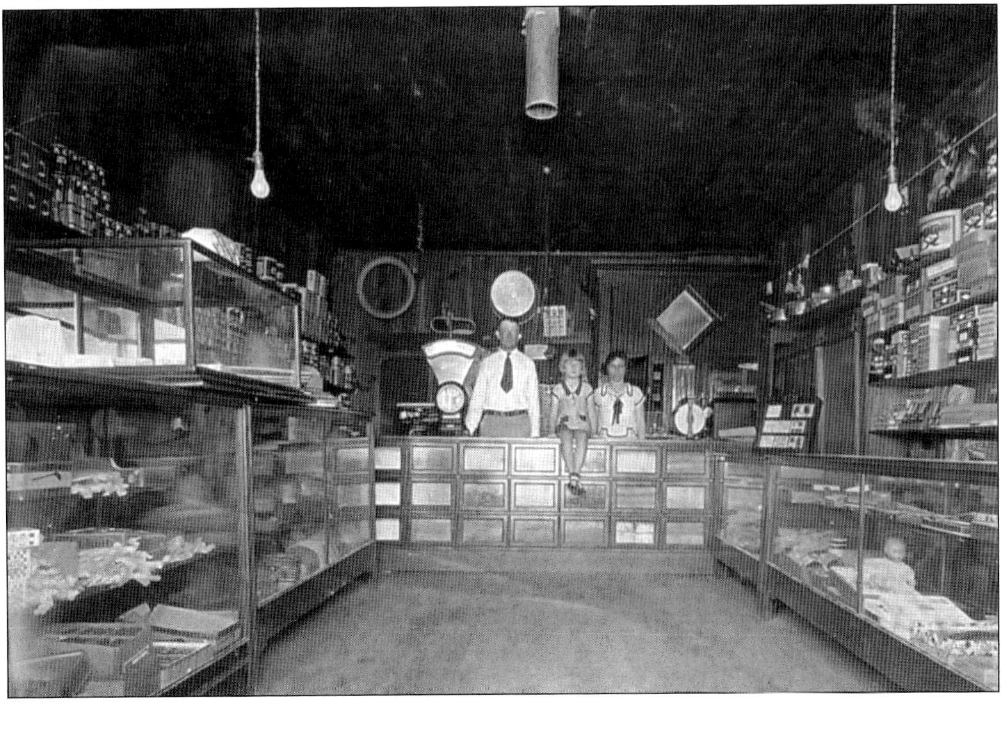

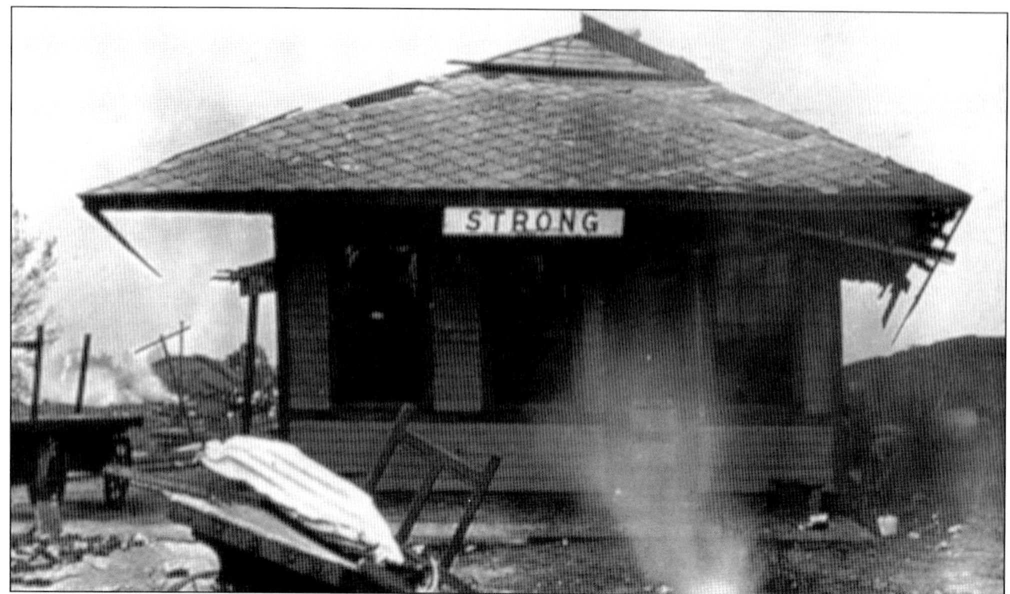

The town of Strong is located 20 miles southeast of El Dorado and was originally named Victoria. It was renamed Strong to honor a railroad man who had helped bring in the rail line. The town became an important shipping center for cotton and lumber, and during the 1920s, eight passenger trains a day stopped there. However, no trains were stopping on May 9, 1927, after a devastating tornado blew through. One confident resident said, "See the name on the station, it is Strong. We'll build back stronger than ever." (Courtesy of Encyclopedia of Arkansas.)

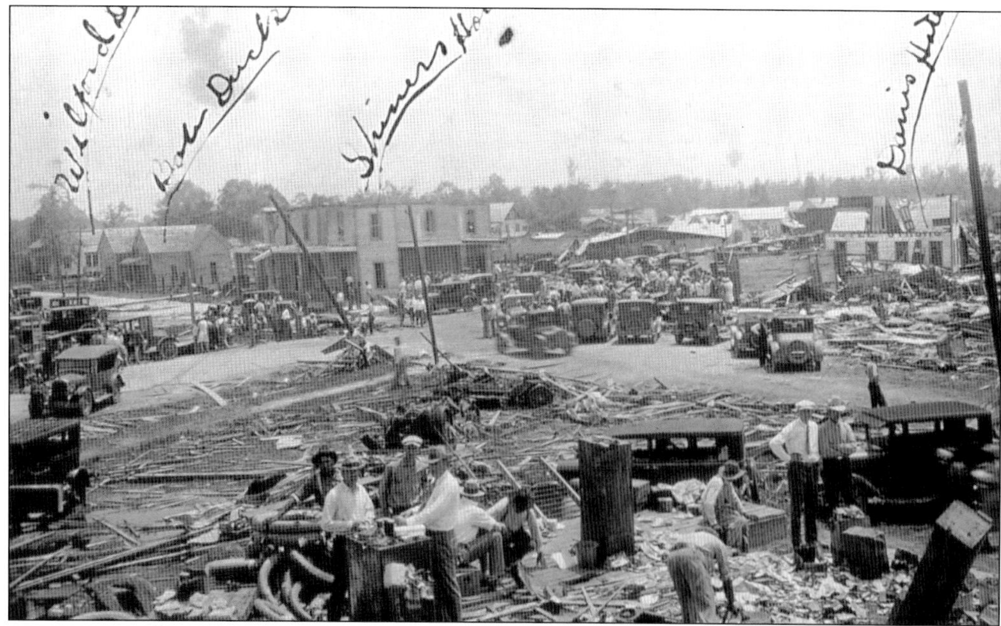

In 1927, a cyclone, as tornados were then called, descended onto Strong without warning. The *Arkansas Gazette* reported, "The disaster at Strong, where 17 are dead, and ten missing, is one of the worst in the history of the Southwest. The twister caught the little farming community off guard, and within ten minutes had leveled all but a few homes. The business district is destroyed." (Courtesy of the Encyclopedia of Arkansas.)

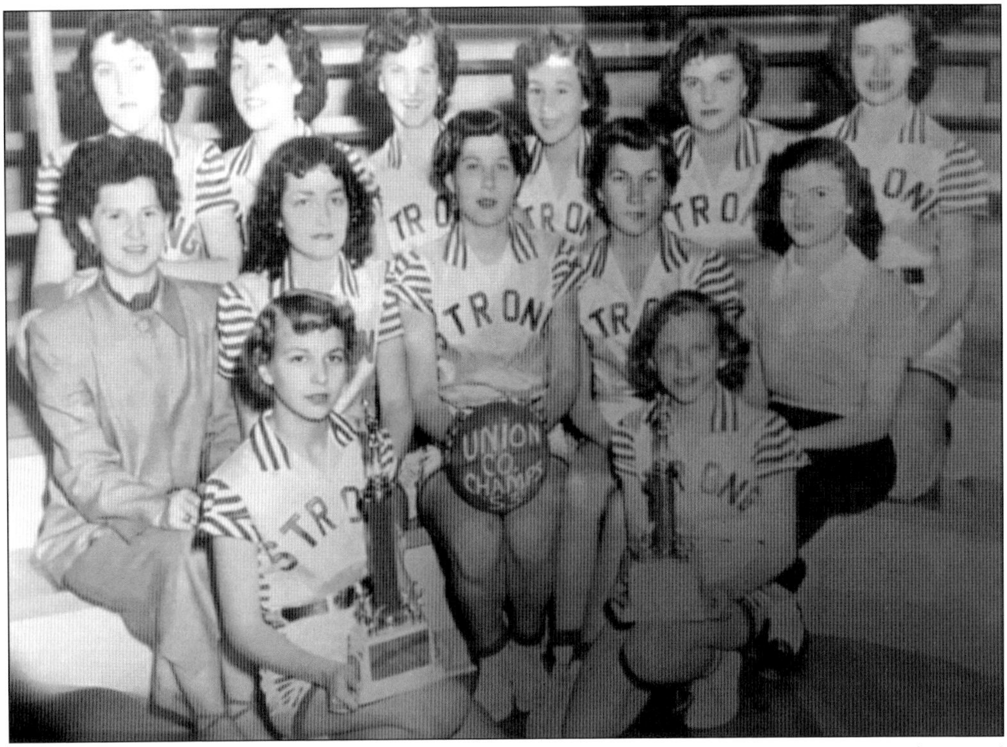

In 1953, Strong High School was proud of its Lady Bulldogs basketball team. Their coach, seated to the left, was Rose George. Players shown include Johnette Taylor (second row, second from left), Peggy Munford (second row, third from left), and Paddie Sue Norris (third row, far right). In the second row on the far right is Betty Jo Taylor, the team manager. Janette Adams (left) and Ethel Duke (right) kneel while holding trophies, and Betty Zane Jerry holds the ball. (Courtesy of Facebook group Strong, Arkansas in Photos and History.)

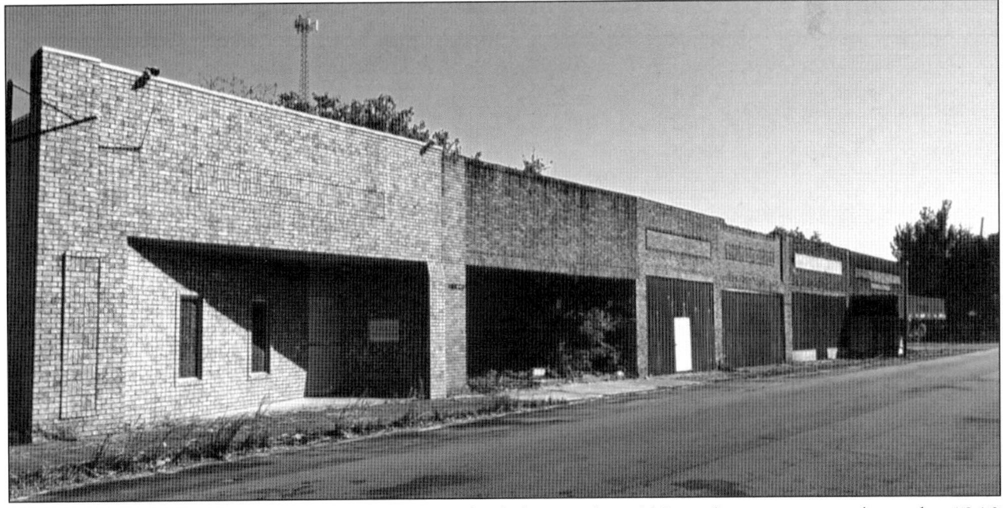

In the 2020 census, the population of Strong had dropped to 410, its lowest since at least the 1910 census, and down by half from 70 years prior. The formerly robust business district is shuttered today, and modern highways allow people to easily travel to El Dorado for shopping. (Photograph by Ray Hanley.)

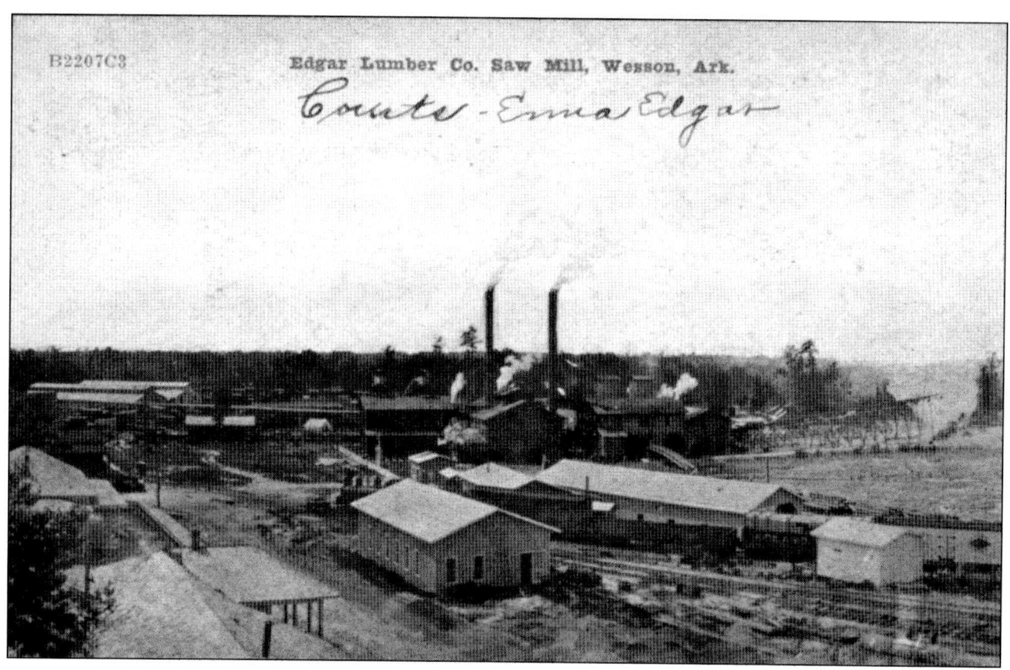

A few miles south of El Dorado was the community of Wesson, Arkansas. The Edgar Lumber Company bought a small sawmill at Wesson in 1904 and greatly expanded it. A short line railroad, only six miles long, opened in 1905 to move lumber from the Wesson mill to El Dorado for shipping. Above is the expansive mill, and below is a c. 1910 view of the office of the company store. Canned provisions are neatly arranged on shelves in the background, while the latest technology in the office includes a gramophone, a chrome-plated cash register, and possibly a typewriter.

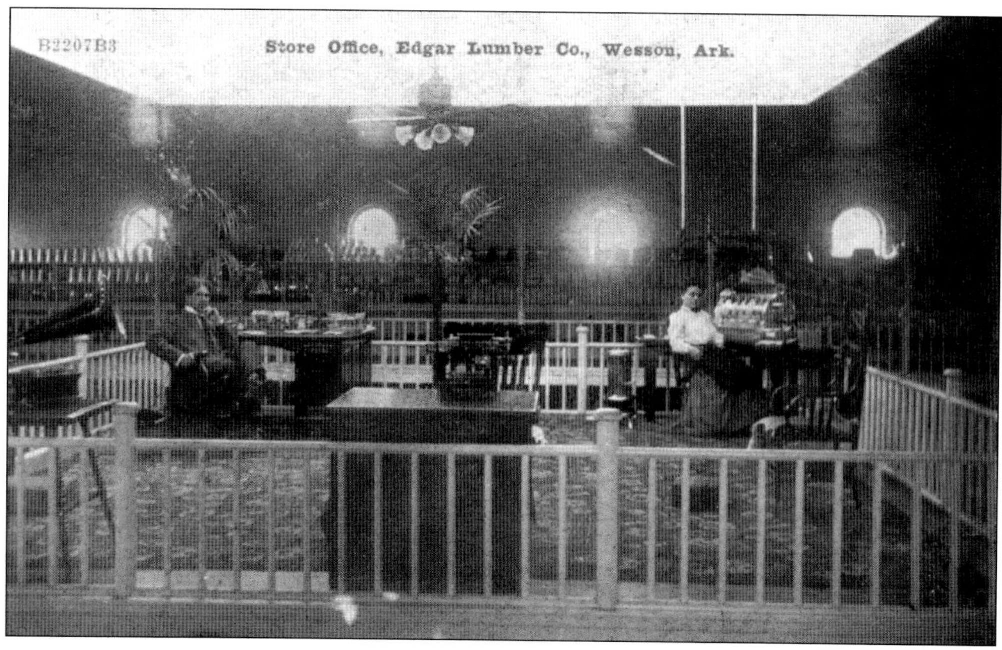

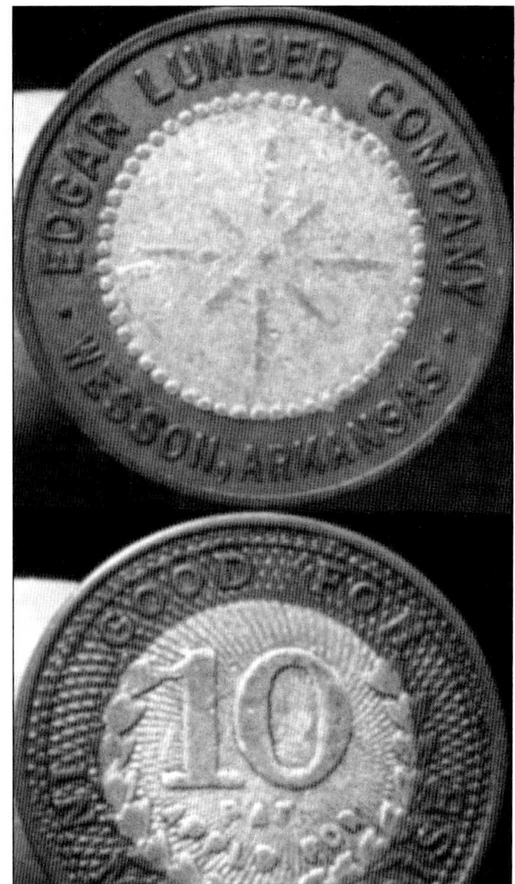

Part of the pay of Edgar Lumber employees was in the form of tokens redeemable in the company store. Such sawmill-made currency was not uncommon in the lumber business, and it helped keep some commerce within the company when employees shopped at the company store.

In 1905, the El Dorado & Wesson short line railroad began to serve the Edgar Lumber mill at Wesson. Against all odds, the railroad spur still operates today. The Wesson mill has shut down, but the short line railroad now serves other industries such as Great Lakes Chemical, located between El Dorado and Newell, Arkansas, six miles away.

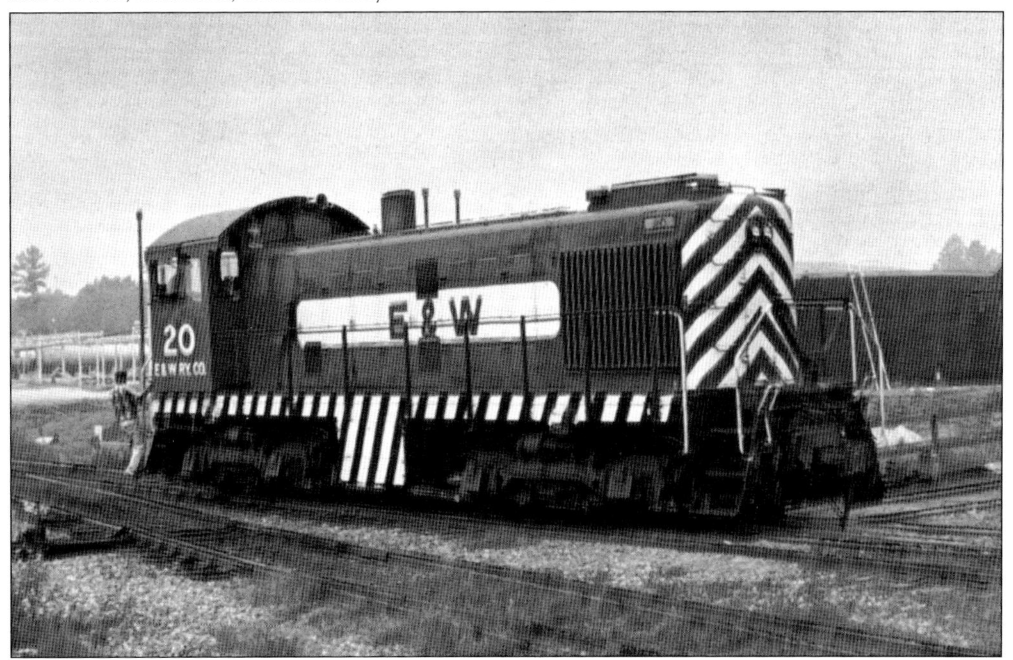

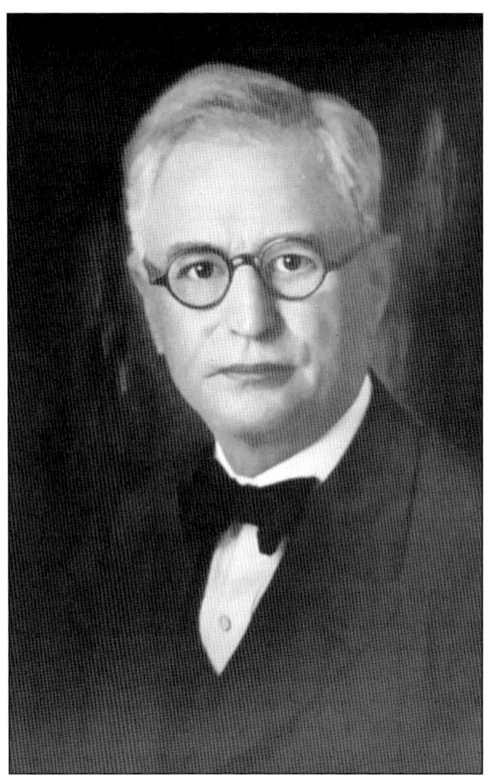

Around 1900, Ike Felsenthal looked at the vast forests of eastern Union County and saw potential for a town. He and his brothers formed the Felsenthal Land and Timber Company, and the town grew quickly to 1,200 residents. Excursion trains brought buyers to town during the timber boom, and the community boasted public schools, three hotels, and even two newspapers. However, as nearby Huttig grew, Felsenthal declined; it was unincorporated in 1911, and by 1919, only 273 people called the town home. Ike Felsenthal moved to El Dorado with the oil boom and became part of the active Jewish community, even helping organize the local chamber of commerce. (Courtesy of SAHPS.)

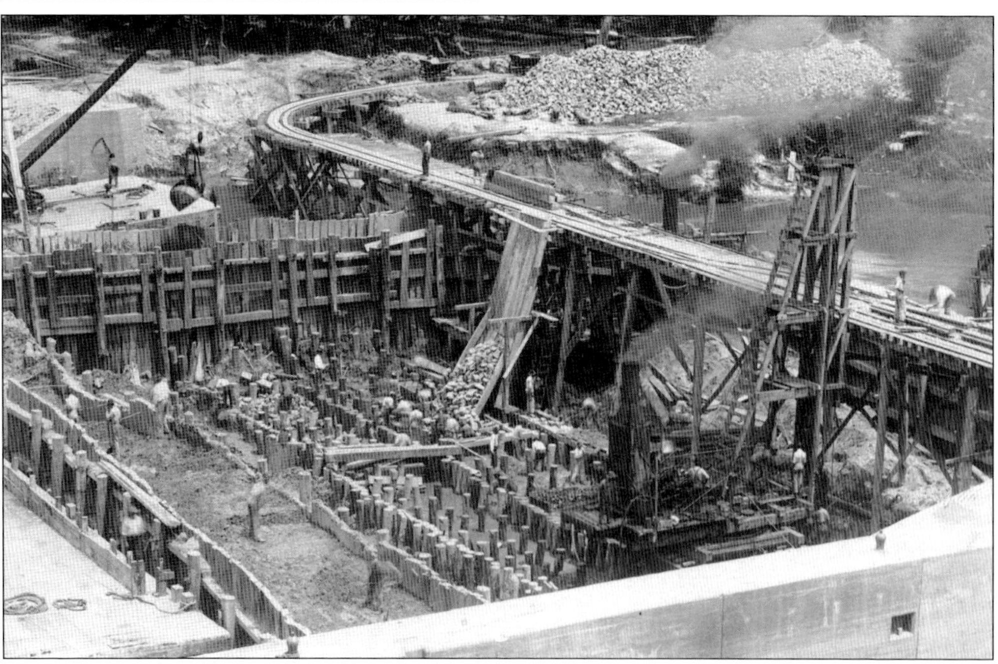

The town of Felsenthal was located near where the Saline River emptied into the Ouachita River. The US Army Corps of Engineers was lobbied to try to tame the Ouachita with a series of locks and dams, making steamboat travel possible upriver to Camden. The construction effort is seen here around 1911.

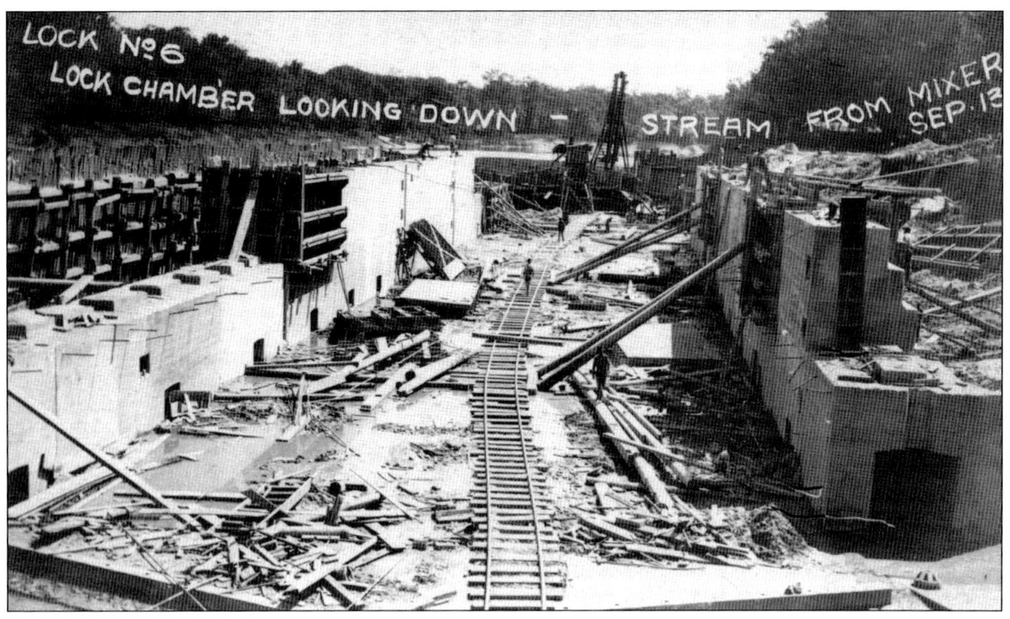

Seen above is Felsenthal Lock No. 6 under construction in 1911. Temporary rails were laid to move heavy loads between what were to be the concrete sides of the lock. Below is the completed Lock No. 8 filling with water. Despite all the effort, the project failed to bring much shipping activity to the river.

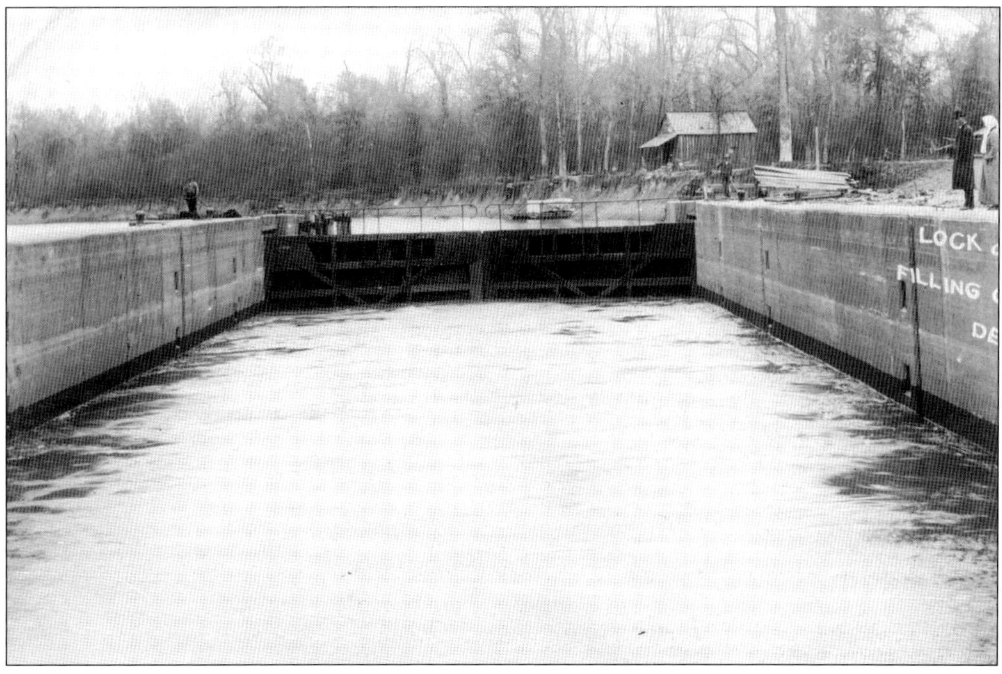

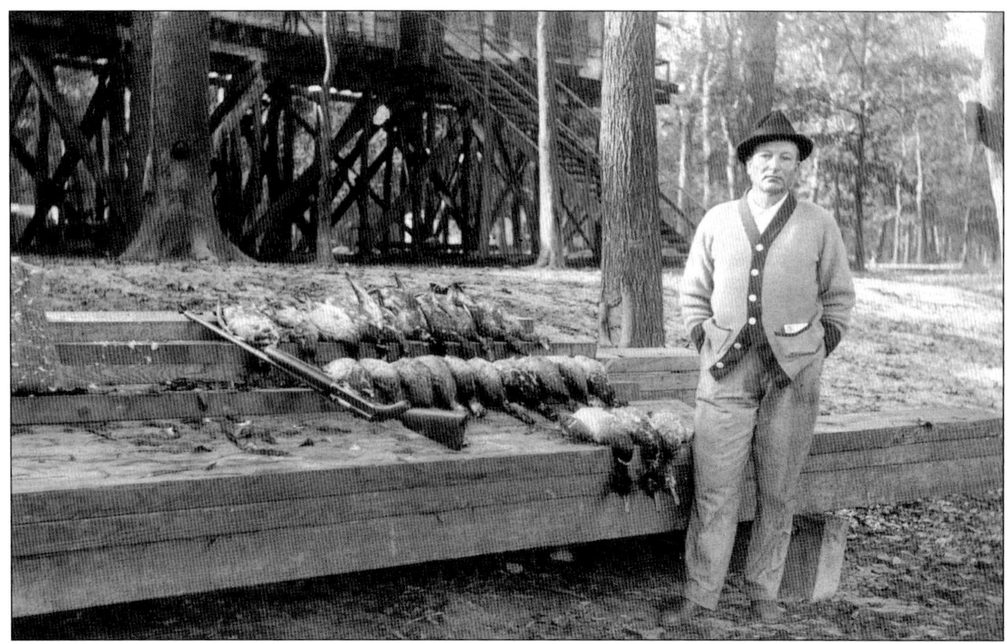

The wilderness around Felsenthal was and is rich in wildlife, as demonstrated by this man posing in 1913 with a number of ducks and his shotgun. Behind him is seen an elevated house, in an area that is often flooded. He wrote, "Was three days coming up the river with our barge. Lots of deer and turkeys and game of all kinds." The man had brought a barge slowly through the system of locks and dams.

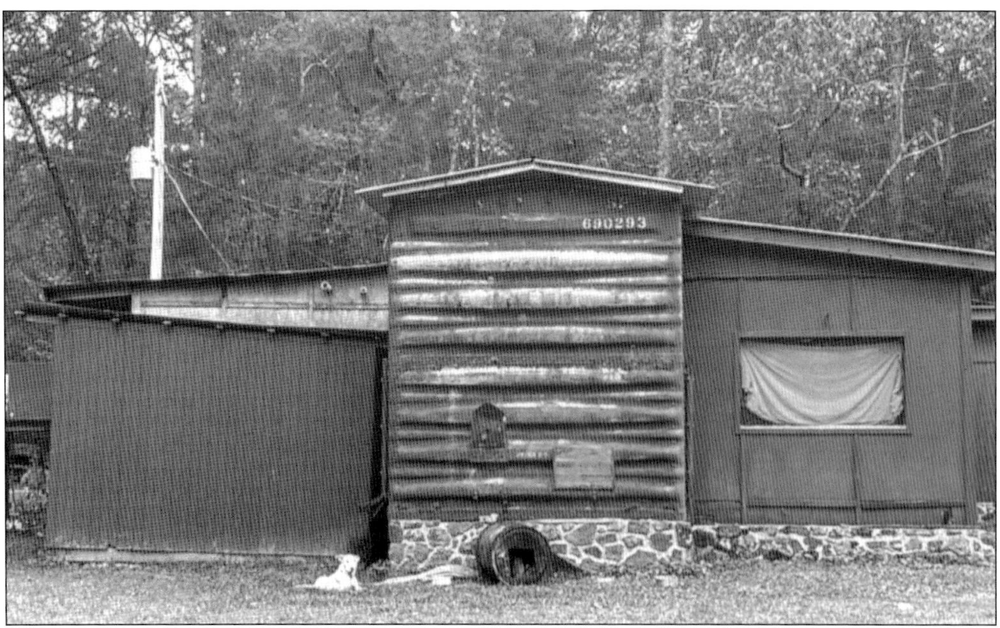

In the 2020 census, the population of Felsenthal was only 85 people. Still, since the 65,000-acre Felsenthal National Wildlife Refuge was established in 1975, thousands of hunters and fishermen come annually. Aside from the many privately owned hunting cabins, one lodging option is the Tracks Inn, a motel of sorts composed of old railroad boxcars. (Photograph by Ray Hanley.)

Seven

Union County, Today and in the Future

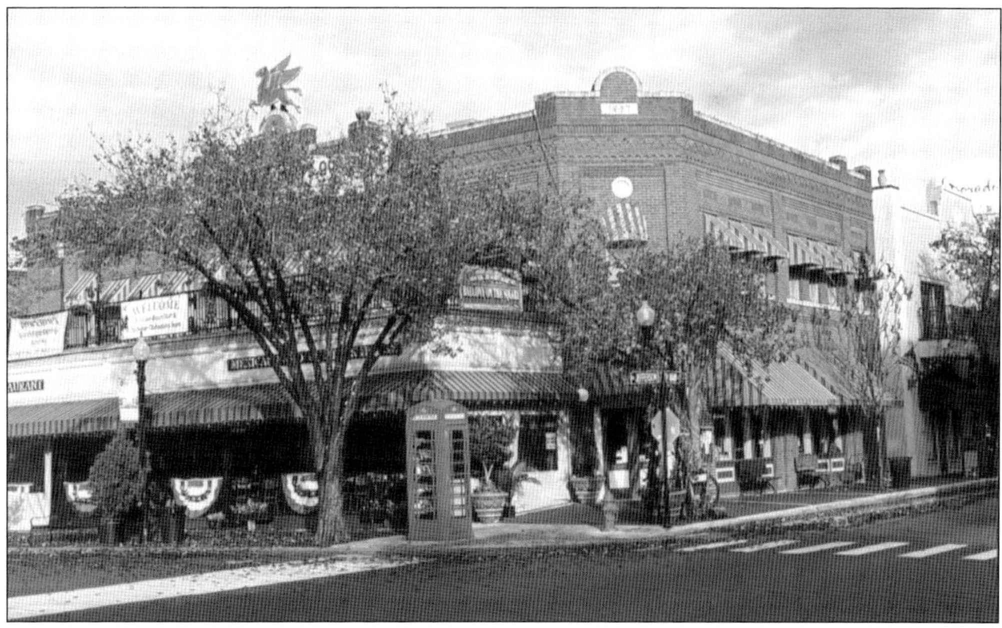

Visitors to El Dorado today are surprised to find a couple of British phone booths located among the shops on the landscaped downtown square. As newcomers enjoy a stroll, they may have little idea how much work, investment, and ingenuity it took to create one of the most pleasant downtowns in America—with even a couple of genuine British phone booths. (Photograph by Ray Hanley.)

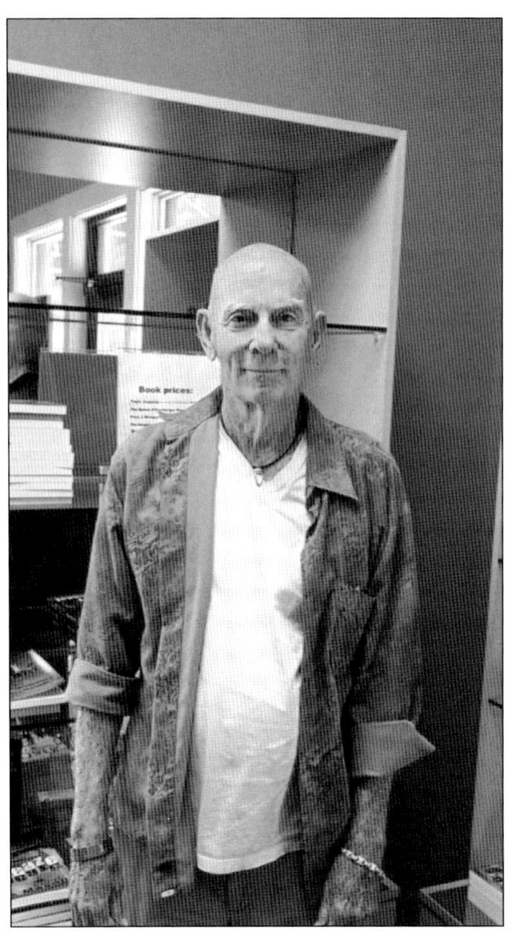

The two people largely responsible for bringing El Dorado back from an empty decaying downtown to a city that became a National Main Street Award Winner are geologist Richard Mason and his wife, Vertis. Richard, seen here in 2024, was born in the Union County town of Norphlet; Vertis hails from Smackover. The couple came home in 1974 after success in the oil business around the world. The Masons saw the empty, sad downtown and slowly developed a vision of what could be. Buying and restoring some 20 downtown buildings, the couple has brought life and commerce back to downtown El Dorado. (Photograph by Ray Hanley.)

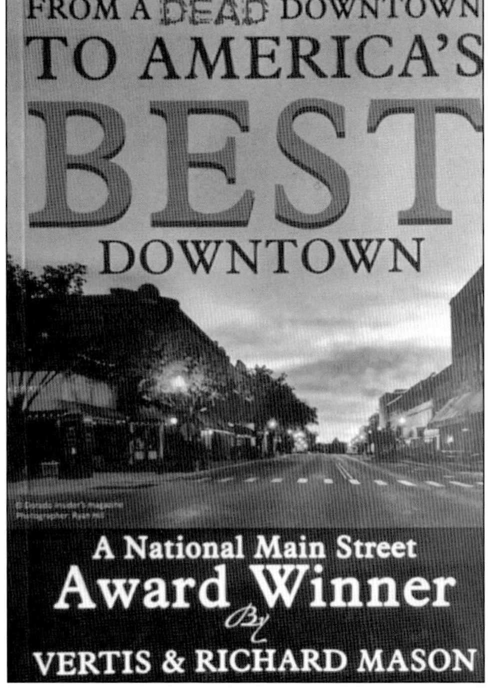

The Masons chronicled the rebirth of downtown El Dorado in their book aptly titled *From a Dead Downtown to America's Best Downtown*. Everywhere one looks in walking around the downtown square, evidence is seen of what has been accomplished. One cannot help but think, "Why can't other towns across America do this?" (Courtesy of Richard Mason.)

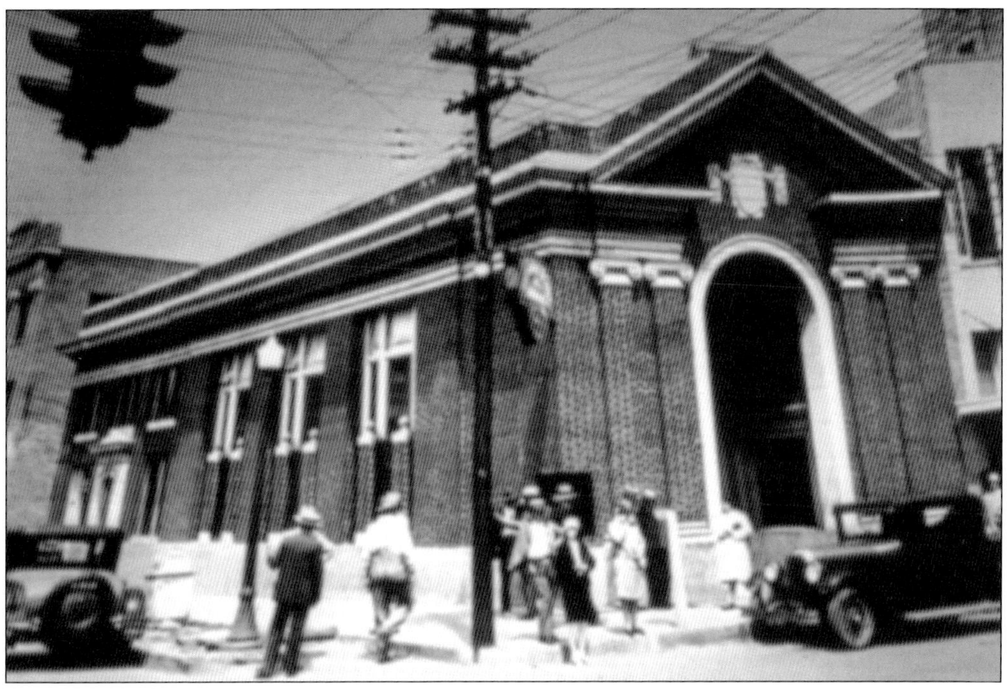

Richard and Vertis Mason, upon their return to El Dorado, built their family's home and then started to look for a place to house Richard's oil exploration business, Gibraltar Energy. They bought the long-vacant National Bank of Commerce building in the center of the shabby but formerly vibrant city. Equipped with a photograph of the original exterior facade (above), the Masons restored it to its 1918 appearance. That was just the start, as over the next few years, the couple bought and restored a number of other buildings in downtown El Dorado. National recognition followed, giving a shining example of how to restore a virtually abandoned, neglected downtown. (Below, photograph by Ray Hanley.)

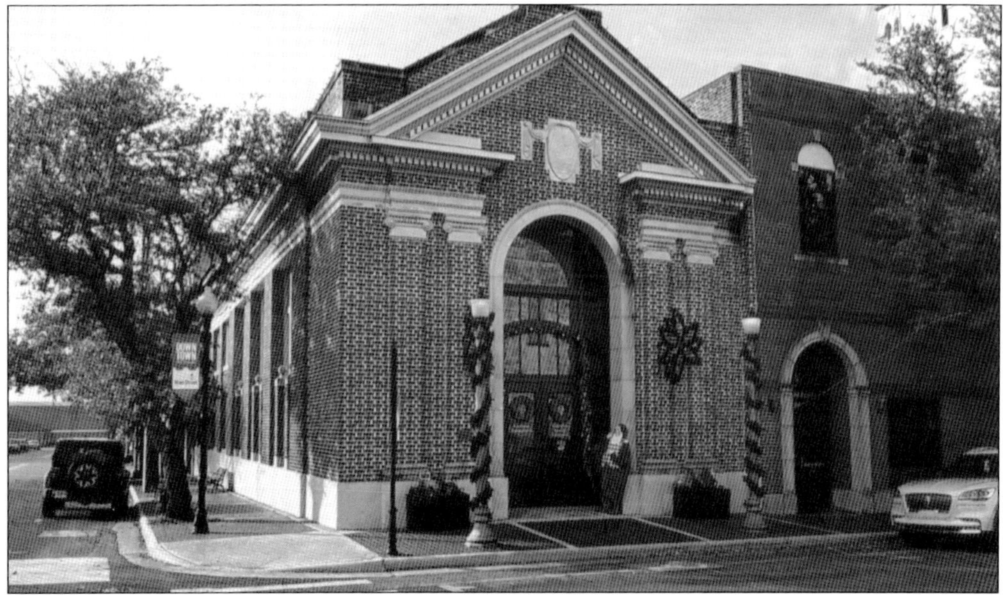

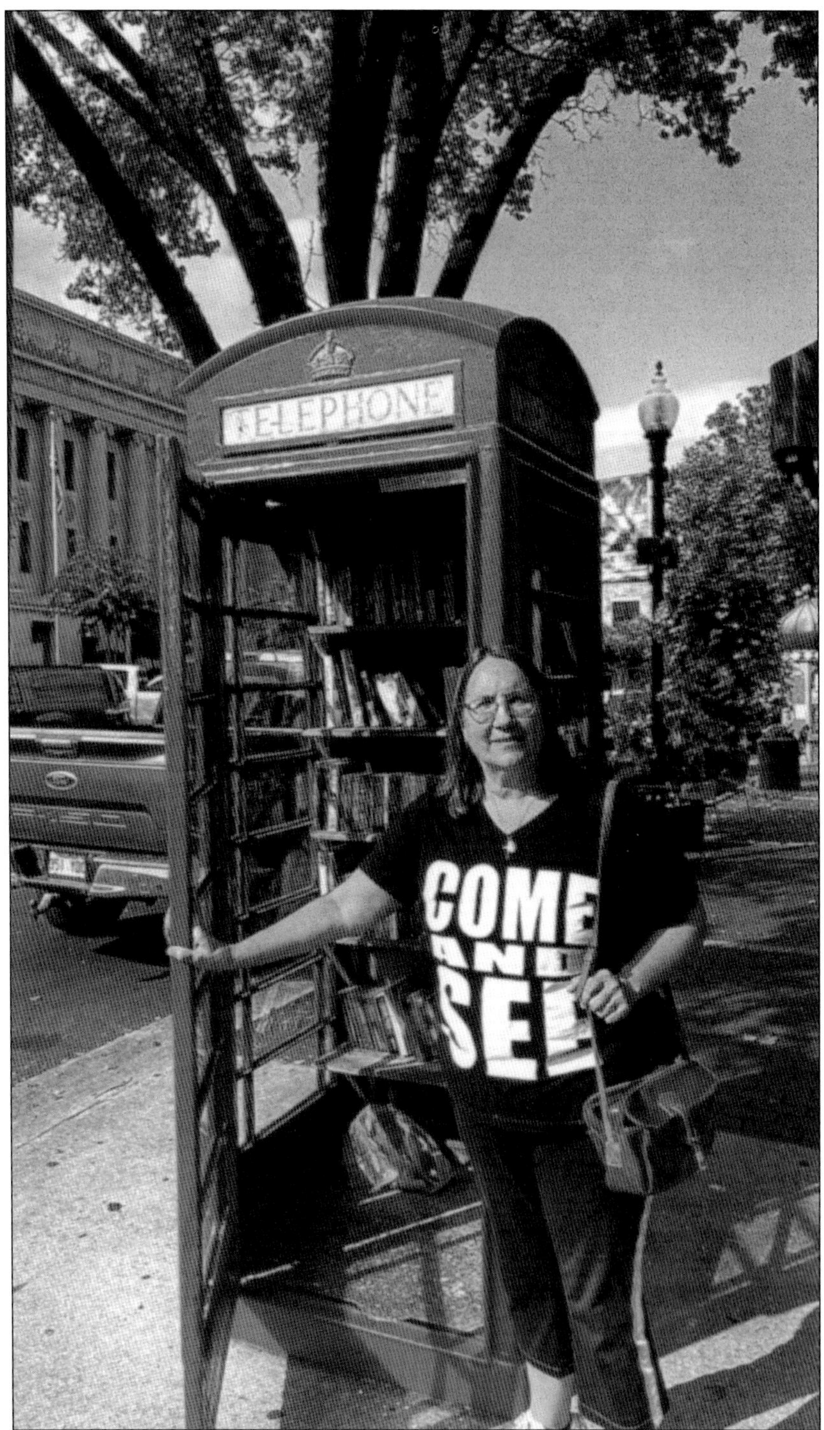

The two British phone booths on the square owe their presence to Richard Mason, who found them at an antique market in Houston. He immediately bought the pair and restored them to donate to the city. At one time, they held actual pay phones; today, they house a free library of donated books, as shown here by a visitor. (Photograph by Ray Hanley.)

El Dorado's history will be forever interwoven with the great oil strikes that put it into the national spotlight a century ago. Some of that history shows up on online auction sites, where an intact, unopened can of Lion oil can sell for $50, plus postage.

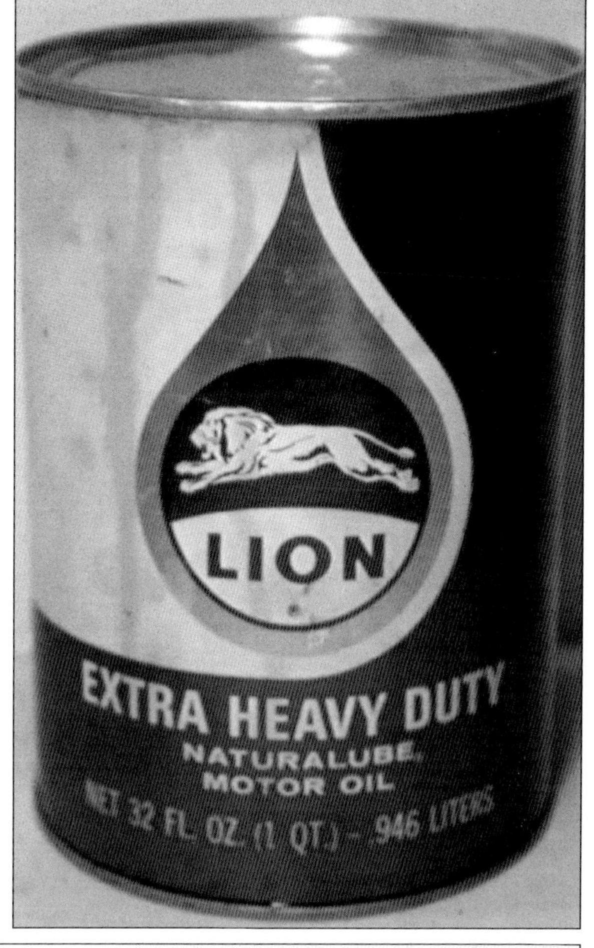

To appreciate El Dorado's past and to equally appreciate the city today can best be done by touring on foot around the downtown historic district, perhaps with this book in hand. Back on page 17, the reader learned about B.W. Reeves and his iconic department store. The town's oldest surviving commercial building still stands today, though greatly altered. (Photograph by Ray Hanley.)

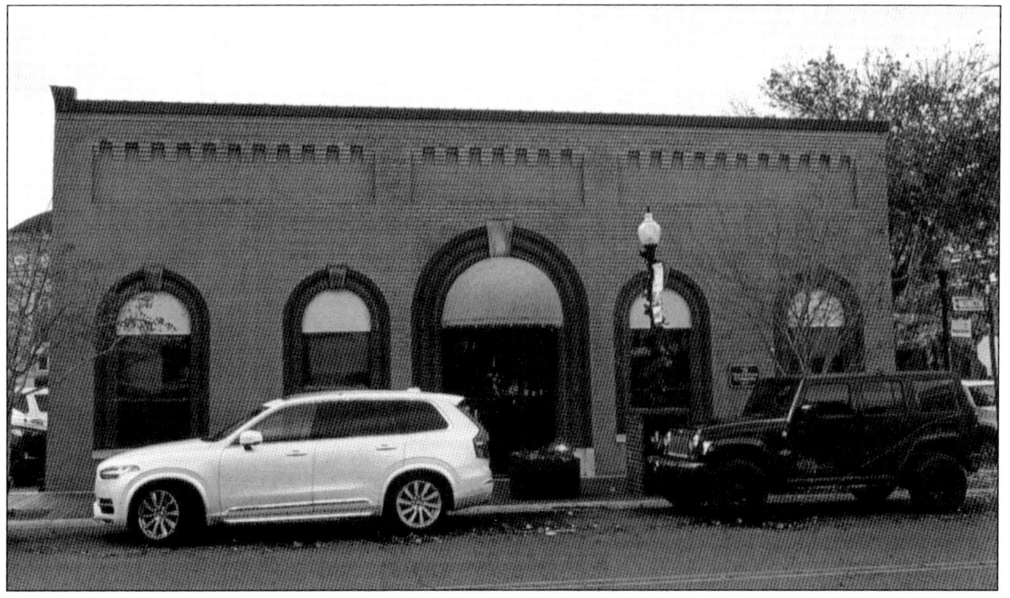

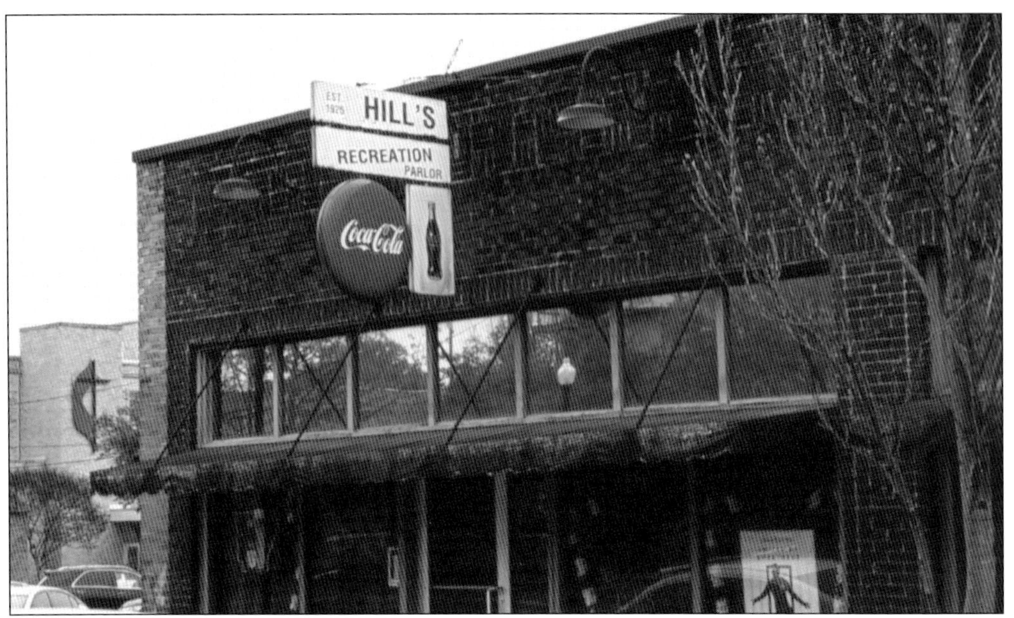

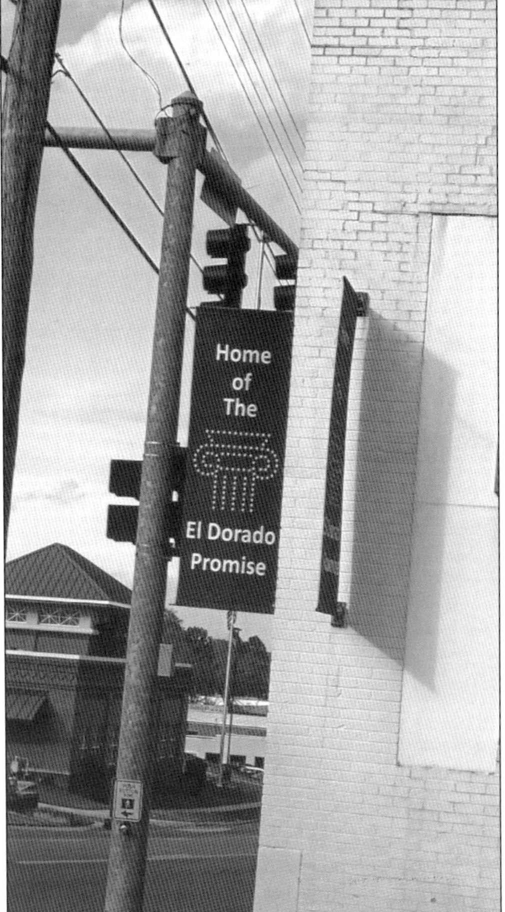

Some history might be noticed only when looking up to read a sign. Hill's Recreation Parlor, a pool hall, boasts on its sign that it was established in 1925. It is perhaps the oldest continually operating business in downtown El Dorado. (Photograph by Ray Hanley.)

The narrow sign hanging on the end of the El Dorado School District's headquarters building is small, reading "Home of the El Dorado Promise." However, that promise looms large in making the town's future. In an effort to halt the loss of population and to give back to its city of origin, Murphy Oil in 2006 put up $50 million for a universal college scholarship program for students of the El Dorado School District. If enrolled by the ninth grade and graduated from the local high school, a student's college tuition and fees are fully covered. The local citizens have stepped up with a millage to further support the effort. (Photograph by Ray Hanley.)

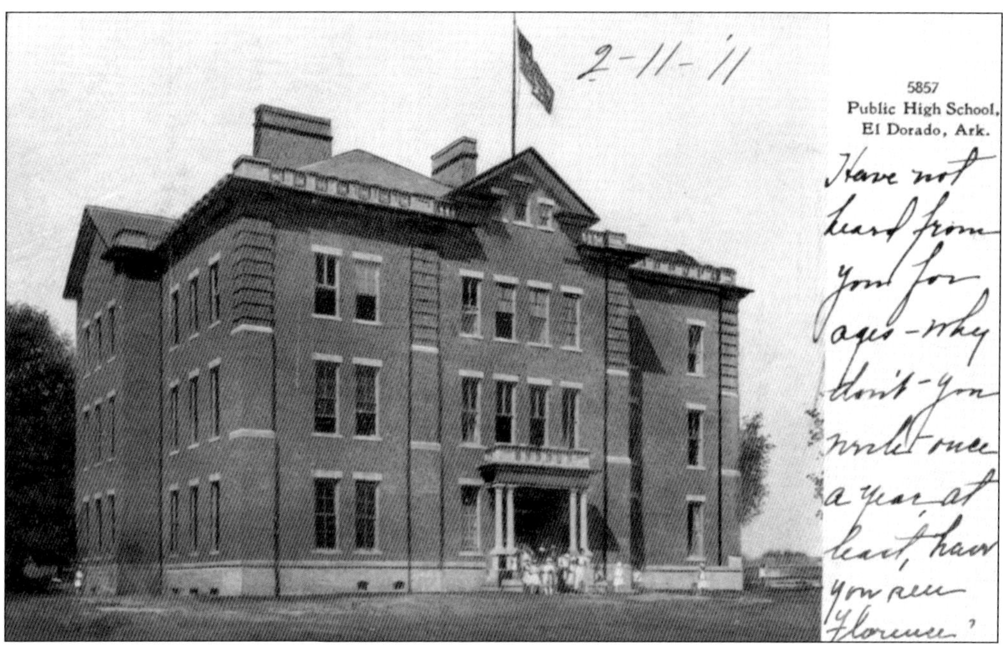

Little better symbolizes the past, present, and future of El Dorado than its 1905 high school building. Seriously damaged by a lightning strike and fire in 2015, it is restored today to house the administrative offices of South Arkansas College. El Dorado's future depends upon the education of its people, and the preservation of a historic education building is something to be proud of. (Below, photograph by Ray Hanley.)

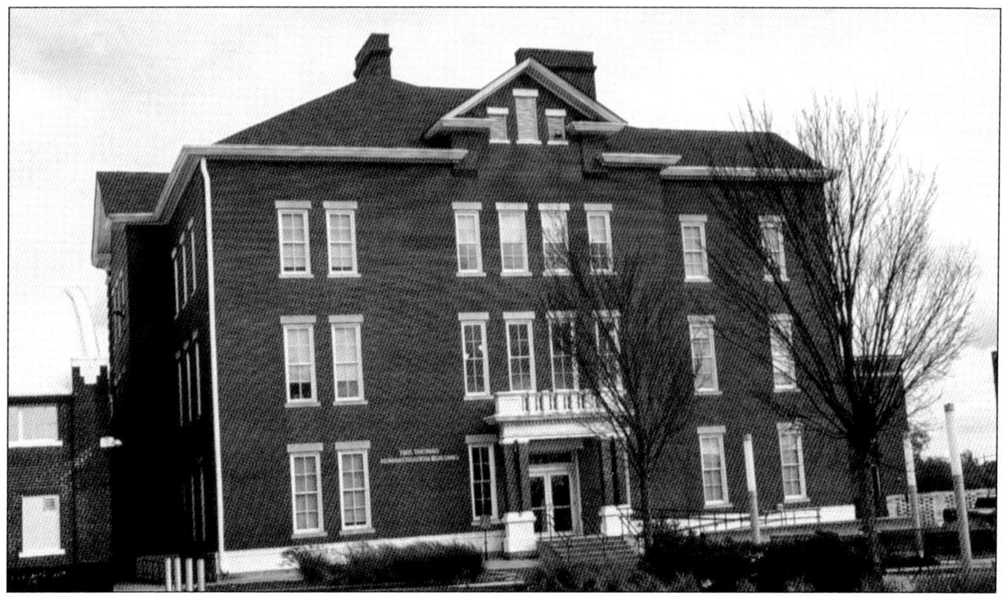

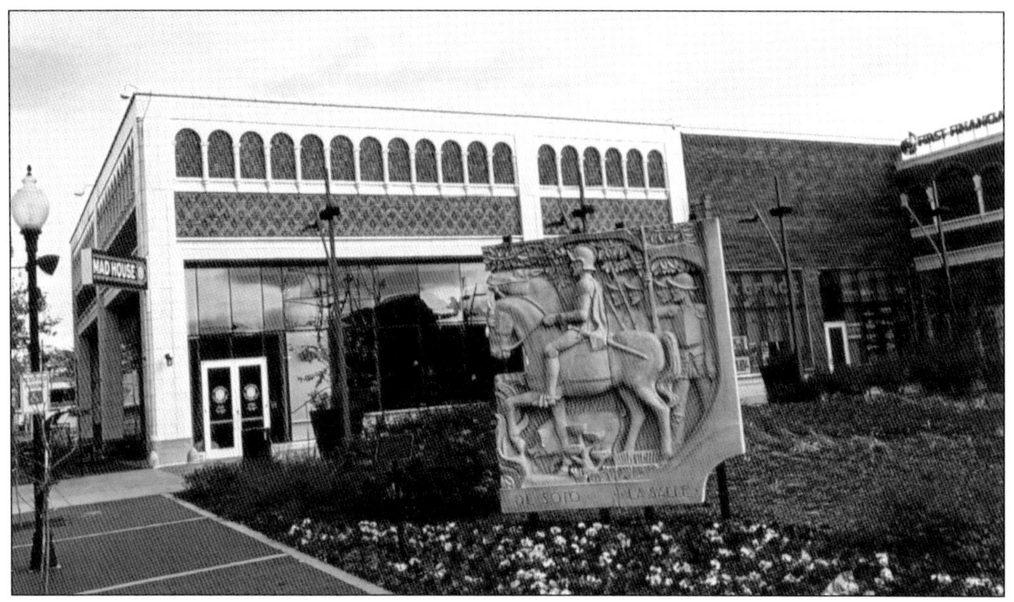

By 2020, El Dorado's population had dropped to about 18,000, and Murphy Oil again wanted to help counteract the decline. This determination led to the creation of the Murphy Arts District, now abbreviated as MAD. The multiphased project turned the 1928 Griffin Auto Building into a dining and performance venue seating 2,000 people. It also developed an outdoor amphitheater accommodating 8,000 people. Bands that have since played at MAD include Three Dog Night, ZZ Top, and the Beach Boys. (Photograph by Ray Hanley.)

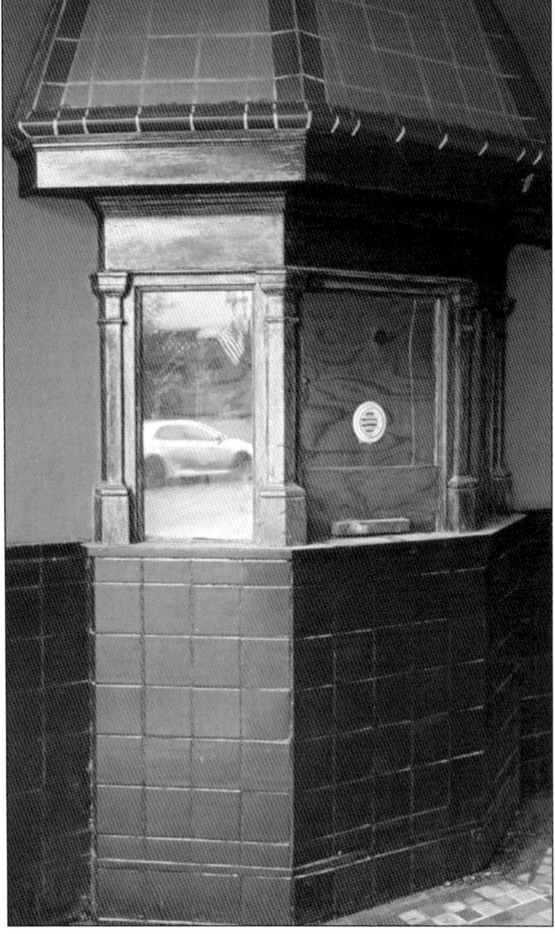

Symbolic of downtown rebirth yet to come might be the boarded-up ticket window of the Rialto Theater. Seen back on page 82 in views from 1929 and 1997, the historic theater is now in the process of a multiyear restoration that will bring further entertainment, life, and enjoyment to downtown El Dorado. (Photograph by Ray Hanley.)

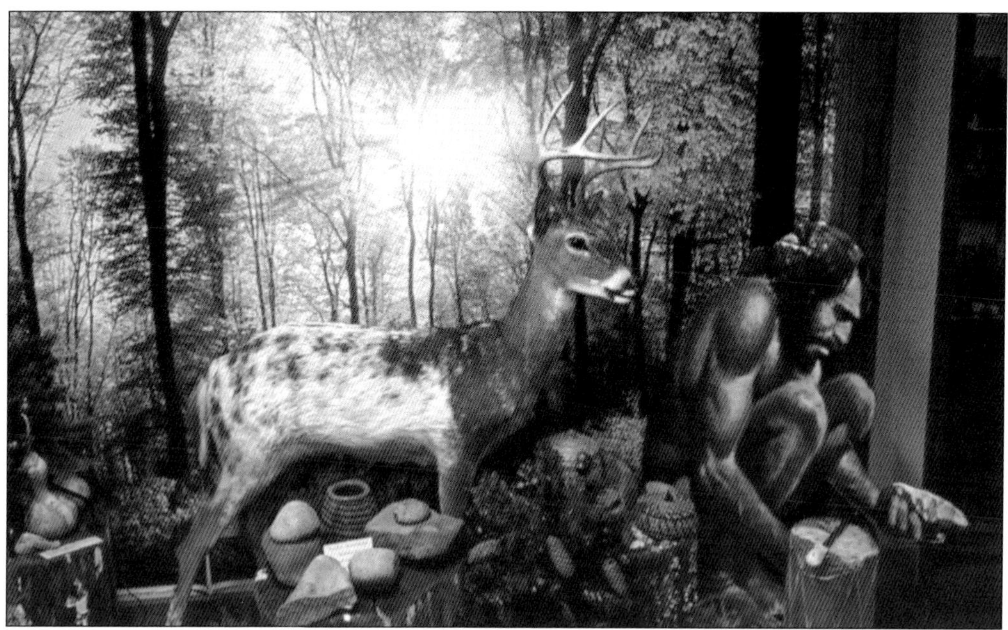

No visit to El Dorado is complete without a tour of the remarkable museum of the South Arkansas Historic Preservation Society on East Faulkner Street, a few blocks from the courthouse square. The professionally curated exhibits tell the region's history through details of Native American life, the area's first settlers, its remarkable oil boom, its sports hall of fame, and much more. (Both photographs by Ray Hanley.)

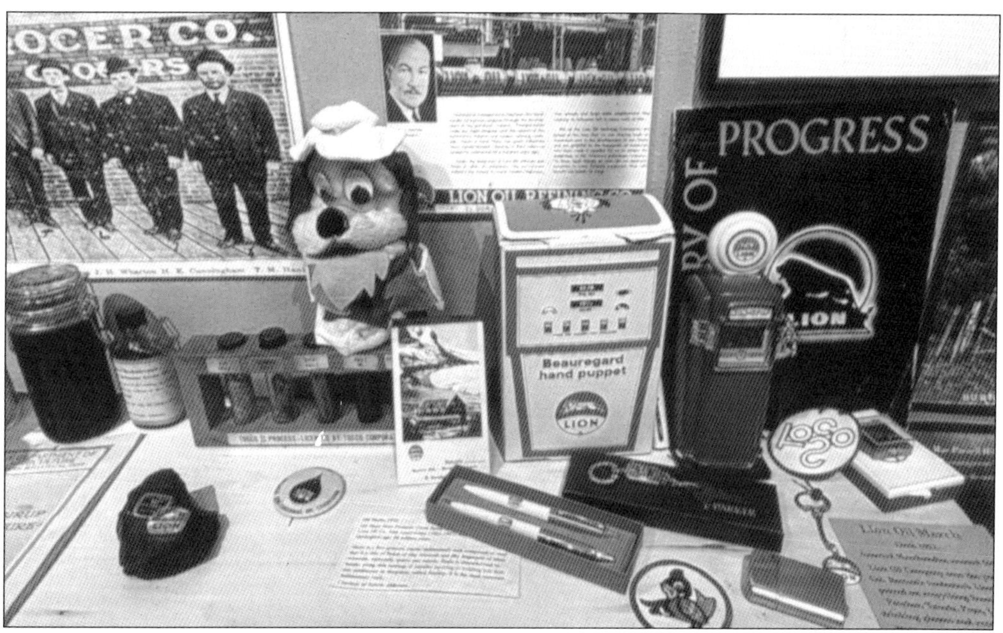

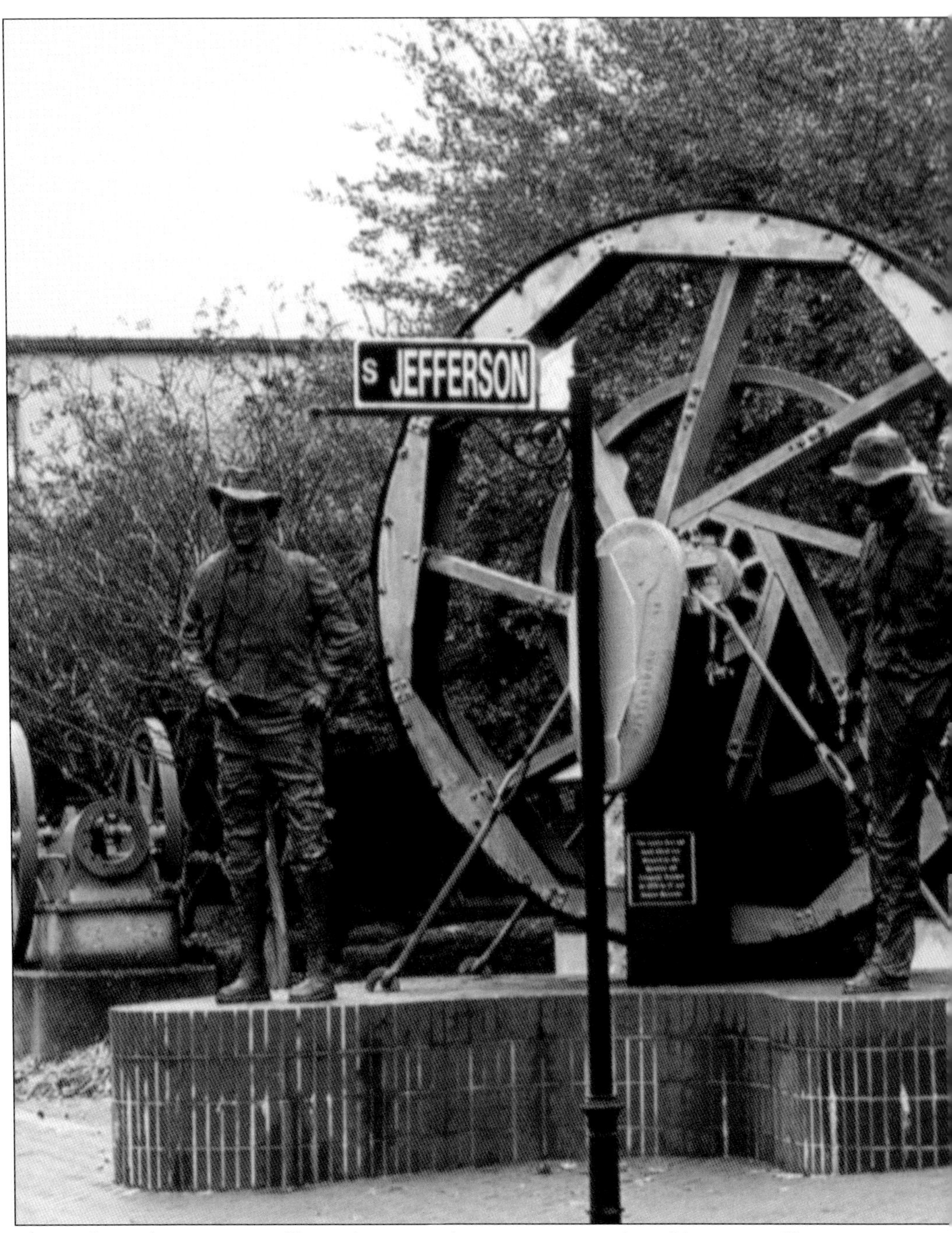

El Dorado marks its unique oil boom history with a monument to the wildcatters and businessmen who gambled fortunes to establish the oil industry in Union County. The formerly sleepy little farming and timber town saw its population peak at 40,000 within two years of the 1921 oil strike. In the boom era, Union County was said to have one of the highest concentrations of millionaires in the nation. Of course, the oil did slow, and the wildcatters moved on to new fields. Recent years have seen a decline in El Dorado's population, though the decline seems to have stabilized at around 18,000. Efforts such as the El Dorado Promise scholarships and downtown revitalization

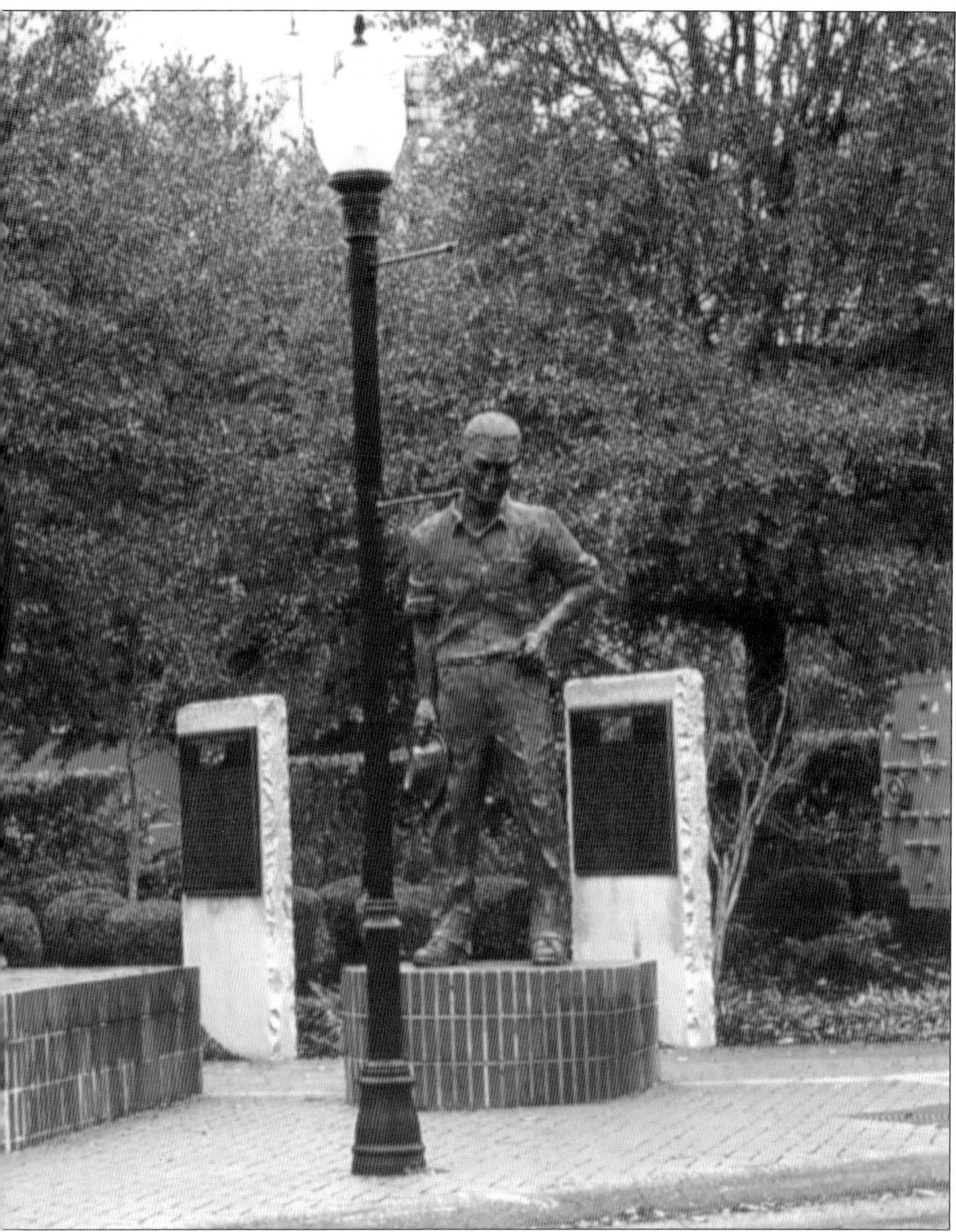

have lifted the hopes of all. The region's future may ride on yet another boom, this time in the vast lithium deposits of the area, which are, ironically, related to the oil exploration of a century ago. Lithium is vital to the production of electric batteries destined to drive much of the world. A large lithium processing plant is planned outside of El Dorado, so perhaps the boom of the 1920s is coming full circle. The rich history of El Dorado and Union County is a proud part of the legacy of Arkansas and will hopefully not be forgotten by those carrying their community into the future. (Photograph by Ray Hanley.)